REDHEAD WITH FIRE
IN HIS BOOTS

REDHEAD WITH FIRE IN HIS BOOTS

My Life in Rugby

PETER HARVEY

FONTHILL

This book is dedicated to my wife Ruth and my children Simon, Louise and Rachael: and our grandchildren, Rebecca, Andrew, Christopher, Amy, Matthew, Adam, Dylan, Esme and Dominic. None of them ever saw me playing rugby, and whilst it was a very important part of my life, hopefully all of the other things I have done will be remembered too.

Fonthill Media Limited
www.fonthillmedia.com
office@fonthillmedia.com

First published in the United Kingdom 2014

British Library Cataloguing in Publication Data:
A catalogue record for this book is available from the British Library

Copyright © Peter Harvey 2014

ISBN 978-1-78155-182-0

Typeset in 10pt on13pt Sabon Lt Std
Printed and bound in England

Contents

Acknowledgements

My very special thanks go to Eamonn McManus, Chairman of St Helens RFC who read the book and wrote the Foreword during a very busy season.

The Saints' statistics used in this book are courtesy of the Saints' Heritage Society, who have their own website at www.saints.org.uk.

The Warrington statistics are courtesy of Club Historian Stan Lewandowski.

Ian Douglas gave me assistance with the Liverpool Rugby Club Fixtures.

I used personal copies of the Loughborough College's Fixture card and various Lancashire Rugby Union Programmes for those results.

Many thanks are due to those reporters who wrote about the matches I played in, like A. W. Croxford and John Pugh and other members of the national press. In particular Tom Ashcroft, a local journalist, who had a weekly column in the *St Helens Newspaper*.

Alex Service helped me so much with the preparation of this book and the presentation of results.

Geoff Lightfoot read the original manuscript, and Katy Sheridan of The St Helens Deafness Resource Centre (DRC), who did the proof reading, and Sean Jenkins who read it as a 'stranger' who did not know me at all, but gave me valuable insight.

Thank you to my good friend, now deceased, Geoff Williams, Press Service of 16 George Street, St Helens for the Wembley photographs.

South Lancs Newspapers for some match pictures.

Frank Barton for his cartoons which were very much part of our heritage.

Foreword

The greatest of many privileges accorded to me as a long-standing Chairman of the outstanding and historic rugby league club of St Helens RFC has been to get to meet and know well many of our famous past players and characters. Peter Harvey certainly ranks as both of those. Being a fellow ginger and having been a pupil at the same school as he, I have a particular appreciation of his path in sport and in life and I feel honoured to script this foreword.

The truly wonderful game of rugby league and the town of St Helens each have a rich and unique history. Peter is very much a part of that having been a great past player in a memorable St Helens team and era in the 1960s, when the sport probably reached its zenith in spectator popularity and national and international recognition. More importantly, Peter is a real student himself of the history of the game, and of the town, and takes an informed, wise and deep-rooted pride in each in equal measure.

I was so glad to hear that Peter was writing his autobiography. His route through rugby union and rugby league was a unique one during an era when the comparative characteristics and social backgrounds of the two sports could not have been more diverse. To hear that he was the first schoolboy from Lancashire, that historic breeding ground of so many great and wonderful rugby players and sportsmen, to represent, let alone captain, England schools at rugby union, and that it was the 1958/9 season before this happened, inadvertently exposes the historic prejudices of the game. Peter was one of the first to break through this historic blockade. His journey through life and through sport is indeed a fascinating one which will educate any reader of his book. It is much more than a collection of sporting memories, although there are many different and illustrious ones: it is also indirectly a great commentary on a rich era of rapid social change in the then industrial North and in the country as a whole.

The town of St Helens and its adopted sport of rugby league are wrapped in incident, intrigue and romance. Peter's own life history, supported by his own knowledge and deep appreciation of local history, gives a wonderful insight into a truly fascinating sport, place and time, which must not be forgotten, nor cease to be appreciated. You will be the wiser and the happier for reading it.

Eamonn McManus
Chairman: St Helens Rugby League Football Club

CHAPTER 1

A Victim of Circumstances

The sound of exploding bombs caused Kate to cower into Peter's cradling arms. The echoes reverberated round the Anderson shelter as they huddled together waiting for the German bomber to pass. Soft words of comfort failed to soothe his pregnant wife who feared for the safety, not only of herself, but also her unborn child. Theirs was not the carefree attitude of those civilians of the cities by now becoming more used to the atmosphere during an air raid, because this was their first, and luckily their last encounter with a night raid. The shelter, dug into the back garden of their St Helens home, was to feel more blasts from falling bombs. The nearby cities of Liverpool and Manchester were the real targets, but Kate's thoughts brought the relative safety of her Scottish home, some way outside Glasgow, there beside them. 'I want to go home—now—*tonight*.'

My father, Peter, paused pensive. 'Alright love, we'll pack tomorrow and I'll take you on the one o'clock train.' That day, a Friday, he reported for his morning shift at the local colliery and told no one of his planned journey. Still black with coal dust he cycled the three miles home, his snap tin rattling against the saddle. His wage packet, snug inside his torn trousers, contained little more than the cost of the railway tickets he had to purchase. Carrying a few belongings in a battered brown case, held together with a fraying strap, they walked the three miles to the station, passing the Town Hall as the fingers on the four-faced clock joined together at midnight. Despite the lateness of the hour the small dusty station bustled with soldiers moving to unmarked destinations, carrying kit bags, which served as seats, on the crowded corridors of wartime trains.

The couple, married barely ten months, said little on those occasions both found themselves awake together. Neither knew whether this journey would be the beginning of a long parting. Each, though accepting the wisdom of the move, wondered about the outcome. She, comforted by the playful kicking of her child, worried about the safety of their new house, so recently purchased with the help of a ten-pound loan from a friend. He kept dismissing the thought that his son would not be born in his native St Helens. His son, yes he was sure of that, would be born in a foreign land.

Johnnie and Annie, his in-laws, had been friendly enough when he had asked for Cathie's hand, little more than a year ago. But did they really feel that this small pitman, with the blue flecked scars on his knees and shins, was really going to care and look after their eldest daughter, especially 200 miles away?

'Do you really come home black and take a bath in front of the fire?' Johnnie had asked when he learned of the suitor's occupation. 'Is it true that you box for money? You say your father is an invalid from the Great War. What does he do? How many children live in that terraced house you come from?'

'Yes, yes a drayman, and twelve,' were the answers which did not allay the unstated worries of the canny Scot, himself a labourer in engineering works, making steel structures. His daughter's eyes had pleaded with him as he turned to his wife, and melting with their desire, he nodded and conceded his precious daughter, to this Englishman's care.

Now my father knew, as his palm pressed gently around Cathie's hand, as the train rattled along to Glasgow, that safety came before birthplace and that his child would be a Scot. 'You were only a victim of circumstances', he would say to me, many times later, but just then he comforted himself by caressing the hair, curled round my mother's head like a crown. After the loving welcome of his in-laws and the relative calm of the week-end spent with them, the lonely return journey, followed by a couple of weeks living alone, left him seriously depressed. The telegram boy rapped the doorknocker, holding his yellow missive nonchalantly, impatiently waiting for the signature. Nervously his small but powerful hands fumbled with the flap. Quickly his eyes flashed across the message.

IT'S A BOY EVERYTHING ALRIGHT STOP.

'Thank God for that,' the words burst through pursed lips. Alone, behind the door, the tough bantamweight boxer, the Pit Boy Champion of England, shed tears of relief and delight. How soon can I get them both home, was the main theme of his thoughts, as he sat down by the warm coal fire.

His telegram in return said, 'Pleased as Punch. Sorry unable to come. All my love to my wife and son. Peter'

Addressed to 54 Craigview Ave., Johnstone, Scotland, it was received in Johnstone 2610 40 which I take to be 26 October 1940. So I, Peter Harvey, was born in Johnstone, Renfrewshire, Scotland 'a victim of circumstances,' a Lancastrian in Renfrewshire.

In fact the telegram had lied. Neither mother nor I were alright. It had been a very difficult birth, and I was a 'blue baby' struggling for breath. Both of us nearly died and to compound events, a German bomber strayed overhead and dropped a bomb less than 200 yards from the house. It was truly a dramatic entrance, to be followed by some months of ill health and depression for my mother. No one could have predicted neither the pathway which my life was to follow nor the dramatic changes which were to come about, because of decisions taken by me and others.

CHAPTER 2

Donkeys and Dangers at Carr Mill

The Anderson shelter had been converted into a huge coal shed, which was needed to house the coal delivered directly from the pithead, as part of my dad's wages. We little boys, Kerry Vose and I, often carried lumps from the front of the house, where the lorry had tipped it, to the back, always finishing up as black as the coal itself. More often than not both Kerry and I would both end up in the washing tub, after the clothes had been washed.

'No good wasting good water.' Auntie Mary would say plunging first one then the other struggling boy into the soapy water. Who could possibly have predicted that both of us would one day take the communal bath in a rugby league club, as the soapsuds made us splutter.

My dad and Uncle Jack worked hard to keep their families happy. Between turns at the pit and the ropery, they laid a lawn, cut from sods carried from the common land, a quarter of a mile away. This field, big enough for a football pitch, with room at the side for another small one, was flanked on two sides by railway lines. One, the main line to Wigan from Liverpool, was the escape route to Scotland taken on that fearful night earlier described. The other coming from Blackbrook and the East, carried freight only, and the dirty wagons clanked up the steep hill, often at no more than walking pace. The third side was the Burghy, the name given to the waste lands of sand pumped out as silt, from the polishing of glass at Pilkingtons. The fourth side was a field that was full of luscious grass, chewed happily by Farmer Moncrief's cows. It was simply called Laffak field, this being the name of the district, home of Haresfinch Rovers, and open to all in friendly matches.

At that time my dad would cut squares of turf and carry them back, a wheelbarrow load at a time, pushing them up the short steepish lane that curved round past the old church, now used as a school. The 'helpful boys', Peter and Kerry were tied to the wheelbarrow with strings to their wrists, sufficiently long to keep us from under his feet, but short enough to ensure our safety. The lawn was laid in the back garden to disguise the rough area left when the shelter had been repositioned, and in the course of time a small wooden fence was built to surround it. Such 'expeditions' were accompanied by Dinah, an Alsatian bitch of superbly gentle temperament, who had acted as the walking aid when both of the boys were toddlers. She responded to a single whistle of her master and was never out of reach of this simple device. The whistle from Peter was to become a common signal for both dog and children as they grew together and began to stray further afield.

A whistle held to the mouth by various blazer-wearing referees, some blasting loudly as they gesticulated wildly, in gestures designed to inform the crowd, would come later. But for now there was no such crowd.

However, from the restrictions of the front and back gardens, we went to Holy Cross School away into town on the school bus. This would arrive at 8.30 a.m. and all of the Catholic children in the neighbourhood would be ushered onto it by anxious mothers. Many Protestant children whose parents wished them to go to the Parish Church School would also go on that bus, as both schools were next door to each other. This ensured that most of the children in the district became friendly with each other and a common bonding was achieved. John joined Kerry and me at school, but Thomas, born as the third boy, was found to be suffering from Hunter's syndrome, and needed his mother's attention at home. A further minor tragedy was felt in the home when Kerry's sister Jean was found to be profoundly deaf, and it was recommended that she be sent away to a residential school in Yorkshire. Boston Spa became the home of my two deaf cousins, and perhaps explains my later involvement with The St Helens Deafness Resource Centre.

Having completed a lifetime in looking after children, teaching them, and offering the best protection I could organise, I look back at some of the things which happened in my childhood with incredulity. It is difficult to compare the freedom, or independence given to us as children, with the constraints of today, when children are taken to school in cars, and rarely walk anywhere.

My infant school life was pleasant with good caring teachers who dealt in the basics of education, bringing together social and academic training. Playtime on the large playground was enjoyable and the rough and tumble of tick, was smoothed out with circle games and even organised skipping. One day however, I was becoming more adventurous, and accepted a piggyback from one of the juniors who took me across the playground as far as the junior toilets. My teacher, hearing of this transgression of the rules, broke a small branch from the privet hedge surrounding the school playground, and gave me a sharp switch across my legs. This small punishment made me cry, not because of its severity, but more because of the sudden realisation that I could not do entirely as I pleased. The same action today would no doubt have brought about an assault charge and the teacher's dismissal.

Perhaps the biggest disappointment of my very young life came when my classmates transferred to the junior school and I was made to stay in the top infant class. It took patience on the part of the headmistress, to explain to me that it was not a punishment, but that as I had earlier been advanced a class because of my academic progress, I was still too young to leave the infant school. In that last year I was to learn the responsibility of looking after the new classmates and progressed to become something of a leader among the group. My tasks included looking after the PE equipment, which I relished, and being a team leader, which I greatly enjoyed. This taste of power was a great boost, and my infantile realisation that I was in some way better than those around me, gave me more confidence in myself.

This leadership ability was to be a fundamental quality in my life, sporting or otherwise. But in the following incident it led me into a greater danger than I imagined.

By the age of eight or nine, it was not unusual for groups of boys to walk the three miles home from school on sunny days, and of course the added freedom gave opportunities for much play and adventure. One day when a group of us were walking home, we came across a small pony (maybe a donkey) tethered in a field. Perhaps influenced by my father's stories of riding bare back in his childhood, on my grandfather's horse Tommy, (used to pull the family cart) I decided that I would ride this pony. Cautiously the gang approached the creature and pulled the rope, trying to bring it towards us. The beast stubbornly refused to move, but shied away when any attempt was made to go close to it from the side. The more we boys pulled, the harder the animal resisted until suddenly it galloped forward throwing us backwards to the ground. Before I had time to roll clear, it ran over the top of me, stepping on my forehead as it passed. I clung to the rope, in the forlorn hope that I could stop it, but the dull ache in my leg and hot flush on my head, caused me to let go. I lay there not knowing if I was bleeding or even dying. My tears were of both pain and fear, as I realised that I would have to explain to my parents what I had done.

After my mother had bathed my wounds and saved me from my father's wrath, I sobbed myself to sleep, vowing never to do anything so stupid again. It is true that since then, I have never been kicked in the head by a donkey, but maybe some of my stubbornness never to give in, was transferred to my head as the huge lump subsided. Perhaps freedom does have its dangers, but I am sure that we have overcompensated in our desire to make the world safe. Time changes everything, except it would seem the weather as seen in this example.

The winter of 1947 stormed in, cold and snowing with frost biting hard on the ground. The adults struggled to keep their children warm. The extra blankets and overcoats on the beds made them the warmest place in the house. My brother John and I now found that our shared bed had benefits beyond the companionship that we were used to. However, snow has great appeal to young children. Snowmen and snowball throwing played a great part in the enjoyment of the short cold days. Now our boots, resoled with wooden clogs clad in rubber, were good and strong. Sometimes as we walked, the clogs grew three or four inches as the snow packed onto them.

The cold weather persisted for week after week and by Christmas Carr Mill Dam was frozen. Of course, this was not the first time it had frozen, but this time the ice was thick. It grew thicker and stronger, until it was generally accepted to be safe. Suddenly it became the Mecca of skating enthusiasts. The home-made toboggan was often in service on the hills of the Happy Valley and the East Lancs Road, despite the real danger of careering across the road into the traffic. However, the opportunity to use it on a lake was unique. My dad borrowed some skates from a friend, and after some practice alone, took us boys, one bright but bitterly cold afternoon onto the open acres of the frozen lake. The atmosphere of a Dickensian Christmas held for a week or so and everyone skated and slid around, buying chestnuts roasted on brassieres at the side of the lake, among the bare trees. Growing in confidence we were towed around by my father, waving at all of the other children equally enjoying their rides. Woolly hats and scarves were quickly knitted and their bright colours lightened the snow-laden skies. Whatever discomfort adults were suffering, all children were wishing the snow and ice would stay. Slowly but inexorably, the days warmed and the ice thinned, until one day it was no longer safe and long thin cracks appeared in the surface. The whole episode came to an abrupt end when an unknown man went through the ice, and was reported drowned, much to the dismay of the whole neighbourhood. The Dam was dangerous, but it was our playground.

As was the 'plot', a piece of rough ground at the end of the road, which had become the regular playground for the dozen or so boys who lived around Laffak, and boys between nine and fifteen, often mixed in games of cricket and football. There was a good community spirit, probably caused by the wartime hardships now receding among the families. Many of the older boys took part in the games, encouraging the juniors and teaching us the rudiments and rules by which to play. One such adult was Ken Finney who was a very good games player; in fact he was a professional footballer and played for Stockport County, the first person that I knew who I saw on television. He was also 'Uncle Ken' to Geoff Pimblett, who also was part of that group of youngsters. From time to time, Ken would play with us younger boys, and his sustained bowling of slow off brakes, mixed in with the odd leg break and googly, gave plenty of opportunity for batting practice for all and sundry. The dirt pitch was worn flat by constant running, and the 'village green cricket' of other areas was enacted there by the side of Carr Mill Road.

When not playing football or cricket on the 'plot' we boys would go swimming in the dam nearby. At first we went to Hollin Hey, a small sandy bay about twenty yards across, where in earlier years we had watched the German prisoners of war laze around sunbathing and noisily swimming. Now we had it to ourselves and I was both incompetent and stupid, far from the intelligent boy I was supposed to be.

I was slow to swim as neither of my parents had mastered the art, and it was too far to go to the baths in Boundary Road, except on a very rare occasion. One day, one of the older boys decided that it was about time that I learned how to swim, so he threw me into the water some yards from the shallow part. Finding myself floundering, and not being able to reach the bottom, I simply kicked my feet and splashed my arms until I reached the sand where the others were standing laughing at me. In a fit of rage I threw myself at my tormentor and received a thick ear for my trouble. Still the deed was done and I could swim, albeit with difficulty.

Those first forced strokes were followed by days of practice, until one day the older boys decided to swim across the dam to the boat house on the other side. Watching them go with some envy, I sat silently on the grass trying to decide if the 200 yards or so were too many for me. That day I dared not go, but their taunts at the evening cricket game angered me so much that I slunk away, determined to do it the next time. The opportunity soon presented itself and this time I set off with the others. The water was much colder out there where it was deep, and the sight of their receding heads, made me feel very much alone. By the time I had got to the middle of the dam the others were clambering out on the other side. My arms were tired and I gulped the water instead of the air. I was frightened and began to shout. They shouted back misinterpreting my cries for help. I went under. The water closed around me and I panicked. I came up gasping for air and thrashing the water. I went down again. As I surfaced, Jackie Cotham, a strong swimmer who had started long after everyone else, appeared beside me. Grabbing a floating log he thrust it towards me. By now I was desperate.

'Grab hold of this lad,' was an order he need not repeat. Hanging onto the log and panting for air I realised the extreme danger my bravado had got me into, but by the time I had been helped back to the side, my attitude had changed. 'Thanks Jack, but I reckon I could have done it by myself.' If I believed that, I was the only one who did. My life could so easily have ended that day, drowned in the Carr Mill Dam. There would not have been any rugby matches at all because oddly it was not played in that district, which produced two Lance Todd Trophy Winners in Geoff Pimblett (St Helens) and Ray Ashby (Wigan).

There were several people drowned in the Dam that year and so I, along with Kerry and John were forbidden to go there unaccompanied. However, some weeks later we did once more go walking with the older boys, without any intention of swimming. As we walked along the stone side of the Dam, just short of the overflow slipway, Kerry slipped and fell. Fully clothed he dropped into the water, and though only feet from the side, he was in great danger of drowning. Between us, Bobby Fish and I grabbed his hair and his clothes and managed to drag him to the side. A bedraggled group went home to face the consequences.

'We saved him dad, we saved him.' John blurted out by way of explanation.

'Did you now?' dad answered as he took hold of his two boys. 'I-told-you-not-to-go-any-where-near-the-bloody-dam.'

Each word was separated from the next by a very firm slap across the behind, and both of us spent the rest of the evening in our room, rueing our disobedience, not at all consoled by the sobs from the next room from Kerry, similarly treated by his father, Jack Vose.

By now the simple semi had become too small to cope with the demands of the swelling families within its walls, and Mary and Jack took their children to the brand new council estate being built at Clinkham Wood. The physical separation of the two families was at first lessened by the wearing of a path through the fields, as we children gradually learned how to do without our cousins. The mental bond remained and was never broken.

Kerry Vose grew up to play rugby league for UGB and was signed by Liverpool City to play scrum-half for a couple of seasons. He is remembered by many for his cheerful disposition and good sense. Unfortunately he developed Leukaemia and died within two weeks in Whiston Hospital, at the age of twenty-nine. Known as Kerry to the family, Thomas to his friends, he was well liked. But to me any form of rugby was well in the future as the local team was Haresfinch Rovers who played football.

By now I was coping with the struggle to emulate my slightly older peers, and as before, a stubborn refusal to give in to an unequal task led me into danger.

On summer evenings, when the light grew too dim to continue with the cricket, we boys took to running 'The Tin Tack'. This was the name given locally to the circle of lanes that went away to Bob Harrison's dairy, the Laffak Cottages where Geoff Pimblett lived, and back to the Laffak schoolhouse porch, which we used as a den. It was quite a common sight to see all of the youngsters line up across the lane and set off in a road race round this improvised three-quarters of a mile track. Puffing and panting, we would return to the school doorway and gather together beneath the warm glow of the gas lamp, atop the green iron post. This would be the signal for parents to come out and collect their children to consign them to their homes. One particular night, the race was run as usual, but I found myself struggling fifty yards behind the others as I came under the railway bridge, running up the deserted lane towards Burkill's Café. A man walking towards me suddenly opened his coat and drew what appeared to be an enormous bread knife from his sleeve.

'I've got you now,' were the words which froze my blood.

Turning in great fear, I ran back the half mile or so already covered, tears streaming down my face, along the way I had come. With mounting fear I cried aloud, as the panic reached my brain. Without going near any of the other boys, I ran screaming to my home.

'Where's my dad?' I shouted, 'Where's my dad?'

My mother, not knowing why her panic stricken boy was standing in the hallway, red faced and screaming, called for her husband Peter. Between tears and sobs, the tale was told, and father and son went to the end of the road to call for the police. The wooden police box, of a type now made famous by Dr Who, stood at the corner. The little door on the side was drawn back, and the report duly made to the unseen face, linked by whatever made the contraption work. Still sobbing, I took my father to the now deserted slip road, and eventually back home. The Police duly came, and an unsuccessful search of the area was made. I was comforted and put to bed and after a few days the incident receded into history. Nothing came of the affair but 'The Tin Tack' run, was no longer the popular finish to the evening playtime. Some said that I had imagined it, but I remain convinced that my ordeal had been real; the unknown man had threatened to kill me.

The war was over, but rationing was still in place, and the corner shops were the key to the local economy. Bob Harrison figured further in the life of the neighbourhood, because being the local milkman, he was regularly to be seen on his morning round. He had a blind horse called 'Queenie,' that daily slipped between the shafts of the milk-cart and pulled the high-sided trap along the pre-determined route, stopping without command at every door. I, along with many of the other boys, helped to deliver the milk, not in bottles but served out in pint or half pints from the milk churn on the float.

We sat high up as the horse clipped slowly along the roads, stopping to allow us to dismount from the metal step. Many a boy learned the lesson of dismounting from a moving vehicle, by their error in walking forward from that step, to pitch forward onto their face, as the float went from under them. Queenie was a lovely horse, friendly to all who came near her. She knew the round perfectly, stopping at every door and moving quietly on. However, she refused to go on once she reached Mrs Finney's door, unless she was fed a crust or two from yesterday's loaf. She would drag the float askew the pavement, as she clattered on the thick flagstones outside the black terraced cottage. Her head would poke through the door into the tiny living room until titbits were provided.

The three penny bit, which I received at the end of the morning's work, was always welcomed, but the example of that blind white horse was to last much longer than any monetary gain. Sadly, Queenie grew older with the boys and eventually had to retire. The lesson is simple, no matter how clever we are, or how good, we do grow old and eventually have to retire.

CHAPTER 3

There's Nothing for Coming Second

One of my dad's expressions was, 'When it comes to 'hey lads hey' you want a fighter by your side.' He had been a professional boxer, known in the ring as Battling Harvey. He naturally wanted his sons to be able to defend themselves and as he had run a boxing club for many years we were taken down there.

Growing now into a chubby boy, I began to heed my father's instruction in boxing. He, in his genuine desire to pass on his enthusiasm and expertise, had taken over the running of a boxing club. Boys of eight to sixteen gathered in the downstairs room of Holy Cross Men's Club on a couple of nights a week and learned the rudiments of the noble art. Perhaps more than the skills themselves, we learned to win and lose with equal grace. No one was allowed to be really hurt, and much confidence was gained in the process of standing facing each other, in the makeshift ring. The huge leather gloves, smelling of the stale sweat of countless hands, worn by constant use, were held high to protect the head. Punches, swung round-arm style, landed with great slaps until each boy in turn, learned to punch correctly, sticking out the left jabs and crossing with the right.

One night my father matched me with another boy of roughly the same size, but a year older and commanded me to fight. 'I can't fight him,' I said, 'He's the Cock of the School.' All of you will know, that the establishing of the pecking order in junior school is built on the process of who can fight who, and the best fighter is acknowledged by all, to be the 'Cock of the School'.

'Have you ever fought him?' Father asked quizzically. 'No, but everyone knows he is the best fighter,' I replied, as the gloves were carried to me. 'Then now's his chance to prove it. Keep sticking your left hand out.' My dad's words were both a challenge and instruction at the same time.

The 'champion' sailed in full of confidence, right hand drawn back. Whack! A right hand thrown from my shoulder and not preceded by the customary left hit him square on the nose. Slightly taken aback he stopped and blinked. Lifted by my success, I sailed in both arms flailing. After barely a minute we stopped. The referee, my dad, looked at us both and said, 'Had enough?' We looked at each other—one with tears in his eyes, the other blinking in amazement. 'Yes,' we agreed as neither wanted to see what would happen in the second round.

Now simple success was not sufficient for my father, after all he was the trainer and referee. His boy had won alright but the style was all wrong. 'Next time you fight him you must hold your hands up and punch straight. Boxers don't just put their heads down and swing like that. Left jab, left jab, right cross, that's the way to do it.

A week or so later the return match was made, and heeding my father's instruction, I stood straight in the middle of the ring. Now with no element of surprise, and little other than a modicum of courage, I awaited the onslaught. My tentative left was brushed aside by his swinging right, which hit me on the side of the head. My own right cross missed as the boy ducked into me. Thud! Another blow struck me in the midriff. Fighting for air I stood up in the boxer's pose. My weak lefts were ineffective in stopping the rushing opponent, and one, two, three, four blows struck me as I stood there trying to look at the fighter. 'Box him son, box him,' was a vain instruction as the heart went out of me. 'That's enough take the gloves off,' was an order rather gladly obeyed as I sucked my swelling lip.

Just then the other boy's mother came in, and seeing me crying came over to comfort me. 'It's not fair letting our Damien fight him he's only little,' she said. 'You wouldn't have said that last week if you had been here.' Father retorted. It was perhaps a hard lesson, but one well learned. Gradually some semblance of boxing skills were acquired, but they were really never developed, and were certainly never put to any test other than on playground fights the next year, to establish myself as 'Cock of the School'.

I was never the street fighter, nor indeed one to start a fight, but I never remember turning away when I needed to stand up to someone. My father was an ex-professional fighter, who could truthfully boast to have boxed at the Liverpool Stadium. He knew people in boxing, and continued with his interest as a spectator, through and after the war. When we were about eight and ten, my brother John and I would be taken on the bus to Liverpool Stadium. We went fairly frequently and grew used to the electric atmosphere: thick smoke, penetrated by dazzling lights that bathed the ring. The colours were intense, the white ring with the blue surround, the red gloves and the satin shorts of the boxers, were experiences etched in my mind.

We watched boxers and fighters, clapping the skilled and cheering the destroyers. The protagonists in this sport came in all shapes and sizes, some brave but foolish, others brave and skilful. The real draw is the one with the killer punch. Like the gunmen of old they met in the centre of the ring to fight it out. One, D. Keersgeter a Dutchman was nicknamed, 'the man with the iron jaw,' because of his ability to take a punch. He was the crowd's favourite for some time, because he was easy to hit, but very difficult to put down. He stood and traded blows until the opponent was spent and then knocked them out. I think that it was Johnny Butterworth from Rochdale who discovered that he had a hard jaw but a soft belly. We watched Stan Skinkiss dance his way to local fame, and cheered Eric Marsden through his first few fights on his way to the British title.

My father travelled further afield, and news of the current champions, and indeed potential champions were often expressed in our household. We went and watched Hogan 'Kid' Bassey train in St Helens, in a tiny gym off Liverpool Road. We met former fighters and walked to the ringside to get autographs from the personalities of the time, threading our way through the serried ranks of the seats, often stopping to chat to Stadium regulars. On one or two occasions we went on a coach trip to the Kings Hall, Belle Vue, for a Championship fight. The heightened tension of such occasions, the drama of the combat, the thrill of decisions, good and bad, built up an awareness of the courage of men who won and lost. The idea that the ring was the loneliest place in the world was often fed to us. On your own, with no one to help, driven to your limit of skill and endurance; many qualities necessary for success, all combined into a philosophy of survival. 'It takes a lot to make a champion,' father would say. 'It's not always the most talented that wins.' Also, his most obvious comment, that in boxing, there is nothing for second. So in our house we were brought up to be winners.

One can only guess at the importance of the final year in junior school, but in my case it marked the beginning of a metamorphosis. This was the year in which the larvae was to pass through the pupae stage and emerge, changed into me. For the last two years of my junior school life, I was strongly influenced by Mr Norbert Balmer who was our games teacher at Holy Cross. Like so many other primary school children, we had a dearth of male teachers in our lives. Few children can chose their teachers, and even parents have a very limited say, in who will develop their children's talents. It was not then accepted that the early development of the basic skills was the way to further progress: we were still working on the 1933 PE Syllabus and drill had been the order of the day since 1905. Mr Balmer changed that for us, as much more games playing was introduced. We were introduced to many forms of playground games and encouraged to take part in a variety of small team games, often improvising our own equipment, controlling hoops, balls and skipping ropes.

The highlight of the week would be the Friday on which we were walked a mile or so to the Bishop Road playing field, for our football or cricket match. Very few primary schools had their own grass pitches, and the long crocodiles of boys and girls, wending their way along the cobbled streets, were a very common sight in St Helens. Bishop Road, the nursery ground of ten-year-old sporting stars, was the Mecca for all of us: many hundreds of children must have congregated to, and dispersed from, its open spaces. Muddied but unbowed we would walk home, the prize sometimes being the loan of the school football for the weekend. When playing we were encouraged to attack, and keep on attacking. Since our goalkeeper could not reach more than half way to the cross bar, it was little use defending. I played inside left, and imagined myself as Albert Stubbins, Billy Liddle or on a rare occasion Stanley Matthews. I enjoyed my football and was made captain of the school team. Probably many boys shared that honour but I don't remember, as naturally enough I was completely egocentric in those days. The taking home of the football was not such a great prize for me because, believe it or not, I had one of my own. At least, one shared with my brother John. It had been a Christmas present. The gleaming yellow leather ball sat in the middle of the room. We stood looking at it in disbelief. We felt like lords. However, we did not have a cricket set and it was with great pride and joy that I carried the batting pads strapped around the new bat, when it was my turn to take them home after the Friday afternoon's cricket at Bishop Road. The whole unwieldy weapon slung over my shoulder. We played cricket for the whole of the Saturday, and many a run was cracked from the willow. We took it in turns to wear the pads, tall and straight and white. Several of the older boys, influenced by our newfound affluence, joined in the game towards the evening. Eventually someone noticed that the bat had a big split in its face. I was distressed, but slightly encouraged when one of them said that he would take the bat home, and bind it for me the next day. 'You won't even see that crack when I've finished.' he assured me. I imagined that a beautiful new strong binding, held in place with clear varnish, would satisfy Mr Balmer, and save my skin. Even that half inch pink tape, so beloved by cricketers of the day might suffice.

Sunday afternoon dragged on as I awaited the allotted hour of five to arrive. Not that I was worried about the skill of the craftsman, it was a case of ignorance is bliss. He brought the bat to the door. 'I think that should be alright young man.' He had kept his promise; I could not see the crack. I could hardly see the bat. His father must have been an electrician because he had used about two rolls of thick black insulation tape to bind the bat from bottom to top over and over again. My heart sank with the weight of the implement in my hand. I nodded my thanks and turned speechless to return home. It felt like a piece of tree trunk, heavy and lifeless. 'But Dad he'll kill me,' I blurted out when I arrived home. 'Who will? It's not your fault. He can't blame you. Anyhow I'll write him a letter.' Though pacified, I spent the evening wondering what the morning would bring.

I took the bat to school on the Monday morning strapped, as before, inside the batting pads. I looked at it on the bus seat. Should I tell him or just leave it in the games cupboard? No, the responsibility lay with me. 'Look after the equipment for the weekend,' he had said. Not, 'Play with it,' or, 'see if you can break it.' He knew we would play with it though, I rationalised to myself, that's why he gives it to us. The doubt was still there as I looked at it, like a leg in a plaster cast, hard and useless. To this day I don't know whether it was the letter, or the nature of the man, but he simply accepted the monstrosity with a shake of his head. 'It could have happened to anyone Peter, don't worry,' he said.

I will not surmise the reaction inside that staff room, but remember him as a man of great understanding, at least on that occasion. Mr Balmer was young and enthusiastic; he nurtured within us the love of games. He encouraged the dash and determination so beloved of my father. He taught us to play fair, and give credit to the opposition, not always the first thing in my mind. He allowed the flower of youth to bloom, rather than nip it in the bud with adult sarcasm and cynicism, born of bitterness and resentment, often seen in older teachers who fail to get promotion. Few will remember Mr Balmer, but he was really important to me and I was so lucky to have a strong male role model, in my primary school experience.

CHAPTER 4

Wearing my Green Blazer

In 1952 I took the scholarship exam (11+) one Saturday morning in the big hall of Windle Pilkington School. We had been preparing for this exam, by doing lots of past papers, and learning about all kinds of sequences, and various other direct forms of answering the questions, in the quickest possible time. We had been working with the 'King's English' textbooks, and learning all kinds of idiomatic expressions, plural forms, specific grammar, and of course practicing our handwriting. We were not to know the importance of this work, but simply went to the school one Saturday, and did the papers which were presented to us. I can't remember the exam, but do remember going onto the school roof at playtime. What a wonderful view of St Helens, a playground on the roof, such lucky pupils I thought. Windle Pilkington School, never a place I visited again, but one of the schools which Ruth, my wife taught in twenty years later.

In due course Sister Gertrude SND, (Sister of Notre Dame) the head teacher, came into our classroom and announced that the following boys and girls had passed the 11+. As I looked around the classroom, I could see some boys and girls crying, as their names were not on the list. I remember staring at her and she asked why I looked so miserable. 'I don't want to go to the Grammar School,' I said. And when she asked why not I said 'Because I live at Carr Mill and like to play around the dam and I don't want to do homework, which I will have to do if I go to the Grammar School.' Neither she nor Mrs Fairhurst, our teacher, was amused, and they told me how lucky I was to be given the chance to go to the Catholic Grammar School. I was told that I had to go home immediately to tell my parents, and get them to sign a form, which committed them to supporting me at this new school.

I arrived home at lunchtime to find an empty house. Mother, not expecting me of course, had gone to the corner shop with my two younger sisters Catherine and Mary. I followed her up there and laughed at her surprise. No I wasn't ill. No I hadn't been naughty. 'Well what are you doing here?' she enquired, the richness of her Scottish accent emphasising the last word. 'I've passed the scholarship': a simple statement in which I had no means of comprehending the opportunity being given to me.

'Oh my god what shall we do?' For Mother it was indeed a double-edged sword. She was pleased—no delighted—by my news, but she also saw the difficulties in buying a whole new school uniform, with five other children to provide for.

Retrospectively, this kind of scene must have been happening in dozens of homes around St Helens that day. Very many working class families were finding, for the first time ever, that their children could compete on equal terms, with those of more affluent means. Schools like mine taking many industrial families from Central Ward, Pocket Nook and Parr, did not get many scholarships but the four or five boys now on their way to Grammar School, with each having an opportunity denied to their parents, were pleased with their success. Some people still argue that for the likes of us to take up such a place confutes the true value of scholastic endeavour, in that we can never be provided with sufficient means to get the best from our education.

Perhaps it is true that many families, without the experience of the degree of support necessary to the advancement of their children; do waste very valuable time and money. However, it is far more important to recognise that because of sheer numbers alone, the vast majority of potentially bright children are to be found in this singularly inefficient mass. Put simply, there are plenty of clever children from working class homes. Even the process of buying the school uniform was traumatic and had to be done 'on credit.' However, I do know that when my dad saw the uniform hanging ready for me, he said, 'Wearing that means he will never have to go down the pit.' I had no idea that this was to change my life completely, to give me an opportunity to mix with boys who came from other areas and backgrounds.

There I was chrysalis gone, resplendent in my green blazer, cap sitting squarely on my head, leather school bag gleaming on my back. As I walked down the road to the Catholic Grammar School, the high wall all along to the side on my right heightened the tension already strong because of the seemingly endless journey. Two older boys met us at the gates. 'Do you want to join the ship club?' they asked, 'Everybody does.' This encouraged us. 'You have to give us half a penny with a yacht on it to become a member, that's the fee and it's a kind of badge as well.' We joined, nearly all of us. Daft isn't it, but no doubt those two characters are successful businessmen now, maybe even sailing on a yacht of their own.

My school, how quickly the identification becomes a part of us, was a three-form entry grammar school. Really quite small by today's standards, to me it seemed huge, I only knew two other boys in my class, and at that stage only about five or six others in the school. Our school, like so many other institutions loosely modelled on the public schools of the nineteenth century, had its initiation ceremony. I had already gone through one and been little the wiser, that truth was to dawn on me much later in conversations with others rooked the same way. The more spectacular and fearsome one followed at the first lunchtime.

I sat on the railings separating the playground from the rugby pitch, only mildly interested in the chasing game that appeared to be going on around the school. Since I didn't know anyone it was difficult to break into the various ball games, all played with a tennis ball, which were going on around me. Eventually someone came up to me and said 'Are you a new boy?' Considering the newness of my clothes an unnecessary question I would have thought. 'Yes' I replied, largely unsuspecting, but slightly disturbed at this newfound interest in me. 'Grab him,' one boy said to the other, but they had reckoned without the extra height given to me by the railings. I stood on the bottom rail and lashed out at one of them. Then leaping, off I ran away around the back of the school. There an awesome sight greeted me.

The playground dropped down about a dozen steps to a gateway in the bottom of the high wall which I had passed alongside that morning. The steps formed a three-sided pit with two high sides and one side made by throngs of boys, mainly second years, standing behind the metal rail. The fourth side was both entrance and exit, if that were possible, to this the 'black hole of Calcutta'. By now most of my first day classmates were down this hole and it was a seething mass of bodies shouting to be released. Further screams erupted each time another new boy was hurled down the steps. There was no escape. Boy after boy toppled downwards until everyone was engulfed in this sea of arms and legs. I suppose I was lucky, most of the other ninety boys were down the steps when I went in, and so my fall was short, perhaps three or four steps and my landing soft, being cushioned by so many below me. The torture did not last long, but for those at the bottom the discomfort was very real, and their cries were of pain and distress, not excitement. This was my initial induction completed and though the memory remains, I have heard of much worse in other schools.

An eleven year old, leaving a football school to go to a rugby school, finds new doors opened up to him. I had no idea what lay behind the portals of Knowsley Road, not half a mile from the school. I had never watched the Saints, or any team better than Haresfinch Rovers, the football team that played on the same field as us, nearby at Laffak. I did read the Wizard and was full of Wilson, but my only heroes so far had been Boxers. Now my world was to change in many ways as my experiences would grow, because I met many new people and challenges.

The school was at the top end of Dunriding Lane, behind the Bird in Hand pub, the Saints ground at the bottom. So it was not surprising that a certain affinity existed between them. Oddly enough, until I attended West Park (the St Helens Catholic Grammar School) I had seen neither. At the first rugby lesson I was one of those never to have played before. Boys from Wigan, Warrington and Widnes had played in their primary school, but I was put with those from Liverpool who had only ever played football. 'Here you, Harvey, play in the second row; it doesn't matter if you don't know the rules, just push when I tell you.' I did for a while and enjoyed the rough and tumble, learning not to get offside and not to pick the ball up in a loose scrum.

The first year team played only two matches and in the first of these I was still playing in the second row. We played on the Rose Bowl, a particularly euphemistic name for a large dusty natural bowl, across the road from the school. The ground was solid dirt with narrow strips of grass along the wings. Legend has it that during one match the referee Billy Bold, known to everyone who ever went to West Park, stopped the game, because a piece of iron was found sticking out of the ground. He insisted that this should be removed as it was dangerous. On finding that it did not respond to a simple pull, the players set about digging it up. About half an hour later the remains of a silver cross pram lay exposed and the resultant hole was far more dangerous than the original piece of handle.

No such event took place on the day I played there. Yes it was a singular experience in more ways than one. The game was closely fought and for me uneventful except in one crucial moment. We were awarded a five-yard scrum and the pack leader called for an attempt at a pushover try. We gradually pushed their pack backwards on to the line where they held. I found myself being bent double as the pressure grew. I lost the hold of my partner and was squeezed out of the pack like a pip from an orange. As I emerged sideways, the ball rolled in front of me out of their legs and I dived on it. The whole pack collapsed on top of me but the referee awarded the try. God bless him.

That was it, the only time I played second row for a team and the only time on the Rose Bowl. Like many of our memories the reality no longer exists. Pilkington's built their Head Offices there and that spot, etched in my memory because of my first try, is now covered by a huge office block surrounded by a lake.

I was found sadly lacking in that position and failed to distinguish myself in any other in that year. However, by the end of the summer term I had found that I could run with the best of them and did well in the school sports. This led to me playing in the backs in the second year, but I was not accepted as one of the skilful players, and was making little progress until fate played its hand.

One games afternoon I was put out of the way at full back, on the less fancied side. I was pleased to get a game and ran backwards and forwards, merrily chasing everything that came near me. One forward, renowned for his strength and directness, was the terror of his peers. His name was Joe Butts, and he played almost as he willed, with the rest of us. He broke through the middle at a mighty gallop, with assistance on either side. I stood flat-footed under the posts knowing that a certain try was on. I bent down as he approached fully expecting him to pass the ball. He didn't, and I clung on for dear life as his muscular body thumped into me. The ball ran loose and at the resultant scrum, the master in charge ran over to me and after checking that I had no bones broken said, 'That's the best tackle I have seen for a long time, very brave indeed.'

That week when the team sheet went up on the notice board, I was there: Full back- Harvey.

I held that position for three years and learned to catch and kick a ball from the hands. I especially enjoyed joining the back line and always relished the opportunity to score tries. However, I was a very poor goal kicker, which did not matter much for the team as others were much better. The master, Brother Steven, felt that for my own development as a full back I should learn to kick goals. 'Saturday's game is one of the easier ones of the season,' he said. 'You will kick the goals.' I instilled into all of my teammates that they must score as near to the posts as possible as I could not kick very well. They being kindly souls obliged. The result was that we scored fourteen times, all under or near to the posts. It was the kind of game in which each time they kicked off we scored. My personal tally was five tries and fourteen goals, this despite the fact that the second half was shortened to save embarrassment. The 1st XV teacher, watching from the touchline, asked for several of us to see him on the Monday morning. Far from receiving his congratulations for such a high scoring display, we were each caned for ungentlemanly conduct, to whit beating the opposition after we had crossed the try-line. He maintained that we should have placed the ball on the ground where we crossed the try line and that beating men in the dead ball area was both unkind and unnecessary.

In fact we were an excellent team and the school magazine reported, 'This has been a most successful season. The team established for themselves a reputation for open football of a very high order: handling, running, backing up and tackling were all excellent. Everywhere they went they elicited praise for the fast open rugby which they tried to play, and although there were outstanding individuals in the team the key to their success was the high standard of team work which they managed to achieve.'

We had the example of the newly formed West Park Rugby Club which provided excellent facilities in their new clubhouse and many of their members were old boys of the school and therefore took a great interest in us though the school magazine.

CHAPTER 5

View from the Terraces

Together with hundreds of other boys, going to the home matches, I trekked with the crowds up Knowsley Road, nipping in and out of the adults, dodging cars and running to get a place near the wall. The Boys' Pen, a singular institution of its time, was always thronged by youngsters eager to collect the goal kicks landing in its midst. Situated immediately in front of the pavilion and next to the tunnel it was near the heart of the action. Access was gained by a path that passed right by the window of the changing rooms and sometimes, if we were lucky, we caught a glimpse of someone in a red and white shirt moving around inside. The thrill of actually identifying who it could be was as important as the game itself.

That glorious smell of wintergreen, wafting across to us as the team emerged from the tunnel, came as a wonderful herald, soon after the first notes of the March of the Gladiators. Obviously many men played, and others will have their favourites, but for me the team always read; Moses, Llewellyn, Greenall, Gullick and McCormick. A great back division, each one a hero and arguably one of the best to have played for the Saints because of the power of the centres, the solidity of the full back, and the complimentary attributes of the wings. I loved the magnificent style of Llewellyn, like his namesake, as a prince of Welsh Wingmen, coupled with the sheer impudent virtuosity of McCormick, that magician of the wing.

Before Jim Sullivan (Sully) came to coach at St Helens, the forwards were known as the 'Easy Six'. But never when I saw them did I think that. There was Ray Cale, the destroyer of opposing backs; Alan Prescott a wing three quarter playing front row, and a variety of strong men, who combined magnificently to challenge all comers. I watched the Saints avidly for six years and marvelled at their strength and skill. George Parsons, Bill Bretherton and Vince Karalius together with Don Gullick in the centre—the mere sight of them was sufficient to frighten the life out of me. Jimmy Honey and Peter Metcalfe each thrilled me with their diverse skills. The blistering acceleration of Honey, the total indestructibility of Joe Ball and the balanced beauty of Metcalfe, were models for me to strive for.

Between them all, they took the town to Wembley in 1953. Literally it seemed that the whole town went to Wembley. As in other towns at other times, those that had been deprived of success reacted enormously to the possibility of some icing on the cake. Youngsters watching the games will rarely have the opportunity to play on the inside of the white lines, but they can dream of the day that they might just get a kick of a stray ball and a smile from a player.

I was twelve and John was ten, my dad told us he had bought tickets to Wembley. Yes, father at a rugby match! I don't think he had been to one, since the Saints had gone to Wembley in 1930. He was but one of many thousands, who embarked on coaches and trains, for the first time in years. We were kitted out in scarves and favours with suitable headgear for the occasion. Mine was a pit helmet painted red and white with a little plywood cup stuck to the front in place of a lamp.

Thousands of fans thronged the station yard at Shaw Street around midnight on the eve of the game. A good natured mass, easily controlled by the odd policeman who organised the various lines of supporters, needed for each separate train. The train was packed with happy laughing strangers, each united by a common cause. I slept in a luggage rack and so was wide-awake as we poured through the huge edifice of Euston Station as it used to be. Six o'clock in the morning is a strange time to see London for the first time. Always conscious of a chance to educate us, my dad took us sightseeing. On foot, for about five hours, a strange amalgam of pitmen, glassworkers and school children, walking in masses around the tourist centres of London. 'Up for the cup?' rang the cries from the indigenous population.

Indeed we were up for the cup. It was a huge and wonderful experience for us and I'm sure that the expense to our family had been calculated in the benefit we would gain in seeing the capital city.

We saw Covent Garden market at 6.30 a.m., interesting enough for us as we looked at the basket laden porters and viewed with awe the mounds of produce. A couple of apples and oranges satisfied our thirst, but we quickly realised that the real reason for our visit was the convenient reality of pubs serving at such an hour. Suitably refreshed we took in all the sights of Trafalgar Square, the Mall, the Palace and Westminster. We did not have a camera to take the usual photographs of the sentries at Buckingham Palace, horse guards trotting down the Mall, but these and other such novelties were being taken all around us. Our feet began to drag and so with the sun still rising in the sky, the road to Wembley was accomplished. We went up to the Stadium itself.

Luckily it was a typical Rugby League Cup Final day with a blue sky and warming sun. We waited outside of the twin towers, until the gates were opened around noon, and progressed to our seats. Wembley stadium was quite the most magnificent sight I had ever seen. Appearing to stretch endlessly into the distance, it shimmered in the sun. Gradually the fans came in, first as a trickle and then a great stream. By two o'clock the concrete steps around us were nicely filled, and sandwiches and thermos flasks had been emptied. The main stage of the pitch had been visited by sundry white-coated attendants fetching and carrying various items of equipment but nothing that we could recognise with any real interest.

Then quite suddenly the Saints party emerged from the tunnel, neatly kitted out in their new blazers, they strolled into the open space. A lady sitting behind us drew out her wooden rattle, used in the war by air raid wardens to sound the all clear, and whirled it in a frenzy of welcome. The clacker whipped across the spool and the unmistakable racket roared out. Crack, it stopped in mid-air as it resounded across my dad's head. Amid profuse apologies she pushed it deep into her bag and there it remained for the rest of the day. For Dad, the afternoon had really started with a bang.

Each player was welcomed in turn by shouts and applause and they reciprocated with smiles and waves. Everyone looked fighting fit and raring to go, we were convinced that winning would be a formality. Little did we know what was to come.

One of the items brought out by the men in white coats, was a very large set of step ladders which was placed in the centre of the pitch. The Guards' band played a series of rousing tunes and then a figure in a white suit came out and climbed the steps to great applause. It was time for the community singing, a central part of the Wembley experience in 1953. St Helens played Huddersfield and fans of both sides mingled happily throughout. In turn we sang a bunch of popular tunes with equal measure of gusto, but there was real passion in the singing of 'She's a Lassie from Lancashire,' when it was our turn to sing that refrain. 'Sally, Sally the Pride of our Ally,' was sung with almost the strongest fervour, as we tried to emulate Grace Fields, that well known star of stage and screen, from Rochdale, on our side of the Pennines.

Cup finals are notorious for controversy and that one was no exception. Huddersfield were fielding a young half back called Peter Ramsden, and many thought that the Saint's experienced combination of Langfield and Honey would exploit the youth and inexperience of their halves. However, with two disputed tries he proved them wrong. Once more the referee had played a significant part in the result of the game. As spectators we were far more than despondent; we felt thoroughly dejected.

The other sensation was caused by a shrewd piece of professionalism and the prejudice of a radio commentator. During one of the back moves at a crucial point of the game, Hunter, the Huddersfield full back, appeared to be coming into the line. Obeying the Rugby player's maxim, to take the man with the ball, Llewellyn came in from the wing and went to tackle him. Presumably the centre saw him coming and missed him out with the pass. Llewellyn, not noted as a destructive tackler ran into the full back more in error than malice. He dropped like a stone and lay still. A penalty was awarded and on ran the stretcher-bearers. Much was made of the incident and the radio commentator Harry Sunderland wrongly attributed the offence to Greenall, who was renowned for a particularly devastating high tackle which often resulted in injury for the receiver. Apparently the commentator, Harry Sunderland a very well-known Australian, described the incident in vociferous terms and was not welcomed at Knowsley Road for many years.

Hunter was carried towards the tunnel and found enough energy to sit up on the stretcher and watch the resultant goal sail in. They must have had a miraculous sponge in the dressing room that day, because it did not seem long before he was running back onto the pitch, with little sign of injury. Whatever the facts, and few if any spectators know them, the game was lost and the homeward journey was more like a funeral procession than a revel.

Honour was to some extent satisfied, when a week later the teams met again, and St Helens put over forty points on the board without reply. Much was made of the change of half backs because Metcalfe and Dickenson took a major share of the praise, but reference must be made to greater authority than I to substantiate or deny this claim. Certainly Peter Metcalfe became one of my all-time heroes, who was acclaimed in a meteoric rise to the top, before being cruelly struck down with a severe and near-crippling injury to a knee cap. He was young and highly talented, famously missing the Wembley defeat, but starring in the Championship victory against Halifax. All Saints supporters will know that Jim Sullivan played the more experienced Langfield and Honey at Wembley, and then changed his half backs to Metcalfe and Dickinson for the Championship play-offs. That change began the run of success with which we have become accustomed to in this town. Unfortunately for Peter Metcalfe his career was ended within two years when his patella split, never to be mended well enough to allow him to play again. He was twenty-four years old and he would have been in the Hall of Fame now if that injury had not ruined his career.

I am really delighted to say that I knew Peter Metcalfe though he probably never knew me. He was in the SS Peter and Paul's Pools and I called at his house in Woodlands Road and stood in awe as he looked for the sixpence needed for his weekly subscription. I talked to him, he was human, and he bridged the divide from the Boys' Pen to the pitch. My eyes probably gleamed as I stood looking at him. Though he may never be aware of me, I will never forget him. Such is the transient fame of sportsmen that few of the thousands that cheer their heroes of today, will know anything at all about this great player, crippled so young.

John (Todder) Dickinson played for many years and still turns up for past player events with Brian McGinn, no doubt still at Holy Cross School at the time I am talking about. Huddersfield figured prominently at that time in Rugby League, but for me they were simply a peripheral detail in one of my less appealing memories. I think that it was the next season that Saints were due to play there in one of the later rounds of the Challenge Cup (3rd March second round lost 5-12) and my dad once more promised to take us all.

I was due to play for the school in the morning, and the arrangements were made that I should join him and my brother at the railway station to catch the special. None of us felt that there was particular urgency in the time, as a comfortable gap existed between our game and the time of departure. I will never know the extraneous circumstances that pertained that morning but two teachers chose that day to meet head on in a point of principle. We only had one rugby pitch at school then, and games were often played some distance away at Red Rocks, on Eccleston Hill. Either pitch would have suited us as we were used to both. However, both Masters laid claim to the school pitch, much the best of any available. We were the junior side at home that day, the other boys being marginally our senior. Each of the Masters insisted that they would play without the bother of us running through the park, round the golf course and up to the cold and windy wastes of Red Rocks, using the pitches which West Park old boys used for their afternoon matches.

We boys stood around as the Masters conducted their argument in private, shut away in their changing rooms. The kick off time came and went and still we waited. Finally, amid scenes of gloom and despondence, the decision was announced to us. Both teams would play at the school, but we would have to wait until the senior match had finished. This may have been a compromise by them or simply pig-headed stubbornness but whichever it was, it completely cancelled any plans many of us had to attend the afternoon match at Huddersfield. Our pleas were to no avail. The decision had been made. In sullen silence we watched as the game progressed knowing that with every passing minute, our precious match was receding from us. Finally we played. More out of duty than any sense of honour we fulfilled our commitment and longed for the final whistle.

Meanwhile dad organised the seats on the train boldly defending empty ones, between hurried excursions onto the platform. The guard chivvied him around as the appointed departure time came. He, completely in the dark, was forced to bring John from the train and watch sorrowfully as it departed. With useless tickets in his pockets, both for the train and match, he proceeded to the hospital where he felt that I must surely be. His anger when the facts became known in the afternoon was bordering on rage. He complained about the lack of consideration, not only because of the loss of money, though this was considerable, but also because of the anxiety caused to my family. In my professional life as a teacher, this incident taught me to be aware of the consequences of such decisions that alter agreed times, especially when alternatives have allowed me any room for manoeuvre.

In true British style Dad wrote a letter of complaint, which stood on the sideboard throughout the weekend. As his anger subsided he decided not to embarrass me by his protest, and the letter was shelved, lest in some way my chances for the future would be jeopardised. Fortunately the Saints lost, and we took some consolation in the knowledge that we had been spared the pangs of disappointment at first hand.

In July, when Sports Day came I looked forward to racing, as I felt that I had a good chance of winning. My father often said, 'There is nothing for second,' which makes sense when you think of two boxers in a ring, but less so in a race. I did come second in the sack race, won by the Warrington Schools Champion, Joe Chamberlain, but I won the 220 yards race and one other, which was good enough for me to be awarded The Lower School *Victor ludorum*.

By this time the allegiance of the boys at school was firm. Each had his own town, and so the daily discourse revolved around several teams, and that year the 'Wires' were to have their day. Many of the boys from Warrington went to Wembley to see the only drawn Cup Final ever and some defied the Headmaster's ruling, to attend the historic match at Odsal Stadium on the following Wednesday. This, some of you will recall was watched by the greatest crowd ever at a rugby league match in England, with an official attendance of 104,000 spectators. Just how many were on and around that hole in the ground has never been quantified, but estimates range upwards to 120,000. It is well known that a great number saw little of the actual play, but those who wagged it from school that day, never accepted that they came within that category of unfortunates. They regaled us with tales of Brian Bevan, Jim Challinor and Co. so much so that fighting broke out on the playground, born no doubt out of frustration and jealousy. Stan McCormick, having been transferred from the Saints, got a winner's medal and often told us (later when I was playing for the Saints), tales of how the game was won.

In 1956 I was one of about 40,000 who crammed into Central Park to see the semi-final of the Challenge Cup between Saints and Barrow, a game of high drama fought between magnificent adversaries. Personalities abounded, men and boys were carried along on continuous waves of applause. As in all the best theatre, the action dragged me to the depths of despair and the heights of ecstasy. Everyone there will have their own memories, but I have two which stood out then and have persisted ever since: the attempted drop goal from Parsons which struck an upright about a yard from the ground and rebounded to him for a try under the posts. It was lucky maybe, but five glorious points on the scoreboard. The other, the fantastic solo try scored by Llewellyn to win the game and take us to Wembley. Obviously the state of the match, and the resultant prize attached influences my judgement, but it certainly ranks as one of the greatest tries I ever saw. From inside his own half with virtually the whole of the Barrow opposition in front of him, he continued to run and passed man after man, to finish with one of his celebrated and spectacular dives from five yards to touch down in the corner. The whole crowd stood on tip-toe and the noise rose in a giant crescendo as he progressed towards the line, running round some, pushing off others, resisting yet more. To a soul we applauded loud and long as he returned breathless to his position.

So our turn, as supporters of St Helens, unfolded, when the annual seeking of the Holy Grail, was once more accomplished. Wembley revisited was even grander. The match was against Halifax, a powerful team of that era. This time from a place standing down near the pitch, I viewed the event with all the composure and experience of a fifteen year old. My tall red and white stovepipe hat annoyed those behind me, and finally I was forced to relegate it to the floor. I remember much more actively singing with the rest of the community, and the great pleasure in joining with others in mutual celebration of an occasion. No sense of division existed before the game and the whole crowd treated everyone with concordance, emanating from the fraternity of the North. The villages and towns of Lancashire and Yorkshire had disgorged their inhabitants to Wembley's mixing bowl and though a veritable turmoil of noise, the separate affiliations which were obvious to all through their rosettes and favours, identified every local club; but still a real a spirit of community existed.

The songs of attachment, to the red and white roses, were sung with equal fervour, 'She's a Lassie from Lancashire,' followed by, 'On Ilkley Moor Bah't at,' and the waving of programmes came as an acclamation to each other, like the great amen. For once the teams emerged, walking like a great centipede to their presentation; they were greeted in singularly parochial terms.

The Chairman, Mr Harry Cook, proudly lead out the team that he firmly believed would win. Alan Prescot followed him, his head held high. He had promised us all that the team would win. We did not doubt him. He was the epitome of a rugby league forward—very fast on the break with a beautiful pair of hands. A former wingman who put on so much weight that he went to prop—a forward with brains and ability, brawn and courage, character and endurance. Captain of his town, his county and his country; an example to follow and certainly he led by example. Len McIntyre (who I recently learned was called 'Inner Tube', think about it!) and Nat Silcock completed a highly mobile front row. Both had played as centres and wings in their time and were proud of it. George Parsons, a hard-tackling Welshman, made up a solid second row with Roy Robinson. The loose forward shirt, often the star position, was worn by Vinty Karalius, youthful and lithe with muscles that bounced as he walked. Not yet the superman he became but well past the embryo stage. No easy six this that coach Sully had produced.

Steve Llewellyn, elegant as ever, strolled onto Wembley once more, this time accompanied by Frank Carlton who was to prove neat, precise and very effective in attack and defence. Both of them scored that day, each in their own individual way. Frank skipped along the touchline before cutting round in an effort to make it to the posts. Steve dived in at the corner treating us to a special. But the try of the game for me was that from Prescott. He charged from about thirty yards out with the authority of a bull, yet with the nimbleness of a gazelle. With three men clinging to his body he stretched out an arm, like an anteater's tongue, and touched down right in front of us. A very young Austin Rhodes, seventeen I think, tacked on two goals and the game was won 13-2.

At a late stage in the game, when losing was never in danger, and the players must have known so, no one better than the master centre Duggie Greenall, his centre parting sharp as a knife blade, his hair gleaming with Brylcream, stood out almost as a throwback to the past. He carried his relatively small frame of around eleven and a half stone on a pair of odd boots. Can one have a pair of odd boots, or an odd pair of boots? Anyway... he had refused the traditional new pair for the final, to march into battle in his old 8 and 10s. Markedly, odd feet were not his only distinguishing characteristics, for he could run on his knees and often baffled adversaries with the ability to recover after having been apparently felled by their blows. He fetched and carried using his 'old headedness' to protect those around him. He was indeed a target for the Halifax players who wished to disrupt the St Helens lines, and he had on occasions been known to react to provocation with a violent response. His opposite number was a veritable giant called Palmer, who harassed him mercilessly, taking advantage of his unusual calm. Duggie bore it patiently, smiling as he picked himself up, shrugging off the pain. He knew the tactics and refused to succumb to the sucker-punch and get sent off—especially after the furore of the Huddersfield final.

His patience was rewarded late in the game when he opened up his armoury and took out his most feared weapon. 'Mammy', like the slang expressions written on the wartime bombs, was a polite euphemism. This loveable word disguised a bazooka of a tackle. Flying in like a guided missile, on the blind side of the player, the side opposite to the flight of the ball, he launched himself at his opponent in a fearsome leap, his arms held short and tight, elbows tucked in, his knees drawn up in front of his stomach. Like a rocket he landed, exploding into the head and chest of the luckless Palmer. Greenall had 'given him Mammy', the kind of cuddle no one ever wants! His brains temporarily addled and his lungs emptied of air, Palmer crashed to the ground. Greenall leapt to his feet standing over the giant like some latter day David. Nowadays there would have been no doubt of the outcome, a quick blast on the whistle and probably dismissal, with the long walk to follow. Then, the penalty in the Halifax twenty-five area was a cheap price to pay for winning the war.

Moses, Finnan and Howard had their part to play as well, and we were treated to a new weapon called Austin Rhodes. He was a boy of seventeen who was to develop into a record-breaking goal-kicker and serve the club with distinction for years to come, including another Wembley Final in 1961. He is now a well-deserved member in the Hall of Fame after a long and successful career.

Alan Prescott collected the cup and also the Lance Todd Trophy, chosen as the best player on the field by the press. I don't remember the team doing a lap of honour but I do remember their homecoming. There are thousands of people who shared this experience and I would hope that this account helps them to remember the thrill of that evening.

The St Helens Town Hall square was packed to absolute capacity. Each person was supported by the others around them, arms pressed tightly to the sides, and feet were trodden on whenever anyone moved. Two hours we waited singing and laughing. Some people clambered up the boards and stood on top of the Queen Victoria statue; others climbed the trees surrounding the square, clinging precariously to their perches, like vultures waiting for a feast. The crash barriers creaked under the strain and still the crowd poured in. Sardines in a tin are free-range fish compared to that gathering!

A great shout of acclamation greeted the conquering heroes as their open-topped bus edged slowly to the steps. Each victorious gladiator was cheered as he mounted them, shaking hands with the Mayor and waving to us.

This time the team had come back with the cup and Victoria's Statue was drowned by the sea of spectators who thronged the Square. The players were washed up onto the highest steps of the Town Hall by the waves of supporters who sang and chanted for them. Then, Duggie Greenall famously 'gave us Mammy', the Al Johnson song, not the bone crunching tackle of the same name, and we all joined with him in raucous tones. The chairman, Mr Cook, held the Challenge Cup aloft as proof that the promise had been fulfilled. St Helens had won the cup for the very first time. The team that Jim Sullivan had constructed had brought home the bacon. The players and officials went into the civic reception and we all drifted happily home. We ebbed away, joyful that our heroes had come home successfully carrying the cup aloft to great cheers from everyone. That team was the one on which the foundation stone of the St Helens Rugby League Club was built. Before them no one had ever brought the Challenge Cup back with them, after them every team is thought of as failing if they can't win the Challenge Cup. That is totally irrational but they had joined the club of cup winners.

At that stage in my life I do not think that I had ever been inside the Town Hall, let alone feel that one day I might be one of those players on the steps, waving to an adoring crowd chanting my name: which was to happen just ten years later.

CHAPTER 6

Family Upheaval

Within a year or so after that wonderful occasion, in the late fifties we moved from Carr Mill and returned to the Finger Post where dad bought a sweet shop from his brother Tom and my Auntie Alice. 43 Higher Parr Street was just a few doors from Alma's Café. Both shop and café have long gone in the slum clearance of the sixties: but many people will remember the name. My father was born in Pitt Street, which was a cobbled street, with very small terraced houses, all blackened with the smoke of half a century of high-density housing. He was taking us back to where he had grown up and was used to living.

We were literally round the corner from Pitt Street and Atlas Street and straight across the road from the Parrvilion cinema and the Co-op shop, which had one of those wonderful pulley systems for dealing with cash and change. None of these places remain any more, some demolished and one, the Parrvilion, converted to A. T. Free's Glass Company. The living room come kitchen, at the back of the shop and the toilet in the back yard, were a definite lowering of standard from our comfortable house and garden in Carr Mill Road.

In part this was an attempt to get away from the coalface, but for a while at least, he worked at Groves Pit, as a day labourer, a great drop in status from being a coal miner. The remnants of that pit can be seen in Birkenhead Road, opposite to the recycling yard. Now part of the Ravenhead Development with many large shops including B & Q and many others, the Groves Pit was also known as Pilkington's mine as much of the coal produced there was used to fire the furnaces in the Glass Works. The two float glass producing plants, UK5 and UK6, now stand very close to where the old pit head used to be. These are a symbol of the loss of 20,000 production workers who worked in the old tanks, as opposed to the 2,000 who work there now.

However, dad thought that it was worth it to get away from the pit. He believed that between them, with mother working in the shop, they could make the shop pay enough for him to leave the pit for good. Living in a sweetie shop could be thought of as heaven for a child, but somehow that is not what I remember. Going to school, doing homework and serving behind the

Peter's father is wearing a black tie as Thomas had just died. John, Mother, Peter, Dad. Front Row. Ann, Catherine, Mary.

counter till eight o'clock at night, doesn't seem to fit the image created when we moved. However, it was there that I began to play records of my own; Elvis Presley was the sensation of the fifties and what an impact he had on our lives. Then there was The Maida School of Dancing, our place of choice on a Friday night, where I met Ruth Twist and learned to dance.

I also remember my brother Thomas dying and being brought back home to lie in his coffin in that kitchen room behind the shop. I was sixteen, and told to look after the other children whilst the grown-ups went out to McComases. This was The Queens Head on Higher Parr Street, named after a rugby player from earlier times. I still remember the anger I felt at being left with my dead brother and the other children as they went out, 'to enjoy themselves.' Now that I know the pain of loss, and the need to share that pain with relatives, the whole ordeal takes on a deeper significance.

We have very few photographs of Thomas and just one of all six children with my mother, taken at the White Cross Home on one Sunday when we all went. That was a very rare occasion for us all to go, though I do remember going with my mum a few times but I was not allowed to go into the ward where he was. So I wondered just what was going on in there that I wasn't allowed to see. The important thing about my brother Thomas was that his genetic condition could just as easily have been one that I was born with, and it would have been me that died at fourteen. I was, for a time, crippled with infantile paralysis, and taken to a specialist who said that I would grow out of that condition. Also it was thought that my brother John had contracted polio and would have to have his legs supported for the rest of his life. Both of our conditions were in fact temporary ones, whereas Thomas unfortunately died of his.

History, they say, has a way of repeating itself. I know that my mother was very upset by having to live in a house with an outside toilet and once more having to wash in the kitchen, as we did not have a bathroom. She didn't openly complain but there was a resignation about her having to give up her lovely semi-detached house at Carr Mill.

However, when her sister Annie split with her husband Ian Cameron, she brought her two boys Robert and John down here, from Scotland, to live with us in Higher Parr Street. Once more the family was sharing accommodation and Cathie was happy to be able to share with her sister. Later her other sister Jean Young joined them and a tiny clan of Scottish people were here to stay. Not exactly a good place to begin the rest of my journey, an over occupied house in a slum clearance area.

CHAPTER 7

Schoolboy Trials and Tribulations

It may be a revelation to some people, but it is very important to know the process which enabled schoolboys to progress in rugby union in the 1950s.

Around the beginning of December each year, young hopefuls would try to spread their wings, and gain a place in the schoolboy side of either Liverpool or Waterloo. These two clubs were by far the two most important on the Lancashire side of the Mersey. It is difficult to imagine now, the dominance that they held back in the fifties. One had heard of Birkenhead Park and New Brighton, but to me crossing the Mersey was indeed an expedition which I didn't want to undertake, but the other alternatives Liverpool and Waterloo were closer to home. These two clubs were considered to be much better connected than West Park Old Boys, which would have been the natural choice for me and the other boys at our school.

Mr Wainwright, our senior rugby master, liked the idea of his boys playing for Waterloo. 'A better class of member you know,' he had told us. We did as we were told and liked it. It would be December 1956 when I played my first trial. I remember making the pot of tea for breakfast on the morning of the trial. It was pitch black as I went outside to dispose of the spent leaves down the grid in the backyard. It was very cold as I returned from the outside toilet and I wondered where this Waterloo was anyway. I was confused because I had been told that I had been offered a place in the under 16 trial team to play at Blundellsands. I had heard of Waterloo (Napoleon had been beaten there hadn't he?) but never Blundellsands. The long journey on the bus to Liverpool and the electric train to Blundellsands station (now I understood!) sticks fiercely in my memory. Even some of the conversation between Keith Northey, the school rugby captain, Mr Wainwright and me, lingers in my ears.

'Just look at that ground Keith, its massive.'

'Look at the stand.'

'What a belting pitch.'

'Now boys you will have to be careful to judge the touchline correctly,' Mr Wainwright warned. 'The stands and that banking are very deceptive you know.' I'm sure he meant well, but it was useless information to us just then, without the experience of ever having played on anything other than a school pitch. Then there was the clubhouse, very grand I thought. 'What an enormous fire! Black coke stacked up in a great banking, smouldering grey smoke curling up the chimney.

The game was not a memorable one for me but I was convinced that I would get in the team. Strangely I waited after the match. For the first time ever I felt that tension built up by waiting. What were they doing in that room? 'Good game son, don't worry you'll be picked.' I was not worried until the flat-capped members told me not to. Here they come. The shuffling of feet stopped. The chinking glasses were held motionless. The man with the team sheet stopped walking, blew his nose noisily, and fastidiously returned his handkerchief to his tweedy pocket. Everyone was looking at him, waiting. My name would be the first one to be read out as I was the full back. I had never played anywhere else, always at the top of the sheet, sure to be first out.

He coughed. 'The team to play New Brighton on the fourth of December is: full back Currie, Merchant Taylors.' Dumbfounded I looked at him. Surely he had made a mistake—I had played well hadn't I? Apparently not well enough, as he continued to reveal the team. 'Centre Northey.' At least Keith had got in, and so he should. He was the best player on the field. I looked at him and he shrugged. Then, to my utter amazement the tweedy man, reading the list said, 'Wing—Harvey, St Helens Catholic Grammar School.' I looked again at Keith and we both smiled. The rest of the team was immaterial to either of us, the selector went through the various positions and I saw heads rise or fall as boys' names either appeared or were omitted.

The congratulations of our teacher were warm and genuine, but his surprise at my wing selection was no less than my own. He, like me, was well aware that I had never, ever played in that position in any school game. The explanation was simplicity in itself. 'We thought you had a grand game and deserved to be picked, but the other boy has club connections and we wanted him in the team.' I now know that it is quite common for the powerful persuasive influence of teachers, or others for that matter, to affect the selection of a team, but then it was a simple matter. I had been better than him and felt I should have been picked. Equally, at least fifteen other boys' names which had not been heard at all by the gathering felt the same. The great heat, of the now deep red fire, warmed our legs as we talked. 'Never mind, you are both in the team and that is what is important.'

The master's statement did not initiate an argument as we both agreed with him. None of us were to know then, just how important for me that switch in playing positions was to be. The trial was only the precursor to the match against New Brighton on the following Saturday.

The match report by W. B. Croxford in the *Liverpool Daily Post* contained the opinion that New Brighton was beaten by, 'quite simply the best Waterloo under 16s side seen since the War.' Heady praise for those not used to seeing their name in print. To any seasoned player, the match reports are weekly events, but to a schoolboy they are indeed a rarity. I used to go to the public library, on my way home from school, just to see if our game had been reported. Usually it had not. To stand and turn the large pages as they resisted in their metal frames was exciting and I was thrilled to find my name in the paper. Often one had to wait while assorted adults, some really interested, many simply finding a warm, quiet place from the cold, flicked casually through the papers. Only the *Liverpool Daily Post* regularly carried a schools' report, but sometimes a column inch or two could be found in the *Daily Telegraph*, and each were scanned for some mention. That particular match report credited me with two tries and a hand in another, and I was said to be 'impressive' in both decision making and anticipation.

More importantly, though I did not know it at the time, a variety of schoolboy selectors had attended that match, and I received an invitation to play in the next Lancashire Schoolboy trial—as a wingman. The value of meeting, and playing with boys from other schools and walks of life, should not be understated. I met one of them fifteen years later, and he greeted me with, 'Do you remember playing with me for the under 16 side at Waterloo?'

The first Lancashire schools' trial was played at Warrington. It poured with rain and the pitch was a quagmire. The old ramshackle timber shed serving as a pavilion, dressing room and bar, bore no comparison to the relative grandeur of the Waterloo Clubhouse, but then the warmth of relationships owes more to the heat of the combat than the opulence of the surroundings. I managed to score again, and was delighted with my efforts against boys two years my senior. I held one of the South Lancashire wing spots, the other going to Bob Ingham—a flier from Cowley, our arch rivals. No one expected me to make the full Lancashire side—and so no one was surprised when I didn't.

However, by the Easter time and the second Lancashire game, either I had impressed some more selectors, or another player had blotted his copybook, as I was picked as reserve to travel, in the game against Cumberland at the Vale of Lune. We played Cowley on 3 April 1957, and as usual it was a hard fought game with no quarter asked or given. The result was close as usual, but more importantly, it resulted in three of us needing hospital attention. For the first time I sat in the waiting room of the Providence Hospital, and came under the wing and care of Sister Duffy. The work that this lady had done in the casualty ward of that hospital should entitle her to the highest award for service which the land can offer. She looked at the swelling on the back of my hand. 'I reckon it's broken—x-ray for you.' She was right. 'A cock up splint and a roll of plaster should see that right. You won't be playing silly games for a few weeks. Serves you right—just look at the three of you, you should all be in school.'

Ever one with a sympathetic approach, not this one, hard as nails but as soft as my cap. Hundreds, if not thousands of rugby players have been treated by this lady. So much so that 'a man and ball' pass in St Helens is known as a 'Sister Duffy'. Sister Duffy was duly honoured when she became a Freeman of St Helens, and I was one of the people who recommended her, when one of the new hospital wards at St Helens Hospital was called the Sister Duffy Ward.

Notification to play in these county matches consists of a small white card with instructions printed on one side. The postcard arrived about a week later: 'Report for the Lancs Schools *vs* Cumberland and Westmoreland on 24 April, at the Vale of Lune.' The terseness of it belied the joy I felt and the disappointment in the immediate knowledge that I could not go. She had said that it would be a minimum of three weeks before the metacarpal healed. I pleaded with the hospital to take the splint off earlier, but rightly they refused. 'Come and see me on the Friday night and I'll see what I can do.' Perhaps her words held just a little hope.

Strapped up with an instruction not to play I arrived at the sunlit bowl, flexing my wrist and clenching my hand. 'It will be all right. If they tell me someone has not turned up I'll play.' I was not really convinced by my thoughts. The team was complete and I was a spectator. Still, that day remains one of my sporting memories because of the beautiful setting. My broken hand was the only bone injury I sustained in over 350 matches and I can still feel the nodule as I type this today.

The sun shone brightly and it was warm and still. The ground framed in a rising landscape was perfect. Several families were sitting on the hillside overlooking the ground and as I watched from the stand, I envied their more spectacular view. I know nothing of that game but I knew I must return someday and sit on that hillside. That picture is still vivid and the ambition unfulfilled. With my brother John, I did watch Lancashire v Gloucestershire nearly twenty years later, in a county championship match; unfortunately in the pouring rain, and certainly not sitting on the hillside.

The next season (1957-58) held better things for me, as by now I was becoming known in the local schoolboy circles, and usually played on the favoured side, often a great advantage. One of the trials was held at Liverpool Collegiate grounds and I can still see now the massive frame of Ray French, one of our biggest opponents from Cowley School, playing Number 8 and pushing the whole pack up field. He was known then as 'Fat Frenchie', but he completely dominated that pack, appearing to hold on to the props and push right through the second rows driving all before him. Ray and I became good friends and I was to meet him in the first Lancashire Trial as we both began our senior career.

I managed to make the county team that year, again as.a wing, though by now I was playing centre for my school. The Cumberland game was at Carnforth and was played on a bone hard pitch on a steaming hot day. We

Lancashire Schools 1958 at Waterloo. Ray French is 5th player from right on the back row. Peter Harvey 2nd player from left on the front row.

won, but I finished up once more in hospital. The x-ray revealed a sprung collar bone, an injury that was to have a strange effect on my future. Nothing was done about it and the bone reset with a distinct knob on the shoulder. Tackling in the conventional way, became very painful indeed as the shock of the impact was transmitted down my arm causing considerable pain.

It is still remarkable that an Under 16 player could be picked for the County Schools side, even if the selectors just wanted to include me for the experience. We should also acknowledge the work done by all of those teachers who spend many hours organising these trials and matches. For example, I still have cards sent to me by L. G. Fluke, Hon. Sec. of the Lancashire Schools RFU (South West Section). These will be replicated by teachers from each of the four areas of the county. I guess that each county will have similar structures, and this represents an army of people willing to spend time to find the talent in the hundreds of schools in the country. I think he was a housemaster at Liverpool College, small and precise, with very neat, but tiny writing. Len, not to his face of course, represented that welcoming body of men, who dedicated their lives to the education of our middle class pupils, and in meeting boys like me, helped the working class as well. Considering what is to come in later chapters I have to say that they and almost everyone else involved in Rugby Union did not understand what it was like to be a working class boy.

At this point I want to say something about my height and weight. No one referred to me as small, because in fact I was just as tall as most of the boys playing in the backs at this time. In fact only my father used to tell me that I was tall. For our family I was tall. My father and grandfather were both only an inch above five feet, and I was six inches taller than that by the time I was fourteen. There was a boy from the Wigan area who went to our school who was a weightlifter. He was allowed into the gym at lunchtimes to practice with the set of weights which we had there.

I started going into the gym, rather than play tick rugby with a tennis ball in the playground. This had two effects, unlike Tom Brophy and Keith Northey both school friends; I did not learn to sidestep very well. I tended to bulk up in the shoulders and upper arms, as we bench-pressed our way through lunchtimes. I knew that I was stronger than most, bigger than many, and so tended to run straight and hard. Philip Knowles, one of my classmates, met me many years later and said, 'You have shrunk; you were six foot at school, what happened to you?' Of course I never was six foot, but I always played as if I was. In my mind, and with the encouragement of my dad, who said, 'You have all the advantages, you are tall.'

I played direct rugby, to the extent that I became a devastating tackler, and was sometimes called upon to sort people out. I have never thought of myself as small. Yes I have short legs, but a normal large body. Many pitmen have this kind of physique, with very strong short levers, with heavy shoulder development. I am making the point now, because reading match reports later, so many of them say that I am small. I have always been six foot in my mind, and people had to be six foot six to appear tall to me.

I had played against Wade Deacon Grammar, the year before and we were thoroughly walloped. Their pack had hammered ours and it was like Custer's Last Stand from where I stood at full back. Both my shoulders were damaged in tackles, and together with the rest of the team, I blamed the 33 points scored against us, on the strong running of their back row. For the first time I had met up with players wearing shoulder pads and felt that this had given them confidence to run into us.

I remembered the lesson and bought a pair myself after the sprung shoulder. The wearing of pads was quite common in our part of the world because of the Rugby League interest. However, certain RU referees would not allow it as they thought, 'It was not the done thing.' The shoulder pads became a regular feature of my apparel and they certainly gave me confidence. Too much for some opponents, who felt that the crash tackle which I developed with them, was in some way unfair.

By now I was a regular member of the first fifteen, and really enjoying rugby. Not surprising really when one thinks that the team contained about nine players who later won representative honours in either League or Union.

Tom Brophy (Liverpool, Lancashire and England and later Barrow) had graduated into the team, despite being criticised for his elusiveness at scrum-half earlier in his school life. Mr Wainright, known to all as Dico, punished him for beating people before he passed, rather than passing directly from the scrum. Scrum-halves were supposed to do diving passes but Tom would take off and beat the back row before delivering to the backs. The undoubted star of the side was Keith Northey (Birkenhead Park and Lancashire, then St Helens and Widnes), who somehow failed to impress selectors but enthralled us with his superb breaks and handling. Both were later to gain county and international honours, one at Union, the other League. Jim Fairclough (Wigan and Saints), Stan McLeod, Jim McCormack (both Wigan), John Donovan (Saints and Oldham) and Joe Chamberlain (Rochdale), were five more from that side who later served professional clubs well. A couple more, like Ray Shuker, made a big impact in junior RL and Bill Lawrenson (West Park and Birkenhead Park), went on to play for Lancashire RU. Not bad going for one team of schoolboys. Chris Hesketh, who later captained a Great Britain RL Touring team in Australia, was also at school a year or two below us, but he played much of his rugby away from Alder Hey Road where the school pitches were then situated.

None of the players mentioned were to develop into forwards and it was in this department that we were weakest. That year 1958-59 we were defeated by Cowley 35-5 and it remains in my memory as the best display by any team I have ever played against. Certainly it was the biggest defeat I ever felt and along with the aforementioned drubbing by Wade Deacon the year before, was the only time I have known the misery of having thirty points scored against me. Nevertheless when it came to the county matches I was still there, and in 7-a-side matches, the school was unbeaten in the Merseyside area.

The world of schoolboy rugby has grown enormously since then and many opportunities, now available, were denied to us. The Roslyn Park Sevens were simply an item in the press, and Millfield School was somewhere posh that got its picture in the *Rugby World* magazine. How insular we were.

Then came Lower Six, and Brother Augustine promoted Keith Northey and I to Prefects. This was an unusual move as no one makes it to Prefect before Upper Sixth. One explanation might be that the head teacher knew that both Keith and I wanted to become teachers, and would be applying for a college place at the end of the year. Both of us were very good at games, and both wanted to become PE teachers. Keith Northey was such a natural ball player, with wonderful hand to eye co-ordination, that virtually every game which he took up looked so simple for him. In team games we complemented each other, but I never had quite the touch of class that he possessed. Keith is just six weeks older than I am, but that age difference, was to become vitally important to me, though I did not know it at the time.

We both applied for college in the Lower Sixth and both of us were accepted, Keith to Hopwood Hall, Manchester and me at Strawberry Hill, Twickenham. But there was one very telling difference between us. I would have to wait a year because I was still only seventeen on the 1 October 1958, the qualifying date for college entry. During that summer we both played cricket, as we had done before and we got this tribute in the Head teacher's Report:

Since Brother Serenus left I have been unable to discover exactly what happened to our cricket team last season, but it looks as if, in common with most cricketers during a very wet summer, they were sunk without trace, although I do recall that between showers, Keith Northey broke two long standing records with the highest individual score and the highest aggregate. I think it is also true to say that Peter Harvey topped the bowling averages and also broke the school record in taking 9 wickets for 13 runs.

I remember another match against Prescot Grammar School, probably the year before, when John Augustitus took five wickets for no runs, and I took five wickets for five runs. Cricket was an important game at our school and we had wonderful practice facilities, with six nets in pristine condition. Keith also played for Lancashire Schools at cricket, and for many years, as a senior at St Helens Cricket Club, he was a mainstay of the team. My wife Ruth's cousin, Kevin Twist, also played for Lancashire Schools a couple of years after Keith.

In the upper sixth, with Keith gone to teacher training college, the school did me the honour of making me the first fifteen rugby captain. Perhaps more surprisingly, the headmaster Brother Augustine also appointed me as Head Prefect and Head Boy of the School. 'Leadership abilities,' he had said 'are more important than academic performance in this job.' I cannot define what he meant but some people say that no one ever picked a fight with me because I was hard. I don't know about that but if I was hard I was also fair. Thank you for the honour Brother, I hope that you did not regret it.

That season 1958/59 someone, somewhere, was pulling for me. I was given the Lancashire Schools Captaincy, this time as a centre, by now my favourite position. But the opportunity of a chance at the English Schools' team was so remote that I never even thought about it. For some reason, Lancashire Schools did not take part in the national competition, and though Mike Lord, the skipper in the 1958 Lancashire Schools' side, had gone for a trial, no one could remember any boy from Lancashire ever playing for the England Schools' side. I have never found out how it happened, or who proposed me in the first instance, but I think it must have come from the Cumberland and Westmoreland game of 1958. For when my invitation came it was to play for the North of England, as a wingman once more—shades of 1895 and the separation of the Northern Union still in force even at schoolboy level.

By now I was well at home at the county level (schools) and thoroughly enjoyed those games. The most important was a game versus Yorkshire, again at Waterloo. The match was played during an intermittent snowstorm and was one hell of a battle, fed by keen rivalry and high standard players, striving with might and mane to defeat each other, which led to a great game. The stand was well filled with spectators, though the dirt terraces were desolate. The spectators shouted and stamped their feet roaring us on. It is funny how in those conditions, the game is played up and down the touchline, under the stand. The game lives only in my memory, but it was one of do or die. One try followed a clean break through the middle finished by a round arm, one-handed pass behind the fullback, for Bobby Edge of Ormskirk to score. One of the penalty goals was a prodigious kick by a very tall second row who fancied his chance from half-way. Their left wing was a boy called Bussey who could really motor. They kept chipping the ball back over the forwards to him, and after several near misses, they scored from the ploy. It seemed that we must lose but we stuck to our defensive positions and managed to score through Mike Beddow, another of Cowley's young stars, later to become a Lancashire cricketer. A late try from George Bridge, again of Cowley, settled the issue 17-9 in our favour. The match reports were glowing with tributes to both sides and apparently I was considered to have done a good job as captain.

Derek Jewell in the *Liverpool Daily Post* wrote:

> There is no denying the fighting spirit of these Lancashire boys nor the leadership of their captain, Harvey, a sturdy, flame haired centre of all round excellence. He breaks through explosively with fierce hand off and hip-flick, tackles surely, and covers with the zeal of one who hates to see his line crossed and who believes that no cause is ever lost. His example drove Lancashire on so that they came from behind three times.

One of the boys who played in our beaten pack that day, was later to rise to be a very bright star in the English firmament. Again from the same match report, Jewell says:

> The men who did most to hold this disjointed eight together were Greenwood, a quick gobbler-up of unconsidered trifles, Hodgson who is also a good kicker, and Bridge. Cheshire I imagine, will give this pack a testing, even if they cannot approach the flamboyance of the Lancashire backs.

It may not have been the best pack Richard (Dick) Greenwood ever played with, but it set him on his way to his England Caps. We will meet again much later though then on opposite sides of the RU/RL divide.

CHAPTER 8

Schoolboy International: Opening the Doors

The invitation to take part in this trial came as a complete surprise. Burton-on-Trent was another unknown pitch to me. Not that one could wax lyrical about the journey and the scenery on arrival, but I do recollect the odour. The rich dark smell of brewing was there in abundance. '119 breweries' someone told us, 'Not all in production now of course, but still plenty to smile about.' I was relatively unconcerned about this staggering figure, but tasted the flavour of a couple of the cans they offered us as a present.

'But I'm a centre,' I kept on protesting in the changing rooms. My disinclination to play wing was ignored. 'Make the best of it, take all of your chances,' was the sound advice given to me by parents and school. I did. When the first try was scored I offered to convert. Some chance of that. The ball lay near the touchline and players simply walked away from it. In the best traditions, all copied from others because I had hardly kicked at goal for years. I teed it up and, with a long run and a mighty heave I managed to miss by a mile. Nobody seemed to care very much. Then a chance really came—a cross kick popped up for me and I scuttled in—for what the papers called, 'A brilliant solo effort.'

Half time and my prayers were answered. The posse of selectors came out and made the changes. Here there and everywhere boys changed jerseys, and hey presto, I was in the centre. So on to the next and final hurdle, I had made it through to the final trial.

I stood and looked at the pictures in the Rugby Club. Old place this I thought, pretty proud members I guess. Dressing rooms aren't too much though—not a patch on Waterloo. Then an odd thing happened. Maybe it happened to everyone—I don't know. One of the selectors called me over and shook my hand.

'You're Harvey from Lancashire aren't you?'

'Yes Sir,' was the only possible answer.

'Pleased to meet you. Come over and meet the other chaps.' Nice bloke this I thought. Then one by one, as in a presentation line up, I was introduced to several distinguished gentlemen. At the same time, I felt that it was a considerable welcome, to take the trouble to make me feel at home. It certainly worked. Years later, I got to wondering about that introduction. Was I in some way the sacrificial lamb: the means of cementing the broken relationships between my county and the rest of the schoolboy country? I don't know, and probably never will.

Trying to recall the game itself, I meet with no success. Neither can I remember how I got there, who accompanied me, how I returned. Funny that. Do schoolboys really take their Masters so much for granted? Maybe it was a straightforward match and journey but I have no memory of it. Only the pictures on the wall and feeling that it was hereabouts that it all started. I fancy there is an inscription on the wall about William Webb Ellis and Rugby School in 1823. I can't say that I even visited the famous Rugby School but I was there at The Rugby Club.

It would be false to assert that I remember vividly the naming of the team, but I do recall standing by an oval table eating sandwiches and drinking tea. The aroma of cigars, strange for me except in one other setting (Saints and Wigan on Boxing Day) was pungent. The idle chatter ceased and ears were pricked. It was explained to us that two teams had been chosen as the match against France had an age limit on it, Under 18. The game against the Welsh Schools was open to anyone still at school. There were plenty of boys already wearing the rose and insignia of ESRFU, those boys had played at the fifteen-year-old level, others had already played previously at the eighteen-year group. They looked very smart and seemed to ooze with confidence.

The teams were read out, and I felt a real sense of achievement, when I was picked for both sides. My pleasure was intensified by the announcement of the two captaincies—Harvey against the French and Trevor Wintle for the match against Wales. We will meet Trevor again later in this story.

It wasn't my first trip to London as I have described my two journeys to Wembley a few years before, but for the first time I had to make it alone. To anyone used to the metropolis it will be difficult to imagine the sense of awe which a visitor feels. To those modern children, accustomed to flying the world on package tours, the episode would be child's play indeed. To me, the bustle of the commuters, the warren of the underground and the steep efficiency of the elevators, combined to make my arrival both bewildering and full of wonder. The challenge, to read the directions of one of those terminal diagrams, is forgotten once mastered. The diversity of clothing styles, languages and types of people become commonplace to the regular visitor, but to me it was a new world.

I emerged from the Tottenham Court Road underground exit and looked around me. When in doubt ask a policeman. 'Could you tell me where the YMCA is please?' He looked at me and smiled, placed his hands on my shoulders and turned me round. 'There it is son, across the road.' Bag in hand and reporting instructions in my pocket I went in. The main item on the

heads were dropping and I slipped into the vernacular, a strong Lancashire accent belted out at them. There was no need for speech making. 'For God's sake let's have some effort, there's still time to win this game.'

The renewed effort began to pay dividends. The breaks were coming now, and play was more often in the French half. Nick Silk playing number 8, started to show his class around the loose mauls. The French chattered at each other. The clock in the corner swept silently on. Again and again we were foiled in our efforts but now everyone was being more decisive. The ball came quickly to the backs and each in turn had chances. Alan Jones on the other wing looked magnificent, tall and well balanced, but still they held out.

The turning point came when Lamb, a very tall curly headed second row struck a penalty following a handling offence in the loose scrum. The French had turned away arguing with each other as the decision was given, each blaming the other. Now the game was ours to take. Several more attacks faltered at the last hurdle and then my chance came. A free kick awarded around the half way line, looked unpromising, but as the French pack turned away once more, I called to Roger Hill for the ball direct from his tap. His long pass came quickly. With the defence still turning I swung outside my centre. The way was open down the right side and running hard I cleared the cover. Like a fox running from the hounds, I crossed the twenty-five yard line and came inside the full back. There was nothing in front of me now, just a run straight for the posts. I made it with the odd yard to spare and flung myself at its foot, clasping the ball tight to me, as I lay for what seemed like an age, beneath its shadow.

I rolled over and the sky was blue and clear. As if through a fish-eye lens the stands stared down on me. Exalted, I rose and walked back to the cheers of the crowd and the congratulations of my teammates. The clock face beamed a broad smile; its finger hand jumped another minute. Just five more left. Eleven points all. The French boys stood around the posts ready to charge. We stood on the half way line waiting for the *coup de grâce*. Silk took untold care to set up his shot and slowly paced out his run-up. He stopped; they charged and kicked the ball away. Mr L. M. Boundy, a senior international referee, whistled and awarded a free shot at goal, no charge could be allowed this time. The huge finger swung another minute. Once more the ball was placed and the run-up measured. Silk started his short run, and once more they charged. Put off by their proximity and the tension of the situation he sliced the ball outside the post.

Our short protest to the referee was waved away and within minutes, the no-side whistle sounded. With mixed feelings of elation and disappointment, we all shook hands and trooped from the field. Few boys exchanged jerseys, for, like me it was their first and for some, their only one in the England colours. Boundy, the referee, later claimed that his French had failed to convey to them the substance of the no charge rule. We all knew the law and they had successfully circumvented it. More likely he felt that a draw was a fitting result and perhaps he was right. I have used many devices since, to ensure that friendship is fully maintained between boys, by allowing, or disallowing, perfectly fair or unfair goals to protect a drawn result when teaching boys to play football.

Certainly there was no animosity whatsoever at the post-match celebration, a dinner at the Bedford Corner Hotel, where I had to respond to the toast proposed by M. Haitse, Vice President of the French Rugby Union. Besides the fine companionship of teammates like Nick Silk, David Protherough, John Tarbit and the rest, my outstanding memory is the rousing singing of *Alluete*, led by the French Team, and enjoyed by the English, who joined in with exaggerated accents. The essence of Rugby Union was encapsulated in that day. An important game played for enjoyment, staged in the best conditions, controlled by a top grade referee; followed by a slap-up meal with official speeches, and completed with a grand sing song for the participants.

St Helens Public Library has never had a more interested schoolboy, than on the couple of days following Easter Monday 1959. Not only were the two regular papers scanned, obscure reports were sought in countless rags. To my delight many papers carried a report either direct from the match or cribbed from another report. I laughed and yet was secretly pleased by the Peter Wilson report. My Father had talked about him many times and I knew that he was a respected sports' writer, though not noted for his rugby reports. He certainly did not know anything of my background or he may well have chosen others to compare me with. Writing about the game he said:

> What's more it had a perfect story-book ending, when Peter Harvey, fittingly enough the England captain, looking like an embodiment of Harry Wharton and Bob Cherry of the immortal Grey Friars School, made a magnificent fifty-yard-plus solo effort to tie the scores with only minutes to go. What an example these youngsters provided for their more solid elders.

Thank you Peter, but really, Grey Friar's School? I had never even seen a public school never mind any suggestion that I might have attended one, but yes here I was the Captain of English Public Schools.

The London rugby buffs were very quick off the mark and the tapping up process began immediately. I have a letter from Lt-Col. C. D. K. Burnaby on behalf of Rosslyn Park Football Club. He writes:

> Each year we ask a few boys while still at school to join this club as schoolboy members and in accordance with this practice our committee have asked me to invite you . . . Trevor Wintle who will be playing with you on Saturday is a member and has already had a couple of games for us. You might be interested to know that two Lancashire County players are members of our current 1st XV namely Arthur Crick and Roy Lightfoot.

I got to know Arthur Crick and his connection with the Guinness Company later but here he was being used as bait for a schoolboy from the North. I played with Roy at Liverpool and nearly bought my first car from him, but that was later. The tapping up process had started even before I played against Wales and it continued later.

The most momentous week of my short rugby life was not yet over. We reported on the Friday to Cardiff in time for the match against Wales. There were six changes from the Monday and so we took the opportunity to work out with our new teammates. Trevor Wintle from Lydney was to captain the side and he took over the running of the session. It is almost unbelievable that an international side, albeit at schoolboy level, should be without a coach of any kind. Perhaps one could argue especially at schoolboy level. Teams need coaching. No wonder that so few of those talented enough to make the England side at fifteen and eighteen years managed to go right through to the full international side.

The present set up is much more conducive to bringing talent through a system operating at all levels. There is real evidence to show just how effective continuous coaching can be as shown in John Griffith's book, *100 Years of England Schools Rugby*.

Jeff Edgar and Trevor Wintle seemed to operate much more smoothly than our half-backs of the Monday afternoon. Perhaps it was their extra year at school but they both seemed balanced and confident with a quickness to set us free onto good ball. At any rate I was happy to fit in as ordered during the practice.

Saturday 14 April 1959 was a beautiful clear day, still and warm, hot even in the shade. The ground, Cardiff Arms Park, was much more open and the stands further away from the pitch. There were 10,000 spectators; twice as many as at Twickenham but being further from us their voices did not carry the same. I do remember vividly that they booed us roundly when we went out for the team photograph. 'A sporting lot these Welshmen,' I thought.

The match was played at great pace with fine play from both sides. They scored first, but we replied with two good tries, both converted. Holding the 10-3 lead almost to half time. Ken Jones, the Welsh captain from Gwendraeth Grammar School, came away from a scrum running towards me. I checked and stood upright ready to swing a short arm at him. This head high tackle was very effective, and since my shoulder injury, had developed as a lethal part of my armoury. He ran on around Edgar and into my domain. The arm cocked, ready, then, in a flash of remorse as I foresaw the effect of the killing blow, I changed my mind. He's their captain, here on the Arms Park, you can't lay him out. Foolishly, I tried to tackle low, but the fatal indecision caused me to miss. I hit him around the thigh with a swinging arm but failed to hang on. The crowd roared as he skipped around me and set up the try. He may even have scored himself.

A black cloud descended on me as I rose from the ground. I may have saved my side's last match, but I felt that I had caused them to lose this one. No one made anything of it but I knew that it was my fault. One never knows but I don't think that ever, after that, I felt in the least bit sorry for anyone who fell foul of that crunching head high tackle. They scored 13 points to nil in the second half and we were defeated. Nothing unusual in that, any Welsh reader might think. We always beat the English at the Arms Park. Let boys have their dreams and old men their memories, if we can affect the course of our personal histories, we must do it with each act that we make, for what is done cannot be undone.

Among the telegrams on that day, two had referred to home and school. The first read, 'Ten thousand Devils.' Rogan. He was one of my teachers at West Park, it did not refer to the crowd, though well it might, but to a saying often heard in pre match briefings at school level. *Play with the gusto or courage or rage of ten thousand devils.* Its meaning was clear, its exhortation precise. Oddly enough the other telegram, from my parents simply read, 'Best of luck, remember Hard Lane, Cowley.' Hard Lane was well named because it was there that some of the most memorable battles had been fought. 'Remember The Alamo' would have meant nothing to me but this invocation was designed to motivate me to fierce action. I was seduced by the crowd and the occasion. Bare fences and cold winds from the cemetery would have reaped a different reward.

Those 10,000 Welsh spectators far outnumbered the ten men and a dog that braved those cold winds of school pitches. The harvest was theirs, and we gleaned only faint cheers from the few English diehards, who supported us. Like husks winnowing in the wind, they were blown away.

It was the greatest week of my school time, arguably of my whole sporting life. To play at Twickenham and Cardiff Arms Park within a six-day period, is a thrill not given to many at any level in the game. I enjoyed the occasions and valued the friendships. The faces fade and names come but slowly to mind. Nick Silk and Trevor Wintle went on to gain their blues and captain varsity sides before gaining full England caps. Alan Jones spent a brief and unhappy time at Wigan RLFC. Roger Hill and I met up again at Loughborough College, before he went on to the Army Education Corps. Jeff Edgar played for the Cumberland and Westmoreland County side for some time. Dave Protherough made his name first as a hooker and then as a coach to the successful Gloucestershire County side. These were boys I met later as men but the rest went away to continue their lives and develop their aspirations elsewhere. Maybe some days there are reciprocal thought waves passing between us, if they, like me, look at their team photographs.

Peter kept the sea out with his finger in the dyke but as far as the England schoolboys are concerned, this Peter opened the floodgates for boys from Lancashire. If it is true that I was instrumental in, or the key to opening those doors for others, I am delighted. If not, the experience for itself was wonderful. I thank all those who made it possible and the rest who made it memorable. My father always said that it was the greatest achievement of my life. Perhaps he realised the enormity of the leap from the coalface to the white shirt of England. Or the length of the journey from Irish farm to Billy William's

Cabbage Patch, for that was the name given to the Twickenham pitch. I know that he dearly wanted me to wear the white shirt of England, with its bright red Lancashire Rose, at the full international level.

Recent research shows that more than 100 Lancashire schoolboys followed me through that door, to play in the England Schools 18 Group, including these from St Helens. Trevor Jones, from Newton Grammar School, so sadly struck down as a young man.

West Park School produced Tim Melia, T. Rhodes, J. L. Metcalfe, S. D. Flaherty and Kevin Simms, who went on to play at senior international level.

Cowley provided Mel Smaje, Keith Hancock, Nigel Yates, David Gullick, John Ireland, Mick Burke, Alan Simpson, Ian Aspinall, Norman Pickavance, Geoff Sephton, David Rignall, Gary Muldoon, Marcus Taylor and John Horton, who also went on to play at senior international level. Ray French insists that there were even more than these I have identified; he certainly worked hard at Cowley to make sure that they had every chance of getting selected, despite the fact that the Rugby Union banned Rugby League players from coaching at all levels. Warren Joyce was also a student at Cowley who played for England Schools 16 Group, who chose to become a professional footballer, rather than a professional Rugby player.

Some of the other boys from Lancashire include Tony Neary, Roger Utley, J. Syddall, A. H. Swift, F. W. Clough, Keiran Bracken, Ben Kay, L. R. Balshaw and Steve Borthwick; every one of them became a full international.

Two other names which should be recognised, from the list of Lancashire Schoolboy Internationals, are those of Joe Lydon and Shaun Edwards, both well known Rugby League Internationals, who have returned to Rugby Union as outstanding coaches. I have included Shaun Edwards as an outstanding player in the 16 Group, but have not named any of the other numerous players who played in the 16 Group, once the Lancashire Schools became affiliated to the England Schools, or the number would approach 200, from my adoptive county. My impact was great and all of these players will have had to follow the path of schoolboy trials and their families will have had to support them through the whole mysterious process.

A couple of years ago when I was invited to West Park Rugby Club, the first invitation in nearly fifty years, to one of Dennis Glynn's Presidents Lunches, a person from the English Schools Union came to present an international cap to a boy from De La Salle. That school is the modern equivalent of the Catholic Grammar School and I asked politely whether I, as the first schoolboy international, might be awarded a cap for my performance at Twickenham, or even Cardiff Arms Park. I am still awaiting a reply. The group that I was invited with included all of those teams who had played in seven-a-side tournaments for West Park. Perhaps if enough of them lobby the Rugby Union for me I might just get my due reward. I of course burned all of my bridges when I became a professional player, but that is still to come in this story.

CHAPTER 9

Playing with the Big Boys

Playing for England Schools made me well known in Lancashire Rugby circles and led directly to a number of opportunities. The first came immediately on 11 April 1959, when Alan Clemison wrote this in the *Sporting Pink*:

The Selectors know all about Harvey

The most promising young player in the country this season has been Peter Harvey, who Captained England schoolboys. Harvey, a tough, square shouldered centre from West Park Grammar School, has planted the memory of his devastating burst of speed and fierce tackle on the minds of senior county and international selectors. His running in the schoolboy international against France was a class apart, according to one critic. It certainly was when Lancashire boys beat Yorkshire in January. Unfortunately neither West Park nor St Helens, his two local clubs, are likely to see much of him.

In a small piece in the *St Helens Reporter* headed 'Star Rises' it reports:

Peter Harvey, the Lancashire and England schoolboys' captain, made an impressive home debut as left centre in the Liverpool team at New Brighton on Saturday. His telling bursts through the middle often split the opposing defence wide open. In conjunction with the two other St Helens born backs, Hackett and Regan, Harvey formed a centre triangle that worked in admirable unison. Harvey is regarded as the best rugby product of West Park Grammar School since the rise of Martin Regan.

And in the *Daily Express* the headline: 'Redhead Pete isn't Reluctant' preceded a very short report which put all three West Park old boys together in one sentence.

With two old boys at the school alongside him in Jack Regan and Tom Hackett, Harvey showed the form that made him this season's captain of Lancashire and England school boys. Next season he will be at St Mary's College, Twickenham, but Liverpool are hoping the Lancashire county selectors will keep an eye on him and bring him north for trials.

John Pugh. Liverpool 16 New Brighton 0
Ripley breaks a leg in Aigburth game.

Liverpool rang down the Aigburth curtain for this season in jaunty style with a convincing victory over New Brighton by two goals, a try and a penalty. It was a performance that contained happy auguries for 1959/60. Hackett feared lost to the game burst breezily in on the scene again as though he had never heard of such things as shoulder injuries. All the old tricks were there together with his fine turn of speed. Alongside him, Harvey, the flame haired schoolboy international, made the perfect foil—forceful and direct with evidence of a shrewd football brain and an uncompromising defence . . .

Recently I wrote a letter to Tom Hackett who was a star player at Liverpool when I first played there, and is now a good friend, part of a continuing correspondence with him. My thoughts as expressed to him are here.

The piece continues but it is the evidence I want to show that I did actually play alongside you in at least one match. I have also found the Liverpool club picture which I am on. Unfortunately it is for 1960/61 and you are not on that particular one. I have two vivid memories of that first game for Liverpool, one concerns Reg Higgins and the other one concerns you. I was so keen to get involved, being my first match in the senior team; I was trying to do everything. Reg Higgins told me in no uncertain terms to get out of the way of the forwards when the mauls were forming, and when the rucks were happening. He explained to me, that forwards liked nothing better that to find the backs in the rucks, first so that they could stamp on their legs to injure them, and second because if they could trap them in the ruck, there would be room out wide if they won the ball. Simple when you have played lots of rugby. But for me this was my first 'senior' match!

Later in the game, Wilkinson one of the Liverpool players, had to leave the field with a gash on his head. I remember Reg going mad and lots of shouting, some of it at me to get out of the way. Later Ripley, the New Brighton player was carried off with a broken leg which was sustained in the ruck and I'm not at all sure that it was accidental.

The other memory was of me making a clear break and taking the ball through to the fullback, looking round for support, and being tackled for lack of the same. I said to Tom Hackett, 'When I make a break I expect you (the other centre) to be there alongside me.' He shook his head and said that he had been held back. A few minutes later he made a clean break and ran to the fullback, stopped and turned round and said, 'Where are you?' a clear lesson to me that Hackett was actually much quicker than me.

I want it on record that I did play with Hackett and Regan as they had been talked about throughout my time in school.

I have been described many times as a confident player. I do remember saying things like that, and shrink now in embarrassment, thinking that I must have come across as a right big head. I did try very hard and did learn to fit into sides as I got more experience, however in my first match for Rosslyn Park I told the wing forward off for not getting to me quickly enough. I learned later that he was an All Black of some repute. But I'm getting ahead of myself.

Rosslyn Park RFC

Lt-Col Burnaby was pursuing me and I didn't mind one jot. In his letter of 25 April 1959 he writes:

> We shall look forward to seeing you next season. Let us know in advance when you are coming down. Don't be put off by the subs on the back of the form. As an 'invited' schoolboy you remain on the nominal sub of five shillings per annum until you are 21 years old, when it is reviewed.

> PS It would be courteous of me to get your head or Master i/c Rugger to sign on the seconders line.

I duly returned the form and on 9 June 1959 he wrote to me again.

> Dear Harvey,
> I wonder how well you got to know Michael H. Clarke—the other centre with you at Twickenham. Presumable quite well as you skippered the side and played next to him.

His letter asks me to write to him at his school (college) to ask if he is leaving and if he is likely to be near London or in the South as you are. I would sooner that you do not mention my name, nor the idea that I put the idea into your head, nor that I know of the intended invitation, because it might embarrass him.
He closes with this sentence:

> Looking forward to meeting you next season. All good wishes,

> Yours sincerely
> Dickson Burnaby

At the time of that letter I still lived at 43 Higher Parr Street; behind the sweet shop, in the house with the outside toilet, linoleum on the kitchen floor and a big Belfast sink in which we used to wash ourselves and the dirty dishes. I'm not at all convinced that Lt-Col. Dickson Burnaby knew that this schoolboy captain of England was not like the others he had dealt with—nor indeed the powers that be at Liverpool RFC, possibly the oldest club side in England, if not the world, for whom I had already played a couple of matches. I referred earlier to the fact that I found The Waterloo Club perhaps a little too public school for my liking, more Merchant Taylor's than West Park.

On my first visit to Liverpool RFC, I was met by George Gummerson, who greeted me in an accent much closer to mine. Reg Higgins was a player of the highest class, having played for England and toured with the British Lions, but he still bridged the gap to a schoolboy like me, with his down to earth attitude and jovial manner.

I was invited to the Club Dinner which took place at the Athenaeum Club in the centre of Liverpool. I went with Jack Regan, himself an old boy of West Park, who luckily for me had his own transport, and was willing to take me in his car. That dinner was the first time that I had ever experienced the strange mixture of the formal and the informal, which is often the mark of such occasions. The guest of Honour was Harry Fry who was President of Lancashire that year. I listened with intent at all of the honours which he had achieved in the game, and watched as Reg Higgins the club Captain, proposed the toasts first to Harry Fry and then to the Queen, or more likely it was the other way round. As the players settled down to the jugs of beer being taken around the room, I managed to get myself to the top table and up alongside Reg, who then introduced me to Harry Fry. I asked them both to autograph my menu which they duly did, and I was really surprised when Fry said to me, 'If you play as well as Reg tells me that you can, it won't be long before we are asking for your autograph.' I remember the sentiment even if I have lost the menu card.

In 1959/60 my father Peter became the steward in the recently built Parr & Hardshaw Labour Club and returned to working behind the bar in that busiest of places. During the summer holidays I went to work on the building site, as I had done before. My Uncle Tommy Harvey (later to become Mayor of St Helens), told me to go and see his friend Jim Forrester who was building houses in a number of sites in St Helens. I went to his house in Lugsmore Lane, near Toll Bar and knocked on the door with some trepidation. I was ushered into a very comfortable room where Jim sat in a large armchair, smoking a cigar and drinking whisky from a cut glass tumbler. He asked me if I had ever done any labouring work before, as I was still at school. Luckily for me I had worked on the St Helens Corporation building sites during the previous two summer holidays. Once on the new Fire Station site in Parr Stocks Road as a general labourer, and once on the new College site as a joiner's labourer.

So he gave me a job as a hod carrier to start work immediately as one of his hod carriers was unable to work. I turned up and reported to the site foreman, Harry Pilling, who was setting out a line of houses in Poynter Street, off Elephant Lane, Thatto Heath. Harry was the bricklayer for whom I was going to work. He already had one labourer, but he was such a prodigious layer of bricks, that he needed two men to keep up with him. Carrying bricks throughout the day, climbing ladders with a full hod of bricks: building scaffolds for the next lift, while Harry was putting in the foundations on the next house: built up muscles which I didn't know that I had. Harry Pilling was a real character of the old school. He was hard working beyond imagination. When the rain came down he would call out, 'Fetch the big hat and coat,' and he would continue without pause. A former Regimental Sergeant Major, he had fought in Burma during the Second World War, with the Chindits in 'The Forgotten War' against Japan.

Harry was a hard taskmaster and made me run around getting prepared for his next job, so that he never had to stop laying bricks. One day he asked me what I wanted to do at college and when he found out that I wanted to be a PE teacher, he ran me around even more. When I told him that I had Captained England Schools, he laughed out loud and said that he must be the only bricklayer in the world who had two England Captains as hod carriers, because his regular man was Alan Prescott, who was off with an injury sustained in the test match in Australia.

Then one afternoon late in the summer, the very same Alan Prescott turned up and approached my Dad. 'Was there anything that he could do for me?' he asked. As he was the Coach at St Helens RFC that was a very loaded question. 'No,' replied my father, 'he is settled and bound for college in September.' Alan nodded respectfully and promised that he would look after me.

Now this was not the first time that Alan had called on us because when it had been announced in the local paper that I was to Captain England Schools, Alan had come to call then. That visit resulted in me wearing a pair of new boots which he had provided, enough to have had me banned for life if it had become known that I was dealing with a Rugby League Club. I had already played my first game for Liverpool. This time Alan told my dad that Mr Cook, well known club chairman, wanted to see me before I went to college, and that he would take me up to the club and look after my interests. Dad was not happy in case I signed a form which would commit me in the future, but allowed Alan to drive me to the meeting with Mr Cook. I remember walking up those narrow stairs to the chairman's office and his jovial greeting both to me and Alan. He didn't say it but he might have thought, 'Come into my parlour said the spider to the fly.' He told me how pleased they all were with recent events and asked me to tell him about my future plans.

He was prepared to sign me there and then on amateur forms, and he would provide a bursary for me through my college years, with my only commitment to give The Saints first option if I ever decided to sign professional forms in the future. Alan asked the Chairman for permission 'to show me the facilities,' and took me off to wander round the pitch, and under the new stand which had recently been built. I suppose it was a highly charged situation, but I was quite happy to talk to him, as I had such faith in him as player and club captain. Actually, it was him as a person, a father figure (perhaps knowing that he would have to answer to my father), that made a big difference that day.

He explained that the Saints were very interested indeed, and would like to sign me there and then, paying me during my time at college, and then signing me as a professional, as soon as I finished there. He assured me that no one would know and that it would not affect my career in Rugby Union, as it was in the Saints' best interests, to watch me develop from a schoolboy to a mature player. Then he said, 'Listen to me very carefully, no matter what I say when we get back into the room with the Chairman, do not sign any forms today.' He then went on to explain that the club would definitely follow my progress, and that scouts would be watching me, whenever I played close to home. If I got in the Lancashire and England team my value would shoot up and they would definitely be after me.

We returned to the Chairman's room and Alan said how much I had enjoyed the visit, and that I was ready to sign the amateur forms. The Chairman said how exciting it would be for me to play centre to Tom Vollenhoven, and play with such world-class players as Alex Murphy. Alan agreed with the Chairman and said that he thought that I should sign and reap the benefits while I was at college. The form was placed on the table, but I had understood Alan quite plainly. I said that I would have to consult with my dad, understandably Alan accepted and we left. He dropped me off outside the Parr and Hardshaw and I was not to see him for some years.

Northern Sevens

I played in the Liverpool team which won this competition for the first time, shortly before I went to college. The team travelled up to Newcastle on the train. We had the bare seven players with four forwards and only three backs. Reg Higgins, who was the Club Captain at the time, decided that we should play with Tom Brophy at scrum-half and Wilf Murphy at stand-off, as Jack Regan was unavailable for personal reasons.

Brophy must have still been at school as I was only just on my way to college. Wilf was a back row forward, but it was decided that we could cover the backs with what we had available. We did very well and though I do not know how the competition went, I know that we did win a cup, because the one thing I remember from that day was what happened after the event. It was a warm dry day, and we had each played every minute of every match, as we had the bare seven to play with. I was tired, no doubt the other six were too, but I got into the shower and was there for some time. When I came out of the shower Reg Higgins asked me did I want a drink from the cup, which he offered directly. He was still in his playing kit and obviously had gone to the bar when I went into the shower. I naturally though that he had filled the cup with beer, as that was quite common for players to buy jugs of ale. I took a draught from the cup and spluttered my astonishment; the cup was full of whisky and burned red hot onto my tongue and throat. I soon got over it after a few jars with the boys. We came back on the train and I can only assume Reg Higgins took the cup back to Aigburth the following week. I still have the bronze medal, which went with the cup, inscribed 'Northern 7's winners 1959'. It sits with all of my other medals, and I am equally proud to still have possibly the only 7's medal won by a Liverpool team.

18/09/1959. Match report, possibly *Daily Post*.
Liverpool 13 Taunton 0
Red Headed Harvey inspires Liverpool.

Liverpool 1960-61.
Back row: Ian Douglas, Sean Lynch, Wilf Murphy, Roy Lightfoot, Terry Kirchen, Gerry Thomas, Geoff Gadd, Norman Colclough, Geoff Stringer, Jack the Rub.
Front row: Peter Harvey, Jack Regan, Peter Kelly, Alan Lambert, Denis Unsworth, George Wilkinson, Brian Unsworth.

Peter Harvey, Liverpool's eighteen-year-old centre and last year's Captain of the England Schoolboy's side, has the stamp of an international, and barring unforeseen circumstances should certainly don an English jersey one day. This lad is going to St Mary's; the teacher's training College at Twickenham and he will certainly be missed by Liverpool. He had a hand in all three Liverpool tries, and only made two mistakes, both in the second half when he dropped the ball. But for speed, thought, enterprise, initiative and anything else which goes to make a star, he had the lot. And he didn't mind going in either!

But the flashes came on the turn around with the red headed Harvey speeding through with a near perfect partnership with Brian Unsworth, Liverpool's only newcomer who played for the Welsh Universities, and last season Captained University College Bangor.

Wilkinson got the second try after a fine movement started by Regan and continued by Unsworth and Harvey, and it was Harvey who got the final try from an inside pass by Regan after Collins had just failed with a wing run.

It has to be noted that Brian (Bunny) Unsworth, was ex-West Park, and though a couple of years older than me, I remember him from school. Therefore Regan, Harvey, Unsworth, the trio in the middle of the pitch, was the product of West Park rugby.

CHAPTER 10

The Coming of Mr Joe Coan

The PE teacher at West Park in my final two years was Mr Joe Coan, and it was he who had introduced Athletics into the summer curriculum, not as competition for the wonderful cricket team, but to offer individual events alongside team games. He was not in charge of either rugby or cricket at that stage in his career, but he had been trained at Simms and Carnegie College, and had encouraged me to apply to the same colleges. He was different from Mr Lunt, the ex-army PTI who had taken us in the early years at West Park, and Mr Wainwright who was the senior rugby master at the time that I attended. He had introduced school camps in the Lake District and I will never forget the first one that I attended a couple of years before going to Simms. The school camp was on the shore of Coniston Lake, a site that was to be used for many years after that first visit. Keith Northey was there of course, and when we asked Joe how we could get to the top of Coniston Old Man he replied, 'Just try to keep the top in your sights and go straight up.'

As a former head teacher myself, I know that no teacher should give that kind of instruction, but we followed it to the letter, and walked straight through farms, across railway lines, climbed over walls, and took the direct route from bottom to top. He was amazed when we came down a couple of hours later and told him that we had been to the top and back. Joe was prepared to take risks and when one of the boys, Ray Connolly, who later became a well-known writer of films and novels, said that he could swim across Lake Coniston we put it to Joe, who was in charge of the camp, and he agreed, with the proviso that we should accompany Ray in a rowing boat to rescue him if he got into difficulties.

Ray duly undertook 'the big swim' and we followed him in the boat. Ray was not one of the best at team games, being very slight in build. He did do cross-country running, and having little weight to carry, was much better at that than the rugby types. The 'big swim' was his way of getting one over on the rest of us, and perhaps adding some lustre to his reputation. He set off and soon found that the deep water in the middle of the lake was very cold indeed. He was adamant that he wanted to go on, though we were pleading to pull him out. He did make it all the way to the other side and sat shivering in the boat as we rowed back to the camp. He has since told me, that he thought that he would die of exposure on the return journey, as we had not taken any warm clothes with us. As long as we returned, Joe didn't seem to mind at all. Ray was the hero of the hour, as was only right. That fact that he did survive is important not only for him and his family, but also because he became perhaps the world's foremost authority on the life and works of the Beatles.

Joe Coan was a Carnegie College-trained PE Specialist which meant that he had a wide knowledge of all PE activities, and also would have studied games playing in the widest context. The self-reliance which he allowed amongst the boys on that camp contrasted widely with the strict, play it by the book, attitudes which had gone before.

At the summer sports day I was delighted to win the Senior *Victor ludorum* shield, winning the hurdles and javelin, both introduced by Joe Coan, as well as the Father Hearne cup for the 440 yards. He was a swimmer, and a very good one, holding college records, for short and long course swimming. After I left West Park, in his second spell there, by which time he was head of PE, he argued for, and got the De la Salle Brothers to build a swimming pool.

Training for swimming included both work in the pool and in the gymnasium. Stamina can be built by working exercises in repetitions, group these together and the basis of circuit training is established. By varying the number of repetitions, and decreasing the time allowed for each circuit a basic unit can be scheduled, depending on the fitness of the person doing the work. The trainer can manipulate the amount of work being done by increasing the repetitions for each exercise and cutting down the time allowed to do them. Cardio vascular fitness can be increased at will, by reducing the recovery time between circuits.

Any decent PE teacher could do this, and Joe Coan had many groups working in this way, both at school and night school, which he did for additional income. It was because he was doing this in the wintertime that he was available when the Saints first came calling. He was a highly pragmatic individual who was in the right place at the right time, and realised that he had a skill which rugby

The Catholic Grammar School Sports 1959. The Mayoress Mrs McDonald presents me with 'The Fr Hearne Cup'. The Mayor Counc. McDonald presented Peter Harvey with 'The Victor Ludorum' trophy on the same day.

players with international caps didn't have, and capitalised on that.

CHAPTER 11

Strawberry Hill Boys

In September 1959, I went to St Marys College, Twickenham, and trained to become a teacher. Commonly called Simms, or often Strawberry Hill, it was one of the best-known Catholic Colleges which specialised in training men for teaching. Several of the people who played at Liverpool had been through the Training College and the quality of the rugby team was one of the reasons which helped me to decide to go there. It was also known as a Wing College, which meant that it specialised in PE, so people could do a third year to get a Diploma in PE. Wilf Murphy, Peter Kelly and Tom Hackett were all Simmerians (ex Simms), playing at Liverpool when I was there. Other students could take a four-year course and come out with a degree to enhance their teaching qualification.

Leaving home for the first time can be a somewhat traumatic experience, and I vividly remember going to Liverpool Lime Street Station accompanied by Ruth Twist, who was herself about to go to Notre Dame Training College in Liverpool. We were courting for a couple of years and were each committed to the other in a solid, if teenage partnership. We walked down the long, crowded platform and stood next to the London train. There were plenty of student types getting on that train, many with mothers fussing around them, and some like us, holding hands wishing each other good luck and goodbye. We promised to write to each other often, as soon as we knew the proper address of each college. Then it was time to get on the train and it slowly moved away.

I remember watching her standing on that platform, a solitary figure, sadly waving goodbye. Both of us were thinking the same thing, will our friendship stand the distance between us, or will this really be goodbye? The train slowly pulled into the Edge Hill cutting and I lost sight of her as she stood till every carriage had passed her. I was to get used to that journey and luckily for me she was to be by my side every time. I was also lucky in a way because Reg Higgins, who was the Captain of Liverpool Rugby Union Club, told me that the club would be happy to pick me, whenever I was available. There was an understanding, that if I was to be successful in my teacher training, especially as a PE teacher, it was fundamental to my course work that I played for the college team.

So I arrived in the closeted world that was to be my home for two years. Two hundred students, each with their own little study bedroom, all eating together in a refectory, twelve to a table, and three meals a day, breakfast, lunch and dinner. I met John Wilcock immediately, because he was in the room next to mine. A lad from Yorkshire who was taking PE, but his interest was cross-country running not rugby. The first two days in college were very sedate as we went through an induction process which was very gentlemanly indeed. Then on the third day all of the older students appeared and everything became much more noisy and chaotic.

Our suits were laughed at and the polished shoes ridiculed, student clothes of scruffy jumpers and old slippers were the norm. Being a PE main college, many of the students wore tracksuits for most of the time, but the college had a rule that tracksuits could not be worn in the refectory, which forced everyone to change, at least into trousers and tops. I mention the clothes because we were there at the end of the 1950s revolution in fashion and music. Students either liked Jazz and all that went with that scene, or Rock and Roll, Bill Haley and Elvis. Oddly enough there was another form of music which was very popular in the college and that was country dancing. There was also a jazz band in which I had no real interest. However, Terry Dillon, who featured very often in my life, did want to audition.

Terry was older than me, having done National Service in the Welsh Guards. He was a bandsman, and very proud of his Yorkshire heritage, including the time spent as a soloist cornet player in the local brass band. He, like me was the son of a miner, but unlike me had actually spent time underground himself. Yes indeed Terry could play the trumpet and he auditioned for the jazz band. He was absolutely flabbergasted when he failed the audition, 'because he played every note exactly right.' Apparently they wanted him to slide his notes, and his training would not allow that.

Tom O'Connor, later to become a well-known entertainer, lived in the room right across from me. Tom was in the year above me and was the social secretary and ran the country-dance band. Being from Liverpool he had a ready wit and a twinkle in his eye, but was certainly not the polished comedian he became later. The country-dance band provided one of the highlights of the college social life, the dances on a Sunday in the Aula or the Big Hall. Not that I frequented these events, expect rarely, when invited by one of Ruth's school friends. Tom O'Connor duly became a teacher and was successful in the school environment, becoming a Deputy Head in a primary school, before leaving for a fulltime career in show business.

In the first couple of days, one of the older students who came and sat on the same refectory table as me was Gerry Millington, a prop forward from

Wigan. We talked about rugby and quite naturally about Rugby League. I told him that I had played for England Schools and was hoping to play for Rosslyn Park while I was at college, and that Liverpool wanted me to go back home and play for them. He looked at me very sternly, and told me in no uncertain terms, that if I carried on talking like that I would have a very rough ride in the College. I should, 'shut up and say nowt', and just play my way into the team, and I would get a much better reaction from everyone. What good advice, thank you Gerry!

Freshers (first year students) have to play in a trial match as the older students run the club, organise the training, and pick the teams. So we were divided into two teams and away we went. It may seem odd that I am talking about a trial match with students at a college, but really they are one of the most daunting matches to play in. No one has played with each other before, and the older students pick themselves with the best players, leaving the rest to fend for themselves. I was playing quite well and beginning to feel at home, when suddenly this little old fellow stopped me in my tracks with a shoulder charge, like the ones Joe Ball used to use: I had met Ron McCarten head on.

Ron was not really an old fellow, but having done National Service, he was certainly not like the schoolboys that I had been used to. No, he was a county player for Cumberland, and an England Trialist, as well as a regular player

St Mary's Twickenham Rugby Team. 1960.
Back row: J. Miller; C. D. Galbraith; T. Dillon; G. Holland.
Third row:?; ?; ?; H. Fearns; D. Power; M. Maybury; M. Jabale; M. Spall.
Second row: ?; B. Dilley, (Capt.); Fr Dunning (Vice Principal); P. Harvey; P. Kelly.
Front row: W. Ryan; R. J. McCarten; P. Conland; C. Rose.

for the London Irish. I got to know McCarten very well, and he is still one of my good friends. Later I learned that he had been picked to mark me as the senior students thought that I might need a lesson. I remembered Millington's advice, and just got on with the game, and before long they had me on the senior side playing inside McCarten at left centre. He was dynamite on attack, sidestepping off his left foot over and over, beating man after man: at that level he was unstoppable.

I got into the College First XV and began to play in the centre quite happily with a group of people I had never met before. Not only was it very different from schools rugby, I was meeting players from different counties, different school backgrounds, and some older players who had been in the army, or done National Service.

I was quite thick set and athletic, and always very confident. I was a PE main student, and the first time I went into the gymnastics class, I saw a chap bouncing around doing handsprings, Arab springs, fly springs and flick flacks. When told to choose a partner, I immediately asked him, David Brookes, if he would work with me. He wanted to know what I could do, which in all fairness was not very much, but he agreed to be my gymnastic partner, as no one else was anything like as good as him anyway.

Over the period of the two years at St Mary's, I worked hard with David, and for most of the time, he was very dismissive of my progress. 'Can you do this?' followed by a demonstration of some move which I couldn't do, was a very regular occurrence. David was a performer who had worked in a circus and had also worked at his local lido performing acrobatics and diving. He was so good that he was able to make everything funny if he wanted to, and often did, causing us all to laugh. I went with him every day, and learned bit by bit to do the standard gymnastic movements. At the same time we would be working on strengthening exercises, doing circuit training, working with benches, army style. A real mixture of strength and endurance work designed and modelled on the Army PTI courses. Of course being a Teacher Training College, this was all tempered by Theory of Physical Education.

Being a Catholic College, there was an odd perception that somehow the students were not as 'hard' as other colleges. This was sometimes in evidence on the rugby pitch when teams would start trying to rough up our forwards, and were very surprised when they hit back. Pete Scrase, Mick Maybury, Gerry Millington, Chas Galbraith, Dennis Power and Tino Bassinie, were all forwards capable of holding their own with the rest of the rugby world. Each of them became county players in their own right and with flying back row forwards like Terry Dillon, Brian O'Gorman, Punchy Kelly, and Skinner Welsh; we had a pack which functioned very well.

None of these gentlemen will be known to people outside of our college, but I can tell of my first baptism of fire which happened on my nineteenth birthday. The college were playing Harlequins Second team, and they brought a big strong team to Strawberry Hill, expecting to turn us over without much of a problem. Our pack stood their ground, never taking a backward step, and were matching them blow for blow, much to their astonishment. The centre I was marking, was really thick set and heavily built and considerable older than me. Probably even a first team player who had been given the job of captaining the side on the jaunt down from Twickenham, a couple of miles away. He decided that the 'kiwi sidestep' was the way to beat me as he couldn't run round me, he never tried to from first to last. I tackled him over and over, even using my favourite hand and foot throw, which really upset him.

Known as the Cumberland Throw, I had first seen players do it while watching the Saints. It used a well-known judo and wrestling principle which used the opponent's power and weight against himself. I pretty much perfected it and used it when forwards ran straight at me. When they tried to hand me off, I would grip the hand or arm and shift my body under their legs, and throw them over. More often than not they would land on their back, or if they were unlucky on their head. I realised that the principle of using my hand and feet together, often toppled big men over. My father's saying, 'the bigger they are the harder they fall,' was proved over and over again, and to great effect that day.

We won the match and my new teammates accepted me, as Gerry Millington had predicted. We spent the Saturday evening at The King's Head in Twickenham, and every one of the team bought me a whiskey, to celebrate my birthday, and the victory. I remember being walked home from The Kings Head, held up on either side by a strapping forward, as no doubt, it would have been impossible for me to walk home unaided. I remember that because it was so unusual, in fact uniquely so and never repeated.

I must recall what will seem to be an odd way to prepare for a rugby match, but it was easily accepted at the time. Since the players came from all parts of the college, and some from their lodgings throughout Twickenham, we did not have a place to meet. In fact we did not have changing rooms as such, and players got changed in their bedrooms, before going downstairs to meet by the front entrance. Not the field as one might think, but by the entrance to the chapel, which was situated right at the heart of the college. Before every home match, the team, fully kitted out for the match, but leaving their boots at the back, went into the chapel to pray. The prayers would be that everyone would be able to do their best and that no one would get hurt; that we would play in the right spirit and that we would not do anything to spoil the good name of the college. Then after one or two communal prayers we would all file out, go to the door by the playing field and put boots on, to engage in battle, whoever was there to meet us.

Having got settled into the college team I contacted Rosslyn Park and was invited to go to the new ground at Roehampton for training. I only went a couple of times, as obviously the college was adamant that they had first call on my playing for them on a Saturday. Unlike McCarten who had negotiated with the college that London Irish would be his Saturday choice, I had to play for St Mary's. Still in the Spring Term, I was able to attend for training at Rosslyn Park, and I was invited to play for their second team at The Honourable Artillery Company, somewhere in the middle of London. I don't remember very much about the game but I do have a vivid memory of the setting. The pitch was completely surrounded by buildings, solid grey stone, multi-storied and seemingly very close to the touchlines. So much so it seemed that every kick for touch would break a window in one or other of the surrounding offices or barracks, I still don't know what they were. It was that day that I shouted at the open side because he didn't get to me quickly enough, when I took the ball into the tackle, looking to turn and release to the supporting man. I was told later that he was a junior all black and very offended by this upstart from the north who shouted at him. He might have been named 'Ironside,' or that may have been his nickname, he was certainly grumpy that day. That apart it was all very grand and not at all like Laffak Field, with Moncrieff's cows lowing next to the pitch.

It was spring and though the days were getting longer, midweek training was still conducted under 'floodlights'. The lights were pretty poor, despite the beauty of the surroundings, and one night I managed to run into the shoulder of someone during the training session. I remember bouncing down his body from shoulder to hip and then his feet, before lying helpless on the ground. I was knocked out for the first time and struggled to get up. My legs wobbled, and my head spun round, then I was sick. Immediately I was taken from the training pitch and told to go back to college. Had I been back in Liverpool, surely someone would have taken me home in their car, but I had to get the train back to Strawberry Hill, and go straight to bed when I got back to my room. I had concussion and was advised that I could not play anywhere on the Saturday, so I decided to come back home for the weekend.

Thus it was that I arrived unannounced at the door of Notre Dame Training College, Mount Pleasant Liverpool, at around nine o'clock on the Friday night. I knocked on the door and waited for it to be opened. I had no idea the impact that simple act would have on those inside. A nun opened the door, and asked who I was and what I wanted. 'I'm Peter Harvey and I would like to talk to Ruth Twist, please.' 'Ruth and all of the other students are going to bed and you cannot see them.' The surprised nun announced.

I explained that I had been injured, and gave that as the reason why my presence was unannounced and unusual. I had travelled up from London and needed to speak to her.

I was asked to wait while Ruth was summoned from the bedrooms, and she came downstairs with her coat on, over her nightclothes and sat across the table from me, with the porter nun keeping an eagle eye on our strange conversation. After explaining what had happened and why I was home for the weekend I left, little knowing the hubbub I left in my wake because gentlemen were never allowed into the college and certainly not at that time of night. Not yet the swinging sixties.

When I went home my dad told me about the time that he had been knocked out in the ring. A clean blow on the chin literally knocks you out and your body falls to the floor. That is what I had managed to do to myself, when I ran into that fellow's shoulder.

One of the things which I do remember about Rosslyn Park was that the Club Secretary would not write to me at my home address, at The Parr & Hardshaw Labour Club. Instead letters were addressed to The P&H Club, Prospect Road, which was far more gentlemanly. I didn't play for Rosslyn Park until later in that season, when I came up with them on the train to Leeds, to play against Headingley. I was really shocked by the Southern mockery, talking about the North in a way that I had never heard before. Loud-mouthed 'rugger' types, bankers who ordered wine with the meal, and then sent it back as a matter of course. I disliked them and vowed never to go back again. I don't doubt that they were an excellent Rugby Union Club, but few if any of the members would have a background like mine.

As the season drew to a close I was picked to play for ULIESA, which stands for University of London Institute External Students Association. They were to go on an Easter Tour of Holland, and play two games over a weekend. We went by train, I think to Harwich, and then by boat to the Hook of Holland, travelling overnight on the ferry. We continued our journey by train and the most notable thing which I remember was that the policemen on the stations were armed. This was 1960 and armed police were unknown in England, unlike today when every train station and airport, seem to have armed officers patrolling, because of the effect of terrorist groups from home and abroad.

We arrived at the sports ground in time for a light lunch and then the game began. It turned out that rugby in Holland was very much a new sport, and though they tried hard, our opponents were not strong enough up front, nor quick enough behind. The scoreboard ticked gaily along and as the match drew to a close, someone said, 'Let's get Satch a try.'

Dennis Power ('Satch' to his friends) played in the second row and had not scored a try all season long. Now was his chance. From a line out which he won, I made a break down to the try line where I stopped and turned round waiting for him to arrive. One or two of the other side tried to smack me down, but I managed to hold up long enough till he arrived. I passed him the ball, and he duly put it down. We all celebrated wildly, though I was looking through a closing black eye for most of the night.

We did celebrate well as touring teams do, but at last we got to bed, being 'billeted' in the homes of members of the opposition. We travelled on the next day and duly played another team, which may have been stronger, or perhaps we were weaker from the day before. In the first five minutes Satch Power managed to score a try entirely by his own efforts. We won the game and celebrated well before setting off on the trip back to London. Not having booked cabins on the ferry, we were in the bars for most of the trip, but I do remember Satch Power trying to do a handstand on the rail of the ship. He didn't fall overboard, but the letter opener we had bought as a present for our Principal, did fall out of his pocket and disappeared into the North Sea. I suppose that had he fallen over he would have followed it in. For the record that same Dennis Power from Bristol later became the first National Rugby Coach to Holland; I'm not sure when or how, but he certainly did. Now unfortunately deceased, no doubt he is fondly remembered as much in the rugby clubs of Holland, as those he played for in Bristol.

It is true to say that I very much enjoyed all of the games that I played for St Mary's. I was growing fitter and stronger, and developing stamina to go with real pace off the mark. When the summer term came and we were no longer playing rugby, I played in the first cricket trial. I was confident that I would be picked, as I had done so well at West Park, where in my final year I had captained the side, and had continued success as an opening bowler. It came as quite a shock when I wasn't picked to play in the first team.

Brian O'Gorman, who had contested for the open side position in the first XV, was the college captain at cricket. He was a public school boy, who had played for Middlesex, who was also a member of the MCC, as was his father. Brian had served as a junior officer in the army in Kenya and believed in upholding standards. Brian became a very close friend, and in some ways a mentor. He was one of the 200 students who did not have a room in college (like Terry and George also), and so very often I shared his company when he came into college, but he didn't pick me for the cricket team.

As a result of not playing cricket I chose to become a member of the athletics team, feeling that I was good enough to become an all-rounder, not the best at anything, but good at quite a lot. It is interesting, because I did work hard at running, both the sprints and the quarter mile. Consequently both my pace and stamina improved and I started to long jump, over twenty-one feet.

As a PE main student I was studying the techniques necessary to perform both track and field, and though I didn't do high jump or pole vault, even those became active parts of our syllabus. In a strange, or lucky, piece of serendipity, my other main subject was physics, and I will explain why that helped. My lecturer in physics was Mr Hopper, who was also one of the first people to use slow motion film to analyse movement in a scientific way. He was using film to highlight the way in which individual movements combined to make the smooth transition to accurate and powerful performance. He was also very interested in the transfer of power, and the application of force, at varying times in relation to improving performance. As a PE student, and also a physics main, he involved me, and to some extent used me as a sounding board, though I have no doubt that the PE Lecturers there at the time, were well aware of what was happening in that physics laboratory. Anyway I became involved with athletics rather than cricket. Not quite the same facilities fought for by Dave Bedford, which are enjoyed by present day students, most recently Mo Farrar, but I can say that I was the official coach to John McSorley, who later was the AAA representative in the javelin and maybe National Champion in that sport.

The college was set in wonderful grounds, and the original house of Strawberry Hill, actually overlooked the River Thames, though we could not see the river at the time I was there. We had magnificent woodlands, and I was always talking about the squirrels in letters home to Ruth. Oddly, though it didn't seem so at the time, we often played croquet on the lawn below my room, which looked out across the landscape to Walpole's Gothic House, the epitome of middle-class England. I had enjoyed my first year, and followed in the footsteps of hundreds of students, who learned how to teach from within those hallowed walls.

CHAPTER 12

Fun and Frolics with the Red Rose County

I had not yet got the call from the Lancashire selectors which I was hoping for. It came as I was training down at Ruskin Drive, using the track to sharpen up: where I met Ray French for the first time in a couple of years, as he was away studying at Leeds University. He was now a very different slimmed-down shape and he told me a story which was both serious and very funny. It involves an incident while working night shift as an agricultural labourer, to explain what had happened to him. But you will have to read his book to learn the secret of how Ray became a 'ball handling second row'.

Sufficient to say here, that he had a nasty encounter with a pea viner that took more than the peas from the stalks, and threatened his very manhood, before nearly killing him. He too was hoping to get the call from Lancashire, and was puffing round the track saying 'Marques and Curry', (they being the two men holding down the England second row positions) who would have to be knocked over for him to get the chance of playing for England. Both of us were hoping for that first call from Lancashire and sure enough it came. Ray was still at Leeds University and I was just about to begin my second year at St Mary's when I got a card to go to Cornwall. This was it – playing with the big boys.

24/09/1960
Cornwall 13 v Lancashire 8

This was my first match for Lancashire and I do not have the match report but I do remember something of the weekend. For my first match for Lancashire I was selected on the wing (as a replacement for one of the wings who appeared in the programme), in what was billed as a friendly. Tell the Cornish forwards that! The first thing that I remember is that we flew down to Cornwall (probably on the morning of the match). We flew from Speke airport on a Douglas DC3 plane, which was most probably used in the Second World War. It was a converted transport plane, with very little comfort, but it was the very first time that I had ever been off the ground higher than a Llewellyn diving try. The team Captain was Alan Ashcroft, an experienced player, and a very well-travelled member of the British Lions Touring team.

We landed at an Air Force base, mildly converted for passengers, and then travelled by coach to Falmouth. My college pal, C. D. Galbraith, Charlie to his mates, had warned how the Cornish forwards would love to eat up their visitors from the far north. That is not what I recall at all as the game was played on a balmy September day, in front of a very appreciative crowd, lusty in their cheering but overall very friendly. I have no particular memories of the match but remember well the aftermath. We were treated to a fine meal, and as we were to stay overnight we went back to our hotel and were told to enjoy the evening. Before everyone dispersed Alan Ashcroft issued this as a command, 'Midnight swimming for all, no excuses be at the dock.'

I didn't go far away, in fact I didn't go anywhere outside of the hotel, but did have a few jars with the rest of the team who stayed in. So about 11.30 p.m. we all went down to the quay for our midnight swimming. We were the Lancashire team, young fit and healthy, so were not at all inhibited at stripping off and jumping into the water. Skinny dipping with a rugby team does get noisy, and so it was with us. I remember there was a rowing boat which we used for diving into the water, rather than climbing the steps to get onto the dock every time. Good fun was had by everyone, until a pair of the local constabulary came down to see what all the noise was about. Spoken with his Cornish accent, his, 'Now then, now then, what's going on here,' made us laugh, before realising that he was serious. I was the last out of the rowing boat and remember well, tying it tight to the ring on the wall, as I watched Alan Ashcroft, our captain and leader, explain that we were the Lancashire Rugby Union team, down in Cornwall for a friendly match. 'That might well be,' said the policeman, looking at the dozen or more people trying to get dressed on the dock side, 'but you can't go skinny dipping in there.'

Then Alan pulled a master-stroke. 'I'm sorry officer, but you will need to take it up with our Manager Eric Evans, JP, who is in charge of the party.' The visiting dignitary was himself trouser-less at that moment, but began to speak as we all scuttled away. 'High Jinks' it was called in those days. The next morning as the coach pulled away from the scene, I was full of remorse, because the boat that I had tied securely to the ring in the quay, was now hanging from the bow, out of the water because the tide had gone out. Charlie Galbraith almost exploded with invective at my stupidity and lack of common sense. Never mind the swimming, I could have ruined the boat.

With the airfield being military, it was not marked on the map, and we had some difficulty in finding the way in. Eventually the coach driver, having asked several locals, who had no idea what he was talking about, did find the entrance. We flew back to Liverpool without further hazard, other than shaking wings, which seemed to be expected on that type of plane. We were travelling in style and it was certainly a new experience for me.

So my Lancashire career began on the wing and with a defeat, more was to follow. There was a story in the newspaper which has the headline, 'Lancashire Rugby Cap for Harvey.' The report begins 'Peter Harvey (Liverpool) gets his first chance for Lancashire against Ulster, in Belfast a week tomorrow.'

What is the saying? 'Better to travel with hope than to arrive.'

The match report by Frank Davies begins:

> Lancashire spent 80 minutes at Ravenhill, Belfast, chasing shadows while a vital speedy, skilful Ulster team ran up a well earned tally of 29 points to an emphatic nothing. Without trying to make any excuses—which they would hate anyway— one must point out that Lancashire were hamstrung in midfield by the absence of Beverley Risman and Malcolm Phillips.

The rest of the report is in praise of Ulster who no doubt deserved everything he said. However, John Pugh in his match report headlines, 'Spare the axe please Lancashire'.

He explained that not only were the two international backs, Risman and Phillips missing but also the midfield trio failed to function, one of them Booth, was in fact concussed and unable to carry on for much of the match. Then Pugh has this to say.

> In the general condemnation of Saturday's team, one must absolve the two wings Burgess and Harvey. The Fylde man revealed international class, and the way he rounded local hero, Pedlow, left Ulstermen goggling. Harvey had a good if distracting county debut—due to Smith's knock, the Liverpool player often found himself facing two or even three attackers.

Little is made of the fact that once more I had been selected to play on the wing.

This county match was played at Ravenhill in Belfast, but we saw little of the city as we were taken direct from the boat, onto the coach and directly to the ground. This time we did not stay overnight but instead came back on the overnight ferry. Most of us did not go to bed but played cards for almost all of the time before arriving back in Liverpool.

As a footnote to this weekend, I must have already been back at college, because Alan Ashcroft took great delight in teaching me how to claim my expenses. Knowledge is power, and Alan knew how to use the system. Thanks Alan.

As a second year at St Mary's we would be expected to pick the teams, do the training, and organise the fixtures for the next year. I remember a meeting very early in the term, perhaps even before the match against Ulster, when the question of who should be the Captain of the First XV, had to be decided. There were two candidates Brian Dilley and myself. I voted for Brian, in the hope and expectation that I would get more invitations to play away from the college. Brian was elected as the College Captain, but I took my fair share of training sessions with the new team. Training sessions were never part of the Lancashire way of playing rugby, at least I don't ever remember having to attend anywhere other then when playing in matches.

The County Trial when all the players who have a chance of playing in the Championship, come together happened on 22 October 1960. I had been waiting for this day since Reg Higgins told me that Liverpool would keep in touch, and Alan Clemison had said, 'The selectors know all about Harvey.' This was the day, two days before my twentieth birthday, so still officially a teenager, when I would know if I could play at County level. True, I had played in a couple of 'friendly matches', but this was the real deal, everyone would be there.

I was down at Simms when the postcard came, and once more I was excused playing for the college, and allowed to travel up for the match. This meant getting a train from Strawberry Hill Station, travelling on the train up to London Waterloo, and then crossing the city by underground to Euston. At Euston I had to buy my return ticket to St Helens via Liverpool, before getting on the train. Then of course there was the question of sustenance as I was allowed to have a meal on the journey. We have to remember that as a good Catholic boy I would not normally eat meat on a Friday, except if I was travelling! Well here I was a traveller.

So when we sat down at the table, in the dining car, me being one of four strangers to each other, I ordered a steak. For me to have a steak was a rare occurrence and unknown on a Friday. My steak duly came, and the waiter being very solicitous, asked if I wanted some horseradish to go with the steak. The businessman who was sitting opposite to me had said yes, so I followed suit. If it was rare for me to have steak, it was unknown for me to have horseradish. The oxtail soup had been very tasty, and of course I had a buttered roll to go with that. So the horseradish was just another garnish which I spread across the meat. The steak knife drew through the meat, and I raised the fork full, to my mouth, together with a nice piece of roast potato, which I very much looked forward to eating. The moment the white horseradish crossed my lips I knew that I had made a dreadful mistake. My nose exploded and I wanted to disgorge the whole mouthful, but tried desperately to drink some water, but with a mouthful of meat and potatoes, fought tearfully to maintain my composure. No one spoke. No one laughed. No one took any notice. But I felt like dying of embarrassment. I had tried to look so clever, so grown up, sophisticated even. I scraped all of the horseradish from the steak, drank copious amounts of water, wiped my eyes and started all over again.

I arrived back at the Parr & Hardshaw Labour Club, now my home, not long before midnight, gave my washing to my mother and went to bed. It was a bright sunny day when we met up at Moss Lane, the home of St Helens rugby union club, around lunchtime. Maybe ten players were to go to Manchester in a mini-bus. Stan Magowan, Jimmy Fairclough, Alan Ashcroft and Harold Bate were some of the party, and of course me. We met up with Ray French and many others when we got to the Manchester club, got changed and played the game.

One of the headlines on the Monday morning said, 'Harvey gets a hat trick.' The piece went on:

> Lancashire's win… was highlighted by a hat trick of tries scored by former England School boy centre Peter Harvey.' Later it said, 'Two fine performances were given by second row forward Ray French and left winger Tony Leadbetter, who each scored a try.

Another: 'The Rest outplayed by Lancashire,' and in that report it said 'The main part of the damage was done by Leadbetter and Harvey, the left wing pair, in the first half. Both had a remarkable ability to make chances out of nothing.' In a later paragraph it said French was one of the discoveries of the trial.

So when the team was picked the back line read: S. Lynch (Liverpool), A. Leadbetter (St Helens) P. Harvey (Liverpool) M. S. Phillips (Flyde), W. Burgess (Flyde), A. B. W. Risman (Manchester), with Frank Booth as scrum-half. I had made the Lancashire County team, a new phase in my life.

John Pugh in his match report for the *Liverpool Daily Post* gave two reasons why Lancashire should be successful this season:

1) The changes made to the forwards since the Ulster debacle…to support Alan Ashcroft in his work in the loose.
2) Harvey, the young Liverpool centre, has established himself as a county player. He is an exciting and clever player, blessed with a sure pair of hands, positional intelligence, and a darting rapier like break. His game is not yet complete – he could feed his wings more, and occasionally he attempts an odd sort of tackle which will harm him more than an opponent-but time and a willingness to learn would cure these faults.

Mick Beddow (ex-Cowley) and Jimmy Fairclough (ex-West Park) are both mentioned in this match report, both playing for the Rest.

When it came to claiming my expenses, I used the lesson taught me by Alan Ashcroft after the trip to Ulster. I took each part of the journey and added up the total train fares, added the meals coming up and going back and gave the total to the treasurer. Jimmy Fairclough, a fellow Lancashire Trialist and former school friend from West Park days, told me recently that he was amazed at the amount that I charged them, as he only asked for half a crown because he had come on the bus from St Helens: and, as he had seen me do the same, wondered what all the expenses were.

With the mention of Jim Fairclough I am reminded that he later went on to sign for St Helens RL before being transferred to Rochdale and then Wigan. Mick Beddow played in the Saints 'A' team.

Looking at that back line above, Tony Leadbetter played just twice for Lancashire before signing on for Leigh. He told me that after his second game for Lancashire, the Leigh directors knocked on his door at the family home in Parr, where the ex-Cowley pupil lived, and over a cup of tea, produced £1,000 in one pound notes, as an inducement to sign professional forms. W. (Bill) Burgess was to play a few more games than that but quite soon was induced to sign for Barrow RL, and later went on to tour with the Great Britain team. A. B. W. (Bev) Risman, had already toured with the British Lions, and having a famous father in Rugby League, went to Leigh within a couple of years of playing in this game.

Of course I went back down to Twickenham on the Sunday night train, a journey I was to become used to, I'm very glad to say.

Does a Dormouse Need a Handkerchief in his Rugby Drawers?

Living in one of the college rooms had many advantages. Perhaps the one I liked most was that I could sleep for as long as I wanted without being disturbed. I was given the name 'dormouse' because I slept so much. I thought that it was mainly to do with recovery time. As a main PE student I was expected to work in the gymnasium or on the playing fields every day. Then there were rugby matches on Wednesday afternoons and rugby training, two sessions a week. College Lectures in Physics, History and Maths were all seminars so I had to attend, but sometimes year lectures in Education might be skipped, and more than likely I would not be missed. However, one of the disadvantages was that I was away from home, and in particular, away from Ruth Twist. She was doing a similar course in Teacher Training at Mount Pleasant College in Liverpool. We wrote to each other every week, and this particular week I was away for my twentieth birthday on 24 October 1960. I got a card of course and was congratulated on being picked for the County team, for the first time, in the County Championship. The match was to be at Birkenhead Park on the following Saturday and Ruth and her friends from her College would be there.

Having been picked to play against Cheshire at Birkenhead Park, I was back up on the train on Friday of the next week. Learning my lesson from the week before, I took a small amount of horseradish, and gingerly used a tiny amount to learn how to use this potent substance. Still I was home again, lucky boy.

There was little by way of preparation for this match, or any other come to that. One cannot imagine how amateur Rugby Union was in those days, even at County level. We probably met for lunch and had a team talk; usually given by the Captain, in this case Alan Ashcroft. Then we were taken to the venue and jerseys and socks were doled out to each player. I was very proud of my number twelve shirt with the Red Rose badge on the left breast, and the new socks, dark blue with the red and white striped top. I knew that I had to give the jersey back after the game but I would get to keep the socks. I had of course bought a new pair of blue shorts for the occasion, but was still wearing the boots which Alan Prescot had given me.

I learned many lessons from people like Alan Ashcroft and Reg Higgins, not all of them about playing rugby. That day I was amazed when Alan, the Captain of the team, started an argument with the kit man as we were all getting changed.

'Can I have a new pair of socks please?' seemed a reasonable request to me, especially as Alan asked with a smile and a knowing look.

'No,' said the official, 'You have had plenty pairs of socks and you know to bring them with you.'

'Well you see, I like to wear them when I am refereeing the matches at school (he taught at Liverpool College) and they get worn out.'

'That's not my problem, you can't have any more.'

With that Alan pulled on a pair of socks with holes in the back and then proceeded to blacken his legs with shoe polish saying, 'It's coming to something when the Captain of Lancashire has to use boot polish to cover up the holes in his socks.'

To much applause the 'kit man' threw him a pair of socks and laughingly said, 'You do me every year with the same trick.'

When we were dressed for the match Eric Evans, this time with his trousers on, told us that we were Lancashire. We were brave; heroic even; we fought like Lions, and played rugby like only Lancastrians do. Henry V before Agincourt was the model for Eric that day, and every day that I heard him speak. The stamping of feet, and the running on the spot was to summon up the blood as we charged out of the door of the Pavilion.

There, right by the entrance to the pitch stood Ruth Twist and her college friends. They had been regaled about this Peter Harvey, the golden boy, who they had never seen, this games playing titan, who had captained his country and captivated her heart. And here he was, the smallest player on the field, in new blue shorts which came to his knees, looking rather ridiculous to them.

So what did happen next? I have only one account to go from but it says that the match was 'glorious'. The full match report was as follows:

> I doubt if we shall ever see a better game than that at Birkenhead where Cheshire beat Lancashire by a goal, a dropped goal (11 pts) to three tries (9 pts). With a big crowd yelling their heads off as one side then the other, threw all into attack, it was real rugby, a match to talk about for weeks afterwards. Lancashire must take credit for their fight against odds, during which they gave us glimpses of their own inimitable brand of rugby.
>
> They were without fullback J. Lynch from the first minute, when he twisted a knee, until near half time, but their adventurous spirit was never dimmed. Soon after Lynch had returned, limping, his stand in J. A. Lambert returned to the pack. Cheshire were hammered back to their own 25 and time after time Lancashire were oh so near to victory. Lancashire's pack deserves the highest praise especially for their scrimmaging, which was tight, tidy and effective, even when it was seven against eight. E. Hughes, stoutly propped by G. St J. Goddard and R Lightfoot, had a slight margin against the head: J. Simpson and R. French countered the skill of M. P. M. Evans in the line out: and A. Ashcroft and S. Wilcock ranged far and wide in the loose. From the chances made by the pack the Lancashire backs should have scored a couple more tries, even against the speed and covering of L. Rimmer and J. F. Billington and the Cheshire outsides.
>
> They are not yet well enough acquainted with each other to sustain unorthodox

Lancashire *v.* Ulster 1960.
Back row: Mr H. Jackson, (Referee); Lambert; Hughes; Conchie; Parker; Lynch; Stringer; R. H. Guest, (Touch judge).
Second row: Burgess; Marsh; Wardle; Ashcroft, (Capt.); N. Shaw, (Lancs. President); Goddard; Smith; Webster.
Front row: Booth; Harvey;

moves by instinct, which meant that fine individual efforts by A. B. W. Risman, P. Harvey, a highly promising youngster, and M. S. Phillips tended to fade: but the ideas are there—that's the big thing and W. Burgess on the wing did have sufficient chances to thrill the crowd many times with his bold running. I like Burgess: give him half a chance and he brings a crowd to its feet.

Yes we had ideas, but we had never played together, and I had to do something about those shorts. Rugby Union shorts were quite different from the ones which I had worn at school, or even at college, where black, blue or white gym shorts were fine for Rugby.

No, these were special Rugby Union shorts which had pockets for your handkerchief. I never ever saw anyone blow their nose during a rugby match, but we had handkerchiefs in a pocket just in case we wanted to. The shorts were also tailored, in that they were cut wider on the hip and were barrel shaped; consequently I looked twice as wide as I actually was. They had a broad waistband and turned up bottoms which were almost twice as wide as my legs. The very narrow red and white stripes of the Lancashire jersey, and those ridiculous shorts, made me look much shorter than my stocky five foot six inches. Something had to be done.

12/11/60
Durham 12 Lancashire 11 at Hartlepool

Under the headline: Lancashire play all of the rugby but still lose, Derek Jewell had this to say: 'Risman looked quite simply the best fly half in the world and this was probably his finest display since he came back from New Zealand'. He also mentions 'a brilliant dummy scissors with Harvey'. However, despite scoring two tries to their nil, we were beaten with penalty goals. He began his piece with this conclusion. 'What is still possibly the best side in the Northern Rugby Union Championship this morning sits mournfully winless at the bottom of the County Table.'

The next match report begins; 'An odd game this Rugby. Lancashire put on their worst championship display…and yet managed to win…against the co-favourites for the Northern title.'

19/11/1960
Lancashire 6 Northumberland 3 Fylde
S. Lynch, W. Burgess, M. S. Phillips, P. Harvey (St Marys College), D. Webster, A. B. W. Risman, F. Booth, G. St John Goddard, E. Hughes, R. Lightfoot, R. French, J. Simpson, J. A. Lambert, S. Wilcock, A. Ashcroft

23/11/1960
North West Counties v South Africa

How can it be that a match, in which I did not play, still rankles with me? As so many times with team selection there is an element of spreading the net to include some faction or another. There were eight players from Lancashire, three from Cumberland, and four from Cheshire. It is true that both M. S. Phillips (Lancashire) and W. M. Patterson (Cheshire), who played in the centres were the Captains of their county side. Bill Burgess, (Lancashire) was as good as any wing in England and Don Staniford, (Cheshire) a powerful runner who was to become a friend later at Loughborough, formed a formidable back line. Both halves were from Lancashire, F. Booth from Fylde, and A. B. W. Risman Loughborough, Lancashire and England, was an outstanding fly half.

I, on the other hand was still only in the eyes of the selectors, and so not automatically on the team sheet. However, I was given a place as a reserve and proudly took my card along with me when I went to see the Vice Principal at Strawberry Hill. Clad in his black robes, Dr Fr Dunning was not very approachable and he scowled when he opened the door to his study. This was to be the one and only time when I was in that room: oak panelled and austere and not at all friendly; after all the Vice Principal is in charge of discipline and he wondered what I wanted with him. Though I had been at the college for more than a year, I had rarely, if ever come into contact with him, and it was quite possible that he had no idea who I was. 'Please Fr. I have got this reserve card for a very important match next Wednesday and I need your permission to take time off to go up to Manchester.' The match was to be at the Manchester City FC ground at Maine Road on Wednesday 23 November. I had been to watch the Saints there when they played Halifax in the Championship Final in 1953, and so wanted to go again.

'Have you seen the Springboks play? They are very big.'

No I hadn't seen them play, but I so wanted to. They were the Springboks. Tom van Vollenhoven was a Springbok, I had seen him play and he was a great player.

'While you are here at St Mary's, I am responsible for your welfare and I don't think that you should play.'

'But I am a reserve and want to be there.'

Handing me back my card, he refused me permission to take leave for the two days which would have been necessary to attend the game.

And so I am in the programme picture, but was never at the match, all thanks to Fr Dunning. Ray French was in that team, but had not played in the match against Ulster, so was not in the photograph which appeared in the programme. It was a seminal match for him and led to his playing for England in the next semester. My good friend Ron McCarten also played against that Springbok side, but he played for Ireland and in my mind's eye, I can still see him tackling the giant J. P. Englebrecht underneath his six foot one inch armpits. Fr Dunning could not stop Ron playing for Ireland, and I dearly wish that he had allowed me to go up to Manchester for that Wednesday in November 1960.

10/12/60
Lancashire 10 Yorkshire 10. Waterloo

There are four different match reports for this match so we should see some different opinions. John Pugh, a great supporter of these parts, began his report in less than glowing terms:

> With triumphant shouts from across the Mersey ringing in their ears, Lancashire can go thoughtfully into hibernation until autumn 1961. In their long rest they can ponder whether ill luck robbed them of a deserved place in the county championship semi-final or whether that same ill luck merely masked the faults of the team. The last game with Yorkshire at Blundellsands underlined the question. For 55 sedate minutes—the disrespectful were calling it the war of the primroses—Lancashire were the better of two mundane teams and achieved a ten point lead by virtue of two splendid tries, tries that excitingly evoked visions of a brilliant Lancashire.

His piece was headed 'Lancashire lack the will to win.'
He explained how the lead had been achieved with two excellent tries but the injury to Wilcox at full back had cost one try, and the resulting withdrawal of Alan Lambert to full back had caused the pack to lose its momentum.

> Adversity reveals the true calibre of a side and this was the moment of truth for Lancashire . . . and in those final minutes of the game and the County season brought to the surface what might have been the underlying Lancashire fault this year—the lack of will to win. Harvey, Ashcroft and French had the victory urge in abundance but individually it accomplishes little. It needs to sweep through the whole team.

Then in a most revealing sentence he discloses:

> And when it is remembered that just how much individual ability there is-five Lancastrians are in the final England Trial on Saturday and three more have reserve cards-one can only shake the head in disappointment at their final place in the county championship table.

I was one of those with a reserve card, but I had learned a great deal from playing with a Lancashire team full of international class players.

Changes in the Game of Rugby Union

As part of my college work I was developing a thesis, 'The back row and half back partnership.' Playing almost exclusively as a centre I had been close to all of the players who were current Internationals in the five key positions named in the thesis.

The arguments were about which player should be in the England team at stand-off, and included Bev Risman, Richard Sharp, Phil Horrocks-Taylor and Mike Weston. All played differently and the shape of the team was affected by which one was picked at stand-off. We were still in the days of being able to kick directly into touch, and often matches were played up and down the touchlines, sometimes with little involvement from the backs. Open side wing forwards were used to try to wipe out the stand-off and to cover across behind the backs in a defensive role to cut down the space. My thesis said that if the inside centre ran into his man deliberately, standing up and turning to pass to the open side, then the back row could, and should be used as an attacking force, as well as a defensive one. There were 5,000 words in that thesis, later expanded to 10,000 words when I went to Loughborough, which explored all of the possible moves which would follow the use of the back row and half backs in partnership. I included all of the running lines necessary, and ways in which coaching would be needed to change the then accepted format, of forward set piece activity and usually separate back line set pieces.

This change of emphasis led directly to what became known as the crash ball centre, taking the tackle deliberately to begin a system of recycling the ball away from set piece rugby, with lots of scrums and line outs, and separate forward and back play. I had the best advice possible from people like Alan Ashcroft, Reg Higgins, Keith Byrne, Bev Risman and lots more international players.

I had a full season to develop this idea, and College Rugby was a fertile field to introduce a game which had far less kicking and much more open attacking play. The argument which we, at Strawberry Hill, had throughout 1960 was about the relative merits of Risman's inside break versus the outside break of Richard Sharp, leavened a little with the unusual, though very effective high bomb used by Mike Weston at Durham, and Phil Horrocks-Taylor playing the standard game for Yorkshire. Richard Sharp held the England position for that season, much to the delight of Charlie Galbraith and the other Cornish warriors who were with me at Twickenham. Bev Risman was completing his Diploma at Loughborough and I played with him in the Lancashire team. Bev had an excellent kicking game, and his ability to drive the opponents back into their own half, took away most of the driving effort needed by keeping the ball in hand. The combination of his inside break and long kicks deep into the heart of defence, forced the open side wing forward to try to take him on an inside curve, to stop him side-stepping. This meant that more often than not Bev would be able to serve his inside centre directly. Also by sending a long raking kick across to the opposite wing, he forced the wingman to be ready to stand back. In essence his play was unpredictable, and therefore not easy to play against. I particularly remember his ability to punt the ball in a long low spiral, which seemed to gain much more ground than other kickers. He also had the knack of making his kicks travel with the end of their flight being into touch, rather than kick too steeply into touch, or not find touch at all. Risman would take the line on, and often sidestepped inside the inside centre, this could be quite devastating if he also was outside the covering open side. Both he and Tom Brophy later, used this ploy to great effect, and I learned to follow them as they broke, my job was then to take on the ball into the space behind.

In Durham they developed a different game which was based upon 'ten man rugby'. The forwards would win the ball and run forward, as the ball was passed back to Mike Weston. He would boot the ball high into the area towards the opposing fullback, with enough hang time for the forwards to challenge in numbers. It was a highly effective form of play as the backs would pick up the pieces, and possession, if the full back failed to catch the ball. The Lancashire back row, determined to stop this approach, made sure that they tackled Weston, even if he had already kicked the ball. This was a very dangerous tactic in itself as it forced the referee to give a penalty, one way or another. Our hope was that he could see that all of the Durham forwards were offside as they were in front of Weston. On the other hand the referee might decide that the back row had not got to him in time and award a penalty for a late tackle. I still believe in this tactic today, putting the kicker on the ground, though they have changed the rules in Rugby Union to say that forwards must not go forward from an off side position and in Rugby League, must allow the catcher ten yards before he can be tackled. Either way, decisions are largely down to the referee.

The rugby story I like about Phil Horrocks-Taylor, concerns Alex Murphy, who played against him when he was in the RAF. The story (probably apocryphal) says that Alex dummied him, and Horrocks went one way and Taylor the other. Actually, he was a very solid traditional rugby union standoff, really 'a no nonsense Yorkshire man'.

I am very proud to say that we at St Mary's College were one of the first teams in England to develop what became known as the 'box kick.' At that time stand-off halves often kicked directly into touch from all over the pitch. This lead to boring sterile rugby, with many matches being played up and down the touch lines in a succession of line outs. We heard of a new tactic which was being used in New Zealand. We had time to practice, and we used it often. Instead of kicking into touch our scrum-half kicked overhead, just beyond the forwards so that they could chase, with a good chance of getting to the break down, before the opposition. I know everybody does that now, but they didn't use to. If the fullback stood close behind the forwards, then lots of space would be behind him, or across on the open side of the field. It was all about making and using space. Most good tactics still revolve around that premise.

Developing as a Teacher and Coach, With Friends Doing the Same in Different Fields

I often took the rugby training at St Mary's and the time was spent largely on fitness training, but we did also practice set moves by the backs, and forwards were expected to know when box kicks were to be used, or a rolling maul be developed, or a back row move with the stand-off was on. I was developing, taking the ball in and using a slip pass to the following back row. Not done in the way that crash ball is now done, but nevertheless needing joint action to be successful. One of the new players in the team was a priest named Mark Jabalé, who played in the front row. He was a solidly built guy who lived out at Ealing and came into College for our training sessions, replacing Tino Basseni, in the front row. I never saw him actually in the College, as he was on a postgraduate

Simms Volleyball Team 1960-61.
Many names unknown for this team as there were few tournaments.
Front row: 2nd left Peter Harvey; John Wilcock; Mr Leary; George Bulman.

course, but he did play with us. Our rugby training was very hard, and as an academic, he felt it more than most. I'm sure that he felt that he was being picked on as a newcomer to the team. He will reappear later in this story.

I must mention other games which we played during the winter season. The college had an excellent football team which I supported from the touchline but never played for. However, I did get involved with the basketball and played often in the college team in one of the London Leagues. I had left Simmeries (St Mary's) before Mr Jagger (father of Mick) came. He was a lecturer there, with an interest in basketball, but nowhere near as influential as Dr Vaughan Thomas, a Lecturer and coach who took the team to senior league level ten years later. He, (Vaughan Thomas) also transformed the PE Department at John Moores University in Liverpool, ten more years after that. In that process he persuaded Wilf Murphy to renew his studies and take his Masters and Doctorate. Who said front row forwards had no brains, certainly not me!

I mention basketball for two reasons, one as a game in its own right and secondly because it was a fine vehicle for rugby training on cold wet winter nights. Actually I got my college colours, so I must have played in plenty of games. I have said earlier, that in my head I was six feet tall, well nowhere was that more apparent than when I played basketball. Essentially a non-contact game, I played either wing attack or centrally as a ball distributor. I had a standing jump of around 33 inches, and though I never could reach the ring, could do a decent lay up shot. One of the players who was interested in basketball, was George Bulman, a student from Liverpool who was very interested in football. However, George had also served in the army for his National Service and he had been introduced to volleyball, a game virtually unknown in this country.

George started up a volleyball club, which I joined as he was my friend. George, John Wilcock and me went down to the American Air Force Base at Bushey Park where we watched them training and playing. When we got back to the college, George was able to start a club, and his enthusiasm managed to get a team together. Strange as it seems, we entered and played in a tournament, the only English team there. I know that this is laughable, but we started talking about being the English team and playing for England. I do know that George stuck with that ambition and spent most of his life supporting Basketball, and in particular volleyball, writing several books on the subject of coaching. George started from no knowledge and became a National coach.

Terry Dillon, who I mentioned earlier as a back row forward, had a very successful career in teaching. As well, he became interested in rowing when he was a head teacher in Nottingham, he managed to continue his interest, to such an extent, that he went on to coach a Great Britain rowing pair to the World Championships in Indianapolis in 1992. His interest helped his family to take up rowing and his son Terence (my godson), got his rowing blue in the winning Oxford boat in 1989, sandwiched between two Olympic Games at Seoul in 1988 and Barcelona in 1992 when he was in the GB eight. Membership of Leander Rowing Club was a natural progression for them both and the continued development of Terry as a rowing coach, owes a great deal to his friendship with Jurgen Grobler. It was Jurgen who introduced a precision into GB rowing that made GB one of the greatest rowing nations in the world. So now Terry has great people like Redgrave, Pinsent and all of the other oarsmen now talking to him as a friend, and by association, on occasion, to me.

Remember Mark Jabalé, the priest who we met earlier? He also had a very successful life as a teacher. He became head teacher at Belmont Abbey and decided that he wanted his school to become highly proficient at playing rugby. He already had Mick Maybury (who played with me at Liverpool and St Mary's), and Tom Fallon a hooker from Birkenhead Park, both county players, as teachers in his school. Fr Mark contacted me and asked did I know Ray French as they wanted to get Cowley on their fixture list. Ray responded positively and over many years the two schools played for the Cowbel Trophy. Fr Mark profited by getting the benefit of the Cowley rugby playing experience and Ray French, finding a summer location at a boarding school for his players to have a wonderful pre-season training establishment.

Talking of school exchanges, there was a team from Argentina, who came over here to play against Cowley and after the match, the master in charge asked Ray if he knew me, and Ray called me immediately. Cowley, playing at Moss Lane, entertained the visiting school with gusto and a grand evening was had by all. The visiting master, a rugby player who knew me from St Mary's College, invited Ray and his assistants to make a return trip to play them in Argentina. Showing all of that tenacity and self-confidence in their organisational abilities, now so well known, they took up the offer, and Cowley went on their first foreign tour the next year.

Fr Mark, was not only the Headmaster at Belmont School, he also became the Abbot of Belmont Abbey, then later became the Bishop of Minerva, (now Emeritus Bishop) During his tenure of the various offices, he became very interested in rowing and ultimately became one of the Stewards at The Henley Royal Regatta. With Terry Dillon being a highly respected coach, Terence, my godson, an Olympic rower, it is not surprising that Ruth and I have on several occasions, watched boats crossing the finishing line from Stewards Enclosure and the grandstand. Once, I had the singular honour of travelling in the umpire boat with Umpire Fr Mark controlling the race, behind one of Terry's crews, as they rowed down Henley's famous straight, cheered on by all those in the grandstand. I doubt any other rugby league player can claim to have done that.

Blackheath *v.* Harlequins at Twickenham 1960-61.
Peter Harvey sitting front left. The only two players Peter knew were Mick Maybury and Chris Cafferata, back row 3rd and 2nd from right end, both from Liverpool RUFC.

CHAPTER 13

Liverpool and Blackheath: Bedrock of Rugby Union

Playing at Loughborough was also an unusual experience which I will develop later, but one aspect was the fitness of the players, and the speed at which the game was played. They were great at sevens play and were very willing to develop the idea of fast breaking back row forwards. The College Captain was a back row player named Roger Pearman, who went on later to play for Wakefield Trinity as a loose forward in their Cup Winning team. John Mantle was also there, and what an athlete he was then, and a great player later at St Helens. So the development of the breaking back row forwards with half back combinations became the feature of our game.

Within the Lancashire team the back row of Lambert, Ashcroft and Wilson, was giving way to Murphy, Jones and Burgess, or Murphy, Keith Bearne and Burgess. Wilf Murphy was to go on and play around 1,000 games for Liverpool moving through from the back row to the front, but I remember him playing at stand-off in the winning Liverpool team at the Northern Sevens, with Tom Brophy as his scrum-half and me playing in the centre with Michael (Owlie) Collins on the wing. Keith Bearne (Cambridge, Liverpool and Scotland) was also a fast breaking number eight. This then was an ideal back row to exploit the idea of second phase attack, using Brophy's inside break, or my hit and spin to release the ball to them. John Burgess (Broughton Park) was a man in the Eric Evans mould. He took to the idea in a full-blooded way and it became the Lancashire tactic of choice. Later players in the Lancashire jersey well remember John Burgess, by then the Lancashire Coach, using the new invention, insisting that the inside centre took the ball into the tackle at every opportunity. Geoff Pimblett has since told me that he was so cheesed off with the move, that having played almost 200 matches for St Helens at Rugby Union, he was pleased to sign for St Helens at Rugby League.

Rugby League was not in my mind the second time that I played at Twickenham. There is no doubt that it was a magnificent stadium and less than a couple of miles from St Marys College, for whom I was playing week in and week out.

In 1960 I played for Liverpool in their match against Manchester the weekend before Christmas. The games between these two sides are always billed as commemorating the first ever match between two club sides. It might as well have been the first match ever played for all that I remember, except for one thing.

It was after this match, with everyone having the usual top ups, from the jugs of beer being passed around, when I was asked to play for Blackheath. I had been asked before, but the time was not right. On this occasion I was asked to play for Blackheath in their match against the Harlequins at Twickenham. Having played six or seven county games for Lancashire, I was invited as a guest, and assured that there was a strong connection between Liverpool and The Club (Blackheath). This was to be one of the big fixtures of their season, and my invitation was to strengthen the team. Knowing that I would not be called upon by the college so early in January I agreed to play two matches for Blackheath, the first against Harlequins at Twickenham, the second, a week later against London Scottish at Richmond Athletic Ground. Both away matches, and so it came about that I can honestly say that I played for Blackheath, but never visited their home ground.

I was amazed when I turned up at Twickenham, to find that I was not the only guest to play for Blackheath. I recognised two others from Liverpool, Chris Cafferata and Mike Maybury, as well as two others I knew then, but have forgotten now. None of us had ever trained at Blackheath, but were expected to strengthen the team by our involvement. The most important point of all was missed by my self-centred approach to being a guest. What was the effect on those members of the Blackheath Club who did not play that day? They would have turned up for pre-season, trained regularly, perhaps travelling a long way on bad nights, and this was their reward. To find, at least five players who had been called in for the most prestigious match of the season, taking their place, in the big game.

It was a bright clear day, with quite a large crowd, with the typical Harlequins support, but I remember little or nothing of the game itself.

I suppose that it introduced me to another layer of the Rugby Union fraternity, the southern brethren, who would have turned their noses up distinctly, at the very idea of professional sport. The game was robust but exceedingly fair and the one memory I do have was just how quick John Young, the Harlequins and England winger actually was. Paired with international centre J. J. McPartlin, they were perhaps the best I had faced so far in my short career. The programme notes, preceding the match say:

> The side they are bringing today is an interesting one. Two players are making their first appearance in The Club XV, both of them Lancashire county caps, P. Harvey, the right centre and C. C. Cafferata at wing forward.

The next Saturday I played once more for Blackheath, with a new centre partner, H. J. C. Brown, (England Trials, Barbarians and Combined Services) and the setting could not have been more of a contrast. The open fields of the Richmond Athletic Ground were nothing like the tall double-decked stands of Twickenham. Neither did the accents of the Scottish players resonate like those of the Harlequins. In fact for me, I was at home with the Scottish burr, and it did not at that time, strike me that I might have competed directly with the two Scottish centres who played for London Scottish, for a place in their national team. In fact that day Scotland were playing the Springboks at Murrayfield, and the club side was weakened by the non-availability of K. J. F. Scotland, R. H. Thompson, I. G. P. Laughland, N. S. Bruce, F. Ten Bos and G. H. Waddell. Still, the man I marked that day was J. A. P. Shackleton, already an international himself. Blackheath were without P. T. Wright (playing for England at Cardiff). I was a good enough rugby player to be guesting for this club, but perhaps I didn't have enough initials to become an international!

By the time that I played that match on 21 January, 1961, I was back at Simms and expected to play for them on Saturdays. R. J. McCarten, having made his arrangements before going to College was playing for London Irish, and had been picked to play in his national team. During that term I, along with many of the rugby players from Simms, went down to watch England play at Twickenham, including those matches played by Ray French, stepping up from the Lancashire team.

England V France 25 February 1961

John Willcox (Oxford & Harlequins) played full back, with J. C. R. Young (Harlequins) on one wing with J. Roberts (Old Milhillians & Sale), on the other. The team had A. B. W. Risman (Loughborough College & Manchester) and M. P. Weston (Richmond & Durham City) in the centres with Richard Sharp at stand-off, R. E. G. Jeeps captained the side from scrum-half. These were the guys I had to have my sights set on if I hoped to play for England. I

RL and RU captains of Lancashire. John with a broken ankle and Peter.

knew every one of them and had played in their company.

In the second fixture, at Twickenham, that year W. M. Patterson (Sale) replaced Bev. Risman in the centre position, and I notice from the programme that Mr L. M. Boundy (Hertfordshire) was the touch judge.

Ray French had broken into the England team and we were all delighted for him. Of course I knew him personally, but all of my teammates at St Mary's did not. However, over the Spring term lots of discussions took place about our international representatives, and naturally from time to time, my ambition to join them. Playing in the County Championship I was playing with or against this class of player regularly. I remember several conversations with Brian O'Gorman, Public Schoolboy, ex-Army Officer, member of the MCC, who became a mentor to me. He talked about many things which I did wrongly, like putting a Windsor knot on a club tie. 'That is the problem with you people, you always want to rebel.' Sorry Brian I just didn't know the form.

He was ever so polite and encouraging and explained to me why he thought that getting a Blue was more important than playing for Lancashire, in terms of getting an international trial. In those days he was right, playing in the Varsity Match was equivalent to an England Trial. However, he was the person most responsible for my odd choice of twenty-first birthday present, still in the future. He pointed out that after every International Match there was a formal dinner and that if I was going to play for England I should buy a dinner suit. My mother was amazed that I wanted such a present, but my father totally understood. I have had a dinner suit ever since, and am comfortable with wearing it, when the occasion calls for such attire. Not much call for that at the Parr and Hardshaw Labour Club.

From March 1961, I have a cutting from the local newspaper which contains a photograph of me and my brother John, which has the caption 'Peter (RU) sympathises with John (RL).' This article tells of how John has been making his mark in the junior Rugby League game, and whilst playing for the St Helens Town junior team at Bobbies Lane, he damaged his ankle in the opening stages of the match against Oldham. John played on and it was not until after the game that he realised that there was a fracture. The sympathy from me was because that fracture caused him to miss the Lancashire Amateur Rugby League match, for which he had already been selected as Captain. The article also tells everyone that the Harvey boys are sons of Mr Peter Harvey, steward of the Parr and Hardshaw Labour Club, who was once well known as 'Battling Harvey' and a boxer of considerable repute. John followed my dad in this respect, taking up boxing as well as Rugby Union, when he served nine years in the Army. He played Rugby Union for the Corps as well as Birkenhead Park and St Helens RU clubs, where he served loyally as a committee member for many years.

Lancashire 1961.
The Photograph of Lancashire Rugby Union Team seems to have odd jerseys for a championship match so it could be a trial team.
Back row: left to right: K. R. F. Bearne *Liverpool*; T. R. Watts, *St Helens*; R. Lightfoot, *Liverpool*; G. V. R. Watson, *Waterloo*; B. S. Jackson, *Broughton Park*; E. Hughes, *Liverpool*; A. Ashcroft, *Waterloo*; G. St. J. Goddard, *Manchester*.
Front row: D. Unsworth, *Liverpool*; W. R. Gibbins, *Waterloo*; T. Brophy, *Liverpool Univ.*; H. Scott, *Manchester*; B. Unsworth, *Liverpool*; P. Harvey, *Liverpool*; T. Pimblett, *St Helens*. Please Note T. Brophy, B. Unsworth and P. Harvey are all from West Park School.

CHAPTER 14

Hard Graft at Loughborough

September 1961 was the month that I went to Loughborough College and what an experience that turned out to be! From the rugby perspective, the season started with a couple of games for the Lancashire Presidents XV, always enjoyable, and never too strenuous. Then came the first big match of the season, Lancashire V Cornwall at Redruth. My mate Charlie Galbraith, a hard nut second row forward at Simms, but soft as my cap as a friend, had always stressed that Redruth was the heart of Cornish rugby.

C. D. Galbraith (Charlie) later muscled up and made it to the Cornish county side, his life's ambition. He played alongside Cyril (Bonzo) Johns in the front row. Charlie described that as being at the business end of a thrashing machine, everything flailing at once. The entrance to the ground at Redruth had a notice which said quite simply, 'Them as Dies will be the lucky ones.' The intention to frighten the opposition was quite clear, but I must say, that on both occasions I played against Cornwall, though the games were tight, they were played in very good spirit. Rather than talk about the match which was a 3-3 draw I will quote from the programme, in anticipation of the match, written by W. G. Bevan about Lancashire:

> Perhaps one of the finest aspects of Lancashire rugby is the friendly atmosphere which exists in clubs, and between clubs, in the county . . . but from the ashes of defeat, the phoenix of success must surely rise again. With retirements, and the loss of players of the calibre of Risman, French, Parker, Leadbetter and Burgess, to the Rugby League, the county is going through a phase of experiment and rebuilding. In this context, the schools committee is playing its part, and in today's side O'Donnell, Harvey, Brophy and Bearne, all played for the Lancashire Schools XV before moving on into club rugby, and the senior side.'

The fact was that seldom did Lancashire put out the same team, on a week-to-week basis. I was obviously pleased to be playing with Malcolm Phillips, an international centre, but on this occasion also playing next to Tom Brophy, at stand-off, making his debut for the county team.

I wanted to apply to Loughborough College to do my Diploma year there. St Mary's also did a Diploma in PE but I felt that there was a bigger challenge at Loughborough. I applied during the spring term and I still have the letter and reference given to me by my PE teacher at West Park. Remember him? Yes Joe Coan. He was suggesting to me that I should go to Carnegie College in Leeds, as they were better at teaching teachers how to teach, whereas Loughborough were more interested in performers. I went up for interview, which was in two parts.

The first, not unusually, was in a sports hall, where we (there were about four in the group) had to perform some gymnastics and then play with a variety of balls. Footballs, rugby balls, basket balls, hockey balls, running and catching, and generally showing some hand and eye co-ordination. We were told that students who could not do all of these things would not be accepted. The second part of the interview procedure, was a formal discussion with the Dean or Vice Principal. He wanted to know what standard we had achieved in our other subjects besides the PE, which would have had to be outstanding, at least in one area. I remember quite distinctly being told that all students were expected to attend lectures on a Saturday morning. He looked at me, with a withering shake of the head when I emphasised, that when I had told him that I played for Lancashire, I meant at senior level as well as schools. He said, 'Everyone who comes here plays for some county or another, we work Saturday mornings, that's final.'

Joe Coan had been right; everyone was a high level performer at something.

I know that Ray French would have liked to have done his Post Graduate year at Loughborough, that year, but this Saturday morning rule came into play, as he had signed for St Helens RLFC. On the other hand, it could easily be seen that as he would not be eligible to play rugby union, he was not accepted. Therefore, he stayed at Leeds University, did not play RU but carried on quite happily at St Helens RLFC. We make our decisions and stand by the consequences.

As the time came closer for me to go to Loughborough, possibly at one of the opening matches of the season, with the Presidents XV, the respected rugby journalist W. B. Croxford engaged me in conversation, in the warmth of the after match hospitality. He congratulated me on my continuing successful performance in the Lancashire team, and looking forward, talked to me about rugby at Loughborough. In particular, he gave me the name of someone who he knew was going to be there at the same time as me. Not a rugby player, but he will help you with your acceleration and general pace. I wrote the name down and awaited any outcome. Eventually, I left my home in the Running Horses, the old town centre public house, which my father had taken on as the licensee, and went to meet all of these people who every-one was telling me were so good.

I arrived at Middle Avenue, at the house where I was to live, to be met by Mrs Barrett, my landlady, and David Brookes, my gymnastics partner from St Mary's, together with Brian Topham, a mature teacher from Sheffield. She told us that one of her students the year before was Berwyn Jones, (who went on to play for Wakefield, Great Britain and St Helens) who was an international sprinter in his own right, and in a most remarkable co-incidence, which would only come to light some years later, she was also the landlady for Cyril Prescott from whom Ruth and I bought our house in Pike Place. He was a student at the College ten years before me.

We settled in on the Sunday and on Monday morning walked the half a mile or so up to the College Campus. During the induction day we learned about the structure of the students, how there were three sets moving from the two-year college course onto the third year Honours Course, and three other groups including those from other colleges (that's me), postgraduates, and mature students (those who have qualified earlier and taught for five years already). Quite a diverse bunch, a total of around 120, roughly six groups of twenty, on the PE Course, and roughly the same on the Handicraft Course as well. To my surprise I had been appointed by the college as leader of our group, how and why I will never know – and my counterpart in the mature students was Tom Farrell, which had been the name given to me by W. B. Croxford. When I was there in 1961/2 there were three parts to the education offered on the campus. I was at the College of Physical Education; there was a College of Handicraft and a University of Engineering. The students were variously known as The Wooden Tops (us), The Chippies (Woodwork) and the Nuts (Engineers). Now of course it is the University of Loughborough, without those distinctions.

I arranged with Tom that we would have our first training session the following week. That first week we were required to attend the Freshers' Evening, where the intention was that we sign up for the various clubs and societies which interested us. I was determined to heed Gerry Millington's advice, say nothing and just show them what you can do. However, I was in for quite a shock, when I did attend the large hall used for the event. All clubs and societies were organised and run by the Loughborough Students themselves, who had been there for two years and were now the senior students. We were very much the newcomers, and though we were welcomed, we were very much finding our feet, perhaps even the underdogs, certainly seemed to be the ones seeking favours.

Each club had its own display table arranged around the room in a grand circle. The ruling students sat behind the table and we, the applicants sat in front.

The first table I came to was the Basketball Club. I asked politely could I join as maybe I could play in the winter if we couldn't get out training for rugby. No it was not that kind of club. This was for those people who wanted to play Basketball for the college. Well yes I said, I can play basketball, I got my Colours at St Mary's playing in the London League. I'm not sure that it was The London League, or a London League, but I did get my colours and that is because I played in most of the matches. 'Well what position do you play?' was a reasonable question, but my reply caused straightforward laughter. 'How can you play guard at your height? You are too small to play centre or wing attack either, so there is no point in signing on.' Having been dismissed I moved to the next table. Swimming, I was no good at that, so moved on. The Gymnastics Club agreed that I could join, and I felt better. At the Athletics Club they asked me what I did. I said, 'Everything, run, jump and throw.' So they rephrased the question and asked again, 'What did I do best?' I said, 'I can jump over 21 feet and triple jump over 46 feet,' they didn't exactly laugh this time but said, 'We have people who jump over 26 feet and 55 feet, so you won't get in there.'

'I can run 100 yards in almost even time and 440 yards in just over 51 seconds.'

'We have 26 people who break even time and a dozen or more who do under 50 seconds for the quarter.'

Somewhat deflated I moved on passed the Football and Hockey tables until I came to the Rugby table. I must get in here I thought to myself as I sat down. 'Well,' said the guy behind the table, eyeing me up and down, 'Who have you played for?'

I named virtually every team which I had played for, and was almost out of breath with the long list.

'Ok,' he said 'We will give you a trial. Watch the board to see when and where it is.'

The fact was, I was a little fish in a big pond, and really felt deflated, but I had got a trial to look forward to. I played in a couple of trials and was given a place in the second XV. Luckily for me I was still being picked for Lancashire on some Saturdays and in December got an England Trial, which led to the comment in the college newspaper asking how it could be that a member of the College Second XV had an England Trial. I have one match report for Loughborough College 2nd XV 12 v Old Lutonians 3.

> Harvey gave a display of rugby which one expects from a county player. He made the openings, found touch with either foot, and his tackling was devastating. The way Harvey looked and went for the interceptions fascinated the Luton spectators. On his first interception, he was pulled back, but his last one, with a run of 25 yards, gave him a try.

I note that Jack Rowell played in this team, and later went to Leicester and played second row for England, so it wasn't only me that struggled with the college selectors.

One of the Lancashire games I want to refer to was that against Cheshire, at Blundellsands on Saturday 4 November 1961. Bev. Risman had gone to rugby league and his replacement was Tom Brophy, listed as Liverpool University. Risman had preceded me at Loughborough, and Brophy was to follow me the next year. But in that particular match, with Tom Brophy at standoff, Brian Unsworth at right centre and me at left centre, there is proof of yet another three ex-West Park boys making the Lancashire team. With a nod to the future, Tom Pimblett (later a Saint) was playing on the wing outside me. Plenty of other West Park players played at various times but I like to point out where we played in threes.

I also had arranged to meet up with Tom Farrell, who was going to help with my speed. I met him on the campus, in running gear and feeling fit as it was very early in the season. 'Excuse me, Tom,' I asked 'What event do you do?'

'Well, I'm just moving up to the Mile as I am getting on a bit.'

That's no good for me I thought but luckily kept my mouth shut.

'Ok, let's do a few stretchers up and down, for starters.'

The Campus was very large and it was possible to run a long ellipse around the side of a quite steep hill. 'Let's run up the hill, walk across the top and run down the other side.' Tom said, and I concurred. Just a stretcher turned out to be almost flat out for me, and two laps had me panting for breath. 'A miler you say, what did you do before?'

I should have known better, leading with my chin, showing my lack of knowledge. 'I am the British Champion at the quarter hurdles, but there is a chap here who can beat me now and I will have to move on.' I did a few more stretchers with him before he started training at speed, and I knew then and there that I would never make an athlete, in the true sense of that word.

I often went down to the running track to do a bit of training, but that would be a rugby player training, not an athlete's training. I would sit and watch our best athletes, like Robbie Brightwell and John Cooper (who was taking over from Tom Farrell) training for their events. The amount of effort and the technical assistance needed to draw out the best performances from them made me glad that I was a rugby player and not an athlete.

We were all athletes but to a greater or less extent, with higher and lower goals, all timed on the stopwatch. For example, Brightwell and Cooper would have sessions when they had four sprinters with them, each one capable of even time or better. Between them they would run perhaps eight or ten laps of the track, with perhaps two-minute intervals. The quick men would run the first and last 100 and Brightwell and Cooper run the full 400. So pressure all the way round the track, all timed, and each daily session more difficult than the one before. Watching them drag the massive track roller behind them as they practiced 'resistance running' was quite frightening. I always thought how easy it would be for the two guys holding the roller back to fail to stop it when the sprinter slowed down. A runaway roller crushing one of our Olympic athletes would have been really bad news for the college. From my experience in my first term I knew that I would not be good enough to compete in the College Athletics team. I had not played cricket in either of the past two summer terms, so I played tennis and golf, and enjoyed them both. As usual at Loughborough, the standard is very high, and the two lecturers who taught us to play golf, were very good players themselves. One playing off a handicap of three was Leicester Amateur county champion, and it irked the other, who played off scratch, to have to admit that for that season, he had lost the title.

The Diploma is only awarded to students who have passed every exam and competency, in every sport and activity outlined in the prospectus. This comes as quite a shock to some specialist internationals who feel that they are so good at their sport, that they do not have to be able to do those other sports which they do not favour. So I, as a rugby player, was also expected to learn to play and coach football and hockey, as well as tennis and cricket, basketball, gymnastics and trampoline, not forgetting swimming, perhaps the most important in personal survival.

I know that Walter Winterbottom, who was the National Coach to the FA, came and supervised our football coaching, Bob Wilson, later to be the Arsenal goalkeeper, was in a different group from me, and we all had to pass coaching certificates, as part of our Diploma. Athletics was such a strong feature of college life in the summer term, and virtually every day some time would be spent in the sports stadium, usually on the running track, but sometimes in the sports halls learning skills, and more importantly, how to teach those skills.

I vividly remember the day that my group went out to learn how to throw the hammer. This was an activity which I had never done before, despite having worked with John McSorley on improving his javelin technique. Mr Stamatakis was one of the key lecturers in athletics at Loughborough College, and he took our group out onto the sports field to begin our instruction. There we all were in our African violet tracksuits, the choice of the last year's President, himself

Loughborough College Rugby team 1961-62.
Back row: A. E. Chapman, *Stockton & Durham*; D. Staniford, *N. Brighton & Cheshire, England Trials & Barbarians, UAU*; B. Myers, *Milom*; D. A. Gillen, *Queens Belfast, Irish Univ.*; J. Mantle, *Bargoed & WSSRU*; R. Bateman, *W. Hartlepool & Durham*; I. W. Jones, *Birkenhead Park & N. Wales*; J. Gibson, *Workington Cumb. & West*; D. Williams, *Tredegar*.
Second row: A. Davidson, *Workington Cumb. & West*; M. Fairburn, *Ilkley*; M. Harrison, Vice Capt., *Leicester & Leicestershire, UAU*; R. Pearman, Captain, *Headingley*; A. G. Smith, *Bedford, UAU*; D. Cavill, *Pontypool, UAU*; M. Donovan, *Tredegar*.
Front row: P. Harvey, *Liverpool & Lancashire, England Trials & ESRFC, UAU*; R. Hill, *Stafford & Staffordshire, Leicestershire, ESRFC, UAU*.

a hammer thrower, who thought that colour made a change from the usual red. He was certainly right about that, but one did have to have a good deal of panache to wear such a bright colour. When everyone was wearing the tracksuit, no one bothered about it at all, but when we went into schools as individuals we got some very strange looks, if not comments. But I digress.

Mr Stamatakis went through the basic routine of hammer throwing with the whole group. He went through how to hold the handle, how to initiate the first turn, and how to increase the speed of the hammer without actually turning in the throwing circle; I managed all these things, well done for starters. We were all told that we must not let go of the handle, as it would be very dangerous. Gradually we got to feel in charge of the hammer, rather than the other way round.

Mr Stamatakis told the group that he was now going to take us through the next stage, and as this was very dangerous, we had to go to the hammer-throwing cage. He said that I seemed to have mastered the first stages very well, and as he needed someone to do the demonstration, he had picked me to perform. I must admit that I felt very proud he had chosen me. So there I was standing in the hammer-throwing circle for the first time in my life, with the other students in the group standing around behind the safety net.

'OK, Mr Harvey, start the pick up.'

So I did.

'Now try three turns around your head. Well done. Now the body turns and let it fly.'

I went through the first two sets of instructions very well, but when it came to letting go, somehow I miss-timed it, and I went spinning out of the circle and the hammer fell right in the middle of it. The embarrassment when everyone laughed, my face was redder than my hair! Luckily for me Mr Stamatakis, though smiling said, 'Remember he was the best in the group, so you know how bad you all are!' For the end of year assessment every student had to perform every activity. So, the hammer throwers would also have to do the gymnastic tests, and their floor routines were very limited indeed.

By then my work with David Brookes was paying dividends. He had also managed to gain a place at Loughborough, as he was exceptional as a swimmer and diver. We lived in the same lodgings, and though I learned to swim well enough to pass the college standard, I learned much more about gymnastics and trampoline, through working with him.

I did manage to get into the First XV and play plenty of matches. One I remember being a big occasion was the match against St Luke's Exeter, which was one of our big rivals in the PE world. Played at Old Deer Park on a Wednesday afternoon in the middle of February, with the touchlines crammed with supporters from both colleges, all more than 100 miles from home. There was lots of scarf waving, singing and cheering with several coaches from each college in attendance.

As usual I can't remember the score, but I know that we stayed in London till midnight and got back to college about three in the morning, all asleep with thick heads from the beer consumed. Being Loughborough, we were all expected to turn up for lectures at 9 a.m. the next morning, ready to do whatever was on the timetable. In that context, I will explain how we got round the Saturday morning lecture problem. It was always Anatomy and Physiology, the one lecture that everyone attended together; there was no roll call as there were so many students there. If I was playing for Lancashire I would go home on the Friday evening and someone would take notes for me (share their own) and we all did that for each other. We have to say that as this subject was just as important as any of the others, and caused more people to fail for lack of attention, that it was careless in the extreme to disregard those borrowed notes.

A Couple of Weeks in my Life

In a letter post marked 15 March 1962, but addressed to R. Pearman Esq., Captain Rugby Football Club, Loughborough College. I was invited to play for the Universities Athletic Union (UAU). The note says, 'Mr Pearman, please forward the enclosed circulars.'

The first problem with this was that I did not live in the college, and Roger Pearman did not know where my lodgings were. It took a week for him to find me and that was too late to accept the first invitation, which was to play for the UAU v Combined NE Counties. The match would be at Darlington on 31 March. Much as I would have liked to play against old foes I had to decline the invitation. Luckily for me there was a second invitation in the same envelope. As St Mary's College was one of the external colleges of London University, I had never had a chance to play for the UAU. This was my only chance and I really wanted to take it with both hands, however, it was not straightforward. The invitation was to go on the Easter Tour to South Wales, with matches against Ebbw Vale, Neath, Bristol and Abertillery, between 20 and 24 April, yes four matches in four days! Each member of the tour would be guaranteed at least two out of the four matches. I accepted without hesitation, we would deal with the matter later.

But that was only the beginning of a rather hectic month, travelling on public transport, as I out line below.

First, I was informed, that as there had been an outbreak of yellow fever in South Wales, I would need to be inoculated: not by my doctor, but at the Liverpool School of Tropical Medical Science, as it was a mainly tropical disease. So I went along, and after it was done and I was getting the necessary documentation, I asked would there be any side effects. 'You may get a high temperature and perhaps dizziness in about seven days' time, but apart from a sore arm that's all.' Remember that I was a student and had to travel on public transport, paying for myself, unless someone else was paying my expenses.

I was at the Tropical Medicine Centre about 4 April and I was due in the Cairngorm Mountains between 7 and 14, attending a planned trip near Aviemore, with our group from Loughborough. On the 6 April, together with another student, Barry Jones, from Wigan, I began to hitchhike to Scotland, for our planned camping trip. A journey of well over 200 miles was achieved through the day and night that we travelled. On arrival we were billeted in a wooden hut, possibly used by the commandos who had done their training up there in the Second World War. It was primitive, but we were there as part of the Outdoor Education Course, and being Loughborough, it had to be thorough. We were there to learn lessons we couldn't undertake down at Loughborough College Campus.

For example we were taught to ski. Now don't think modern ski resorts, posh gear and après ski. We were taken onto the mountain and quickly learned to snow plough, parallel ski and stop. After one morning lesson we were set free to see what we could do. Many of us learned to ski on the nursery slopes, and I was quite proud to manage about 100 yards and stop at the bottom. As in any group, and in particular, any group from Loughborough, there were students at all levels. Some of them were of a very high standard, and immediately went up on the ski lift, which had recently opened for business. One or two others skiing to a moderate degree, attempted more than the nursery slopes. I can still see now one of that group flying down the hill, trip up, summersault, pitching head first and leaving a round hole in the snow, where his head had punctured through, before completing the somersault, landing onto his skis again. It would have been impossible to do that as a trick, without breaking his neck. I was happy to get back to our wooden hut, eat the dinner, and even share in the washing up of Billy Cans, metal plates and dishes.

The next day we had to plan a walk to the top of the mountain and back to the hut. We gathered together around a table in the hut and our lecturer taught us how to use the map and compass, in particular how to take a bearing, between two points. Then he said, 'OK, let's see what you can do.' We were split up into two groups of about ten and got ready to walk to the top of one of the highest mountains in Scotland. Just before we set off he said to me as the group leader, 'What is the bearing from the top of the mountain to this base?' I admitted that I did not know but would be able to take that bearing when I needed to at the top of the mountain. 'And what if there is a white out and you can't see this hut from there?' Realising that it was an important step I took the bearing and made a note of it.

We then set off up the foothills until we got onto the mountain proper, and sure enough the snow began to fall thickly around us. We persevered, and I battled on, despite a thumping headache, the result of the injection. By the time we got to the top of the mountain, it was indeed a white out, and I was staggering around and shaking, but still aware that I was group leader and had to get everyone down safely. We decided that we were walking around in a circle, and that we should bolt for it, off the top of the mountain, using the bearing I had taken earlier. Within quarter of an hour we came out of the blizzard, and found ourselves on the same side of the mountain as the ski slopes, thus saving a very long walk home. After a week of such activity, including walks and some rock climbing on practice faces, we were told that we could go home. I took a very long day to hitchhike back home arriving about 3 o'clock in the morning, following our 9 a.m. start.

The next day I was due to play in the preliminary rounds of the Middlesex sevens, but was excused on the grounds that I was at a College Camp.

18 April was Ruth's twenty-first birthday and we wanted to celebrate with family and friends. So on Saturday 21 April we went to Liverpool with a group of her college friends who had travelled from all over the north of England to be there. I think that we went to a musical, and I did well to stay awake, after my exertions in Scotland, and my sore arm from the yellow fever injection. I especially wanted to be there, and I was, despite the fact that the UAU had already gathered at The Westgate Hotel in Newport.

I travelled down the next day, and on Easter Monday made my debut for the UAU at Bristol, playing at centre with a group of people I had never played with before. The next day I was picked to play on the wing at Abertillery, but managed to work it so that I played centre. Looking at the team sheets I was the only player from Loughborough College on that tour. I don't remember who I was marking, but whoever it was got injured before half time. The reshuffle meant that Alan Pask, ex-Loughborough and Wales back row, came out to mark me. I really didn't mind as I could stand him up and run round him, much to his chagrin.

We had a pint or two afterwards with Hadyn Morgan, who said that he would have ripped my head off, if the captain had put him out in the centres. Two red heads together, though I would have tried to run away, not take him on, unless I really had to. I enjoyed my couple of days with the UAU, though I never actually wore my blazer with the Unicorn emblem, too many blazers, but I was pleased with the honour.

The next Saturday I was due to play in the Finals of the Middlesex sevens. However, I had also qualified in the Finals of the National Trampoline Championship, also down in London on 27 April, and as I had not played in the preliminary rounds of the sevens, Roger Pearman decided to stay with his team and send me to the gymnastics finals.

That Loughborough Sevens team was the fastest side that I ever played in, but hey ho, competing in the English National Trampoline Championships was something that I never thought I would achieve, even if I did come near the bottom of the list.

My hectic schedule was not yet complete, because on Saturday 28 April, whilst Loughborough were down at Twickenham, I had the honour of guesting in the R. F. (Bob) Oakes Memorial Match, played at Hartlepool Rovers Football Club, New Friarage, Hartlepool.

To quote from the programme about this Fiftieth Anniversary Match:

> Yet another milestone is reached today when we celebrate the Jubilee of the first Rovers-Oakes game—which took place at the end of the season 1911/12. Such are the roots of this event that it has survived the cataclysm of two world wars, albeit with some little dislocation, to remain the end of season game in the North.

The programme lists over forty international players who have guested in these matches and talks about the stars who have filled each position. No pressure there then for me as the centre partner of J. M. Dee, recently selected for England and the British Lions. The opposition was the services' champions, The RAF, with H. J. C. Brown (England Trials, Barbarians, Combined Services and Blackheath), and J. Keepe (Irish Trials and Ulster), playing against me and Johnny Dee. Actually the most important man on the field, who tore us to pieces with magnificent play through the middle, was L. A. C. CO Williams, do you recognise him?

At the time I played that game I did not know who this guy Williams was. Advertised as Barbarians and Cardiff, playing alongside L. A. C. Booth (England Trials and Gloucester), they were so much better than our halfbacks, we never stood a chance. It is never fair to say that we never had a chance, but that day Johnny Dee and I were chasing shadows, all of them caused by this guy Williams. He was strong running, and always ahead of the chaser, but more importantly he could stop on a sixpence, and change direction to lose his marker, and draw in a centre to tackle him, leaving a space for someone else to run into. What a day he had, he totally dominated the match and the RAF ran out winners.

Because of the strenuous time that I was having, I had to get back to St Helens straight after the match. I mean immediately, that means going into the changing room and taking off my jersey, saying goodbye to my teammates, and getting into the chairman's Rolls-Royce to go to the station at Hartlepool to go home. I still have the ticket for the dinner at the Masonic Hall, West Hartlepool as I never used it. I didn't join in any celebrations or meet up with the opposition to sink a few pints, as was the normal procedure. No, I climbed into the back of the Rolls-Royce, I don't know what model it was, but it had a large open access at the back, rather like the one which the Queen uses, and set off for the station. My train back to St Helens was due to leave in less than half an hour, and so it came to pass that for the first and only time in my life, I got stripped in the back of a car. Off came my rugby gear and boots, on went my trousers and shirt, socks and shoes, and with a quick comb of my hair I was ready to catch the train back to St Helens. I didn't get to meet L. A. C. C.O. Williams, to congratulate him on a devastating performance. I didn't get to exchange pints and commiserations with Johnny Dee, but I was to meet both in the future in very different circumstances.

I had the Sunday and Monday at home in the Running Horses and went back to Loughborough College, on the Tuesday, to complete my final term there.

One of the most unusual guest appearances, for which there was no honour, no blazer badge, no write up, happened on a Sunday, but is perhaps the best kept secret of my rugby career. I was invited to play in the Past Match at St Mary's College, and lined up with a number of Liverpool stalwarts, and amazingly, Martin Regan. Perhaps the most recognised product of West Park and St Mary's was playing at fly half, by special invitation. Retired from his contract with Warrington RLFC, I was delighted to play with one of England's finest. Furthermore, he took the trouble to detour on his way back to the northwest, to take me back to Loughborough on his way home, and he talked to me about his time at Warrington.

Before we leave Loughborough College, I want to say something about coaching. Virtually anyone who gets an Honours Diploma from Loughborough, Carnegie or St Luke's will be able to coach the commonly played school sports. I will go further than that and say, that such well qualified people will be better at coaching than most international performers. There is so much common ground, in training for fitness and endurance, seeking and finding space, attacking and defending, practising for restarts and set play situations, that each becomes part of every game. More detailed knowledge of very technical aspects of individual performances will require very specific knowledge, but coaching games requires more dedication and time-consuming effort, rather than the ability to actually perform the skill being coached. The realisation that this is true has led to the massive change in attitude in modern day coaching. International players can make good coaches, but good coaches need not have been international players. It is no surprise at all to me to see how well Joe Coan did when he took over the coaching at St Helens. Both Don Gullick and Steve Llewellyn were qualified PE Specialists, but both had been denied multiple Senior Caps because they left Rugby Union to come to Rugby League, so it fell to Joe Coan to pick up the opportunity when it was presented to him, without any caps at all. We can talk again about the timing of that move, but I was never surprised.

I failed by one match to qualify for the Rugby Colours at Loughborough, but given that I took so long to get into the first team, I must have played the vast majority of the rest of the matches. I can't possibly have played in them all, but I remember, with great pleasure, the general gusto with which the games were played. Fast flowing rugby was the order of the day, and though John Robbins was a lecturer there, we very rarely saw him in a coaching capacity. Roger Pearman, having played at Wembley in 1963 for Wakefield Trinity, took up coaching Rugby League in Australia, and invited me to follow him over there in 1966, but my mind was set on other things then. Australian Rugby League was desperately short of coaches, and not going was certainly a big decision.

CHAPTER 15

A Year of Decisions

Saturday 30 September 1962

Young Men of Rugby. At twenty-two Harvey is already a veteran.
By John Pugh

At the age of twenty-two, Peter Harvey, the Liverpool and Lancashire centre is a veteran. Behind him lie years crammed with rugby. (He was) Educated at the great Rugby academies, West Park, St Mary's Twickenham and Loughborough, Captain of Lancashire and England Schools, a UAU Player with 16 Lancashire Caps. Most of this has been packed into four strenuous student years when in addition to playing rugby twice a week Harvey was training to be a Physical Education Teacher. It is hardly surprising that last season a reaction set in. Although superbly fit he was subconsciously tired and his play lost the fine cutting edge of efficiency. Now Harvey has put away his student days. He is a teacher at Ormskirk and with the strain eased he is back to the form that many think should earn him an England trial alongside his Lancashire colleague Malcolm Phillips. Harvey has all the qualifications, speed, strength, courage, bubbling enthusiasm and a Rugby brain. In defence Harvey has few equals. His tackling of heavyweight forwards sometimes borders on the suicidal. His rugby brain – one eminent critic still rhapsodises over his deployment of an inferior Lancashire schoolboy team so that they routed Yorkshire.

Size Problem

Yes, Harvey has all the qualities to take him to the highest places, all except one – his physique. It is Harvey himself who raises this doubt. At 5ft. 7inches and 11 and a half stone, he is on the small side but this writer has never seen it place him at any disadvantage. But in Harvey's analysis of the way Rugby will develop (he is a great theorist) there is no place for the small centre. While at Loughborough, he wrote a thesis. His subject was the back row forward; a man Harvey believes will become an increasingly dominant force in the game. Set piece attacks by the threequarters will be out. The centres will be big, strong players who will invite the tackle and as they go down will slip the ball to the roaming wing forward who has then a clear way through. Then there is second phase attack, in which the wing forward tackles and has a colleague alongside him to snap up the loose ball. Centres in this context are finishing forces.

New Strategy

Harvey himself is already playing this sort of game for Lancashire. One of the most notable features of the county side's successful new strategy is the Harvey-Phillips strike. Harvey chasing hard after a kick ahead or a loose ball tackles an opponent in possession hard. If the ball runs loose Phillips is up to gather and streak through. (This way Lancashire scored their first try against Cheshire.) It is hoped that when the selectors see that Phillips is scoring tries again, they remember who is making them for him. And in his new role Harvey appears to have solved the problem of his size. By his anticipation, speed and fierce tackling, he is playing the part of a super wing forward.

By the time that the county season was drawing to a close at Fylde on 24 November 1962, Malcolm Phillips was the only three quarter who had played with me from my first match, though as I have shown he didn't play all of the matches. Both he and Tom Brophy, who was at fly half, were still there for the next match, the decider against Yorkshire. I played in all the county games that season and was rewarded for consistent enterprise.

Harvey and Hughes get England Trial
By John Pugh

Two Liverpool players, Peter Harvey and Ted Hughes, have won places in the first England Trial to be played at Carlisle next Saturday. First of December 1962.

In the match report the headline was: England's new tactics suited Peter Harvey.

Liverpool's Peter Harvey found the new England RU tactics to his liking in the first trial at Carlisle on Saturday. The emphasis now is on kicks ahead with forwards and backs following up at the double in an attempt to harry the opposition into error. These are the same tactics which Lancashire have employed this season and Harvey was in his element. He made one try for the Colours with a neat kick ahead, and had a hand in the second when he crash tackled the Whites' full back Hosen. The ball ran loose to Dee who scored.

Harvey's county partner Phillips, playing this time on the opposite side, also paved the way for a try, with a cross kick, and generally showed the selectors reassuring glimpses of his old speed.

9/12/1962 Lancashire v. Yorkshire

The match which was due to be played on this date was postponed because of bad weather. The weather in the north of the country was much worse than that in the south. As this match was to be a decider in the Northern Area Championship, and thus affect matches in the semi-finals it was decided to play it at Twickenham on Saturday 9 March 1963. I had played in every Lancashire match since September 1960 and enjoyed immensely the fact that we always played 'the Lancashire way.' Not always the most effective way of winning matches, but since I never lost my place in the team, I was certainly not responsible for those losses. One notable newcomer to the team sheet in that county decider at Twickenham was blindside wing forward, J. R. H. Greenwood (Cambridge University) a good player, and enough initials to become an international.

I do not remember the details of the match but I think that we lost something like 3-6.

What I do remember about this trip was the train journey back to Liverpool.

By now I was a regular traveller up and down to London on the train, coming backwards and forwards for rugby matches. This time I was not alone on the train, as the whole of the Lancashire team, going to Liverpool, were travelling back together on the Sunday. We were all playing cards, as usual, and were gathered around the entrance to the carriage when the door opened and in walked Cliff Richard. He was very polite and asked to be excused as the game had to be stopped so that he could walk through the passageway, which he did, accompanied by banter from the gathered players. He walked on down the long carriage and sat down beside a figure that we could not see.

After half an hour or so he came back, this time to be greeted with much more comment around the idea that he should sit down and play cards with us so that we could get some money from him. To no avail as he returned to his seat, possibly in the first class carriage down the train. Maybe I had lost the pound which I was prepared to lose, or maybe I was just curious, but anyhow I decided to go and see who the person was that had caused our newest pop star to come to visit them. I walked down to the other end of the carriage, went to the toilet and came back up, specifically to find out whom the person was, that this glamorous young man had come to see. Harry Webb, aka Cliff Richard was born just five days before I was, so we were both young men, at the beginning of our lives. I had bright red hair; a fact often referred to in the newspaper reports, and it was this that caught the attention of the woman sitting facing me as I looked at her. Her question, which followed my far from casual look at her, was 'Whereabouts in Scotland do you come from?' Her strong Scottish accent was not strange to me, and I smiled as I said, 'You won't know it, as it is a little town called Johnstone, which is not very far from Glasgow.' She nodded in obvious understanding and said, 'I ken it well, and where do you stay?'

Then I said 'How did you know that I come from Scotland?' As she indicated to me to sit in the seat so recently vacated by Cliff Richard, that it was still warm, I told her that I was born on the Howard Road. I was amazed when she said that she knew it well. It was an accident, caused by the war, but my mother was really from Johnstone and had been born in Houston Square. 'Indeed,' she said 'and where would that be?'

I had heard the tale so often that I knew that she had been born right in the centre of the town in Houston Square. I said to the lady 'She was born in Houston Square.'

'So was I,' came back the reply. 'What number, Houston Square?'

'Number four,' I said, and she replied 'I was born at number two.'

Now that is quite remarkable in itself, but even more so when you realise that number two is the downstairs house to number four upstairs, my mother and this lady were born in the same building.

She was older than my mother but I recognised her as an actress from TV and she referred to the visit from the young Cliff Richard, as if she had known him all of his life.

Remarkable as this story is, it is not quite complete. She gave me her name and address, and invited me to call, 'Anytime you are in Weybridge.' I never did get to Weybridge, but the story is true.

My mother was not at all surprised when I told her the tale when I got back home. Yes she knew Renee Houston had been born in the same building, and that the Square in Johnstone had been named after the Houston Family for many years.

About three years ago I was back in that very building when my mother's youngest sister Mary died. The square has been remodelled and rebuilt in latter years, and the building number four, is in fact the undertakers' premises, so she was born in, and buried from, number four Houston Square, though she lived all of her life at other addresses.

I never did meet Cliff Richard or Renee Houston again but I haven't forgotten either of them.

I certainly don't remember all of the county matches but they were very important and we took them very seriously and strived to win. However, rugby union was not professional and was still very much a game for players to enjoy, both on and off the pitch. I remember once when we were staying overnight at the King's Arms, Whitby Bay, after the match of course, when someone challenged me to a competition. This time it was not a drinking game though we often had those, he challenged me to see who could 'stand on their hands for the longest time'. Having spent half of my time at Simmeries and Loughborough, doing just that, I knew that I could win that challenge. We 'stood' on both tables and chairs and walked to settees, before collapsing on them, before someone bet me that I couldn't 'walk round the bar on my hands'. I took up the bet and still remember falling off the bar as I tried to turn the corner at right angles, not once but twice, before I managed the feat. Would a professional rugby player have done any of that? I definitely think not, but we enjoyed it immensely.

My time in the Lancashire County team was enjoyable from the first game to the last, but it really was quite chaotic, playing with different players almost every match, and never once having a training session together, no matter how important the fixture was supposed to be. To perhaps explain this situation I will offer this quotation from the Centenary booklet of the Lancashire County Rugby Football Union 1881-1981:

> Probably the most important events in the mid-sixties occurred off the field and were partly in response to a run of defeats and comparative lack of success in the championship, and partly as a result of forward thinking which has characterised Lancashire rugby. In June 1966 a coaching sub-committee was set up and began work with a view to improving the quality of rugby played at all levels. At this time the term 'coach' was viewed with great suspicion by many traditionalists who felt that the coach would lead to a 'win at all costs' mentality which would be detrimental to the traditional spirit of the game.

Another train journey I remember for quite a different reason followed the England Trial which had been switched from Gloucester, down to Torquay, because of the bad weather. It was strange to see the palm trees and the sand blowing in the breeze, when back home we were in the mighty grip of winter. My travelling companion that day was Richard Heaton Guest, Dickie to his friends, ex-England winger, and now an England selector. It was a long journey and we talked of many things, but only one of them sticks out in my mind. We were talking about the difficulty of moving the trials around, and the close proximity to the International matches, when he told me, 'The selectors will not pick you, because they think that you are going to go to Rugby League.' We did not dwell on the subject, but he was proved right when I was selected as reserve for all of the International matches to be played that season. I got on with playing, knowing that I was good enough, and hoping that my time would come. Maybe I would be selected for the tour, if not for the five nations. There was one more game to play for Liverpool and this is the match report.

Headingley 6 pts Liverpool 16 pts. 16 March 1963
Headingley humbled by M. H. Stevenson

Having started his piece by saying that there was only a small crowd to watch this match, Stevenson says in his second paragraph:

> Those who turned out must have been compensated to some degree for their team's mediocre display by the versatility and brilliance of Harvey, the Liverpool and Lancashire centre. He possesses bright red hair but his all-round skill, speed, elusiveness and tactical intelligence, coupled with sheer dash, would make him conspicuous in any class of Rugby even without this distinguishing feature. At half time Liverpool led 6-3, slightly against the run of play, but Harvey's probing thrusts had often tested the Headingley defence. Indeed it was his enterprise that took play up to the Headingley line where Bearne, following up like a Sherman tank, crashed over for an unconverted try.

It is not mentioned in this piece but this was to be my last Rugby Union match in Yorkshire and just five days before the Tour trial which was to be played at Leicester. I felt good about my game and I knew exactly what I was doing.

I was teaching at St Bede's RC Secondary School in Ormskirk where I was head of the PE department. My head teacher Mr Collinge was delighted with the progress I was making with Lancashire as he saw to it that the reflected glory would shine on the school. When I got the England Trials he invited me in for coffee and told me that he had been contacted by County Hall to tell him that they were aware of my progress. I had also been selected to be one of the demonstration teachers at the National Conference of The Gymnastic Association.

The short tour of Australia and New Zealand was announced to take place during May/June 1963, and I was picked to play in the Final Tour Trial of thirty players, from which twenty-three would be picked to tour. The trial was to be played at Leicester. I needed to make arrangements with my employer to take time off, and was duly granted two months' leave of absence with pay.

I borrowed Uncle Joe's red Mini and my dad and Uncle Paddy accompanied me on the trip to Leicester. The journey followed the same roads as I had become used to in Tom Farrell's Mini and Roy Wood's estate as they had ferried me back and forth to Loughborough. This time I was driving, my dad and Uncle Paddy sat petrified in the back seat as neither were used to motor cars. My dad said that he felt that we were flying, and anyone who remembers just how close to the road surface passengers in a Mini were, will understand the fear element as well. I, on the other hand was thrilled. Excited to be driving myself, confident in my playing ability and knowing all of the players who were to play in the match, I sailed along quite happily.

The game itself holds virtually no memories for me, which is not at all unusual, as few matches stand out, even one as important as that. I played

well and was happy with my performance. The team was to be picked later
and as it was late, we drove home largely in the dark. The only thing which I
remember clearly was my dad saying, 'You don't hand them off as well as you
used to do.' My reply that they are much bigger now than last time you saw
me play was accepted without comment.

Somewhere, there is still a *Rugby World* magazine, which has pictures of all
those who played in that trial, maybe because of dates going to press, it was
not possible to wait for the team to be announced. When it was, I was very
disappointed not to be selected. I have the letter sent to me on 2 April, which
tells me to stand by as a reserve. Since I had stood by as a reserve for every
International that season it was little consolation.

Dear Harvey,

You will have received a letter from the President telling you that the selectors
wish you to stand by as a reserve for this tour. Some time must elapse and
many games be played before 11 May—the date of departure and so I think it
desirable that you should be prepared on all counts to step into the breach at
the last minute. Accordingly I send you the circular which I recently sent to the
touring party and would ask you to complete the pink sheet and return it to me.
Please take any steps that maybe necessary with regard to your passport and
vaccination history so that the passport and International Vaccination Certificate
can be produced at the eleventh hour.

Signed Secretary

The luggage label which I received from the RFU and the itinerary for the tour,
which would have taken me all around the world, are perhaps the saddest
things which I ever chose to keep.

The players chosen were all known to me, except G. C. Gibson (US
Portsmouth), who played well in the final trial, but I don't know where he
came from or went to later. At fullback Roger Hosen (Northampton) was
being capped for the first time, as was John Ransom (Rosslyn Park) who
played on the wing. R. F. Read (Harlequins) who was selected as a stand-off,
was also without a previous international cap, though the other three half
backs, J. P. Horrocks-Taylor, Simon Clarke (Cambridge University) and Trevor
Wintle (St Mary's Hospital) each had four. The other backs were F. D. Sykes
(Northampton), Malcolm Phillips (Fylde), Mike Weston (Durham City) and J.
M. Dee (Hartlepool Rovers).

I guess none of these looked like they may go to Rugby League.

Meanwhile back in Lancashire I was playing for Liverpool. Match reports
from the *St Helens Newspaper and Reporter*.

Match report Tuesday 9 April 1963:

Liverpool 6 pts St Helens 3 pts

'Harvey intercepted for Liverpool and fed Chesworth. A long chase followed to the St Helens line but Pimblett tackled him short but from the resultant scrum Liverpool scored a push over try.

This is Tom Pimblett who also got an England Trial and later signed for the Saints.

There is a match report for the game at Ruskin Drive: St Helens Recs.0 Eric Evans XV 36. This was to be my last game in Rugby Union and was reported 4 May 1963.

Having said that the Eric Evans' side were about two stone a man heavier in the pack which was expertly led by John Burgess from open side, the report had this to say about my play:

P. Harvey, the England Trialist Centre, had a grand game, covering the ground from start to finish and turning up all over the field like a red fox.

The Recs. backs usually received the man and ball at the same time and were effectively blotted out. Though soundly beaten the younger members of the side should benefit from their experience against top class opposition.

Scores and results list England's points tally first. (Source: Wikipedia)

Opposing Team	For	Against	Date	Venue	Status
Wellington	14	9	18 May 1963	Athletic Park, Wellington	Tour match
Otago	9	14	22 May 1963	Carisbrook, Dunedin	Tour match
New Zealand	11	21	25 May 1963	Eden Park Auckland	Test Match
Hawke's Bay	5	20	28 May 1963	McLean Park, Napier	Tour match
New Zealand	6	9	1 June 1963	Lancaster Park, Christchurch	Test Match
Australia	9	18	4 June 1963	Sports Ground, Sydney	Test Match

I'm sure that I would have enjoyed the trip at the time. Now I am sure that our lives would have been so different had I gone, that it is impossible to say that I wish I had.

I have still never been to Australia or New Zealand, and perhaps I never will. Certainly I will not be going to play rugby; though I would still like to see an England side turn those defeats into victories.

CHAPTER 16

Playing for the Saints

I began teaching at St Bede's RC Ormskirk in September 1962, as head of PE, teaching football and gymnastics. I got an Honours Diploma from Loughborough with distinctions in gymnastics and teaching, and credits in the other subjects except swimming, but I did get my coaching certificate even in that, my weakest subject. I still played Rugby Union through that first season, being involved in all of the England Trials, and being the reserve for each of the internationals, without being picked for any of them. Then in April 1963 the final England Trial for the Tour to Australia which would take place that summer. I was not selected for that tour and decided that I would become a professional Rugby League player.

Great interest was shown by both Wigan and St Helens and at a very late

Saints *v.* Australia 1963.
Back row: K. Coslett, K. Northey, C. Williams, M. Mooney, G. Heaton, Tom Van Vollenhoven, P. Harvey.
Front row: C. Watson, J. Tembey, B. Dagnall, D. Huddart, R. French, K. Ashcroft.

stage, by Castleford. The connection with Castleford was through a man in Blackpool, who I later came to know was Alf Ellaby, perhaps the first Saints superstar. Wigan had been following me for two years, but as I was training with the Saints in July 1963, they were the favourites to get my signature on professional forms.

As an important aside, my life has been marked as a teacher and later a head teacher rather than as a rugby player, but never the less rugby has played an important part. In June 1963 Mr Clinton Sayer, the Principal at Loughborough College wrote to me to tell me that the post of rugby master at Rugby School was vacant and that he would recommend me for the position should I want to apply. I wrote back to him and told him that I had decided to sign professional forms, though at that moment I wanted it to be a secret. He wrote back to me and wished me every success in the future but naturally understood that I would not be applying for the post. I don't think that I have ever regretted that decision but our lives would certainly have been different had I filled in those application forms, and become the rugby master at Rugby School.

I don't recall the exact circumstances of the first time that I went to train with St Helens, because it seemed perfectly normal to me. Mr Cook had reaffirmed the interest from the club and I was invited to train with them, to meet the players and see how I got on. For many people it would have been a big deal, but the fact that I already knew Keith Northey and Ray French, meant that I was greeted as an old friend, rather than as a stranger coming from Rugby Union. The fact that I was still officially a Rugby Union player, and that training with the Saints would automatically mean a lifetime suspension, should anyone 'tell on me', was not mentioned.

I was there to be part of the squad from the very beginning. I went straight into the first team dressing room and got changed alongside them. They introduced me to Cen Williams, who I had played against when he was in the RAF team, I don't think he remembered me; but along with Kel Coslett, Len Killeen and Tom van Vollenhoven, there were at least six players who knew the position which I was in, and the danger I was courting.

Stan McCormick was the coach and he welcomed me warmly, old connections with Alan Prescott eased the way, and I was out training with them all within ten minutes of my arrival. Training with Stan McCormick was less than rigorous and rarely involved much more than a couple of warm up laps of the pitch, and a few sprints down the touchline, followed by a game of touch and pass, a game at which Stan still excelled.

I fitted into that group as if I had always been there. There was the other aspect of the team, the pack, to be considered. Meeting characters like John Tembey, Bob Dagnall, Cliff Watson, great names like Dick Huddart, and young guns like Doug Laughton and Keith Ashcroft, alongside club Captain Bill Major, was all part of an easy mix of rugby players.

I was fit and quick, and could play tick rugby with anyone at that stage. Stan McCormick was naturally interested in what position I played and was intrigued when I said stand-off or wing. I had made my name in Rugby Union as a centre, but had played wing for Lancashire on a number of occasions. I had never played stand-off in senior rugby but saw myself in the Jimmy Honey or Peter Metcalfe role, rather than the Duggie Greenall, and still less the Don Gullick model. Both were hard-as-nails centres, both had made their name in the rough tough game of the fifties. I don't think either had a side-step or body swerve and neither would take a backward step when it came to sailing into the 'trouble.'

Both were still around and the comparisons would always be against me. I had spoken to Keith Northey almost a year before I signed for the Saints. The conversation was about the difficulty I would face in playing centre. This was not about rugby but in fact about competition for places. 'No problem,' said Keith, 'they sign people all of the time and there is always competition for places, that's just the way it is. We can both play in a number of positions so can easily play alongside each other, come if you want to.'

Even the intervention of Joe Coan with suggestions about training, still very much the junior partner with Stan McCormick, was simple compared with what we were to become used to later. Joe had been utilised in the previous winter so that the players could use the gymnasium which Joe was using for rugby training for the West Park RU team. Now he was there to assist Stan in pre-season work. Joe wanted to use a stopwatch and count the sprints and record times and such. Stan, encouraged by the old heads like Mick Sullivan, would rather talk about the racing results, in between the short, and getting shorter sprints down the touchline, before the inevitable touch rugby.

Tom van Vollenhoven was the first choice right wing, a player of effortless grace, and absolutely blistering pace, serve and side step, a master of the art of wing play. Mick Sullivan was there as the left wing, with his remarkable scoring record and unmatchable international honours. He was one of the most dangerous players in the game, and certainly one of the most vicious tacklers in rugby league. Indeed he was notoriously hard headed and a most fearsome opponent. He shared the left wing shirt with Len Killeen who was making a real name for himself. Sullivan was not fit to play at the time that I arrived, but he was certainly around with his huge personality and presence affecting the team. He and Tom van Vollenhoven had played in the great side which won the Challenge Cup in 1961. Brian McGinn was still in training but his centre partner from that day Ken Large had been transferred, as had Austin Rhodes who had played full-back.

The centres were Keith Northey and Cen Williams, both class players who could hold their own against any pair in the game. Half backs abounded with the truly great Alex Murphy and the up and coming Billy Benyon, great club man Wilf Smith and hard working Jeff Heaton, already having many honours with the club. There were many others in the 'A' team squad who I didn't even know about, more about that later. I played touch rugby with all of them, and learned to play the ball after the tackle, in a couple of minutes of cursory instruction. It wasn't exactly a secret that I was training with the Saints as this piece appeared in the *Reporter*:

Tom Ashcroft: Sportsman's Diary
Tuesday 13 August 1963.

RU STAR TO HAVE SAINTS TRIALS

Peter Harvey, Liverpool, Lancashire and England RU Trialist centre, intends to turn professional and will play a series of trials for Saints, according to yesterday's Club announcement. The new player is a former West Park Grammar school player and has captained the England Schools RU XV.

Saints, I understand, intend to play Harvey at out half. He is 23 in October, is 5 foot 7 ins in height and weighs 11 st. 6 lb, an associate of Keith Northey at West Park in his school rugby days. Peter went to Strawberry Hill College in London, and did a year's PE course at Loughborough College. He has made more than 20 appearances for the Lancashire RU team. Last season he just failed to gain selection for the England Rugby team which went to Australia and New Zealand. A member of the teaching staff of St Bede's School Ormskirk, Harvey is the son of Mr Peter Harvey, licensee of The Rifle Corps, Duke Street.

[See my dad was more famous than me!]

Henry Tomlinson cut to the chase as he was wont to do. He had spoken to me during the week before the Huddersfield match and made it quite plain that he didn't feel compelled to keep the secret. He knew that I had played in the regular pre-season game, loosely named first team against 'A' team. There was no match report of that game but I remember just a couple of things about what happened. I cannot name the teams but I do know that I played number 6 to Alex Murphy at 7. The opposing half back pairing was Jeff Heaton at 7, with Bill Benyon at 6, and as Stan McCormick had told me before the game, they had been good enough to get winner's medals in the Lancashire Cup Final the previous season. The game was played on a virtually empty Knowsley Road ground. The only spectators were the Directors sitting in their seats in the stand.

This was my very first game of Rugby League. I had watched many matches since those days in the boys' pen; I had followed the team to two Wembleys; I had cheered them on with great gusto on the Town Hall steps, but I had never

ever actually played a game. Not at school, because Rugby League was not for the likes of Grammar School boys, not at College as the national game was Rugby Union and no one would have then suggested that there was any cross over between the two codes.

During that first match, on a still summer evening, with no crowd, the stands echoed with the calls of the players. Few people realise just how much talking goes on as the game progresses. At some stage in the game there was a scrum near the 25-yard line, on the left hand side, in the shadow of The Edington Stand. Alex Murphy came away from the scrum running right, on the open side, he ran between Heaton and Benyon, and I was able to run wide of Benyon to score by the posts. Before the goal could be kicked, Murphy had run 60 yards to the Directors' Box and shouted, 'That's another thousand pound you owe him.' Mr Cook was not present and no one else had the authority to pay me what I was asking.

It is said that Alex Murphy did not like RU players, because he was paid so little to sign on, whereas they were paid so much. I don't believe that to be true. He did indeed get only a pittance (said to be £80) as his initial payment, but no doubt added to that on a regular basis as his career progressed. He was indeed critical of those players who he did not think were worth the money which they got up front – but if they were 'worth their shirt', I never heard him complain. However, I do know that he thought that grammar school boys were slightly effete, and not as tough as the secondary modern types that he was used to. They had all played through their schools' system and Rugby League in schools was the normal in this area. Boys had a chance to play representative rugby in Rugby League just as I had done in Rugby Union, but perhaps because of the Rugby Union's non-acceptance of Rugby League there was a natural barrier from those with a Rugby League background. I have no idea what else happened during that game, but I seemed to come through without injury, and had fitted in with those around me. I have since learned that Jim Fairclough, who also played at West Park School, in the same team as Keith Northey and me, played centre against us, in that same match. Apparently, Henry Tomlinson had also viewed the match because he called me and told me so. He recognised me as Peter Harvey, Liverpool and Lancashire and England Trials, and wanted to know what was going on.

After that 'secret trial' I had a conversation with Stan McCormick about what was to happen next. Stan put it to me this way:

> If you are confident that you will make it as a first team player, why would I play you in an 'A' Team somewhere in Yorkshire? If you are not confident of making the first team, we are not going to sign you anyway. We may play you in the 'A' Team to get to know the game, but you will have to be better than that, and I'm sure you will be.

With that in mind he picked me for the home match against Huddersfield, having let the away match at Liverpool City go by. My friends from the Liverpool Rugby Union Club, like Brian Unsworth, felt that I had compromised my position by doing this, in their terms, 'They had me over a barrel as I would never be able to play RU again.' True, but I had worked that out for myself. What was the point? They would not pick me for the England Team because they thought that I would go to RL, so here I was playing Rugby League. It was to be nearly fifty years before I got an invitation to attend a rugby union club function again. No honours rewarded, no caps presented, no recognition whatsoever of what I had achieved. Perhaps worse than that, even in my teaching career all support from county and national PE organisers was withdrawn. Even my own head teacher felt that I had brought some kind of disgrace to the school, rather than the credit he had expected to continue.

I played my first game as an unsigned player and had I got injured in that game, I would have had nowhere else to go. I didn't see that risk, but only the opportunity; I had three clubs watching that match and I would sign for one of them: Wigan, Castleford or St Helens.

The Saints kit man, Walter Jones, must have thought that I was staying because he gave me a pair of boots. Not new ones of course, but a pair which had belonged to Tom Vollenhoven. They were Foster's best, with a split sole, very light with kangaroo skin uppers, very classy. Walter used to use little brass tacks to write the initials of the player into the heel part of the sole. He converted the TV into PH and I was extremely pleased, stepping into the boots of one of the greatest players of all time.

For the first time I was to play in front of the crowd at Knowsley Road, strangely not centre to Vollenhoven, nor stand-off to Alex Murphy or even with Keith Northey by my side. I was stand-off to Wilf Smith and had Mick Mooney at centre, partnered by Cen Williams, with Vollenhoven and Killeen on the wings, the ever-present Kel Coslett was at full back. To me it was just another match, not even a big match, important but no more than that. The touch judges came in to examine our hands and make sure that rings were taken off, and to look at our boots to see if the studs were in order. I recall the silence before the game; the hustle and bustle of players getting changed, the ringing of aluminium studs on the concrete floor, McCormick's words of exhortation and then the silence. The referee banging on the door, time to begin, this is it; we came out of our 'underground shelter' into the light of day. I followed Wilf Smith, behind the Captain Bill Major as he ran down the tunnel and out onto the pitch, to the strains of The March of the Gladiators. The game kicked off and I was a Rugby League player.

Lost Saints 7 v Huddersfield 10 24/08/1963. Att. 9,100. Weather blustery.
Tom Ashcroft wrote that Saints coach Stanley McCormick was surrounded by last minute team problems for the opening game.

To these dicey questions another one was posed when Saints saw fit to put in Peter Harvey with the task of converting himself from Rugby Union and from centre play to the tricky job of professional out-half play all in the day as it were. Saints tempted providence in too many ways. The Fartowners took a tremendous bruising but when they were mown down and left for dead, spirit alone got the casualty to his feet again.

The fiery headed Harvey, quick to pounce on a loose ball, twice rattled the defence. He got Vollenhoven away nicely on the first occasion and it took a supreme effort to hold Coslett who went for the inside pass. Tembey might have made more of Harvey's next thrust but he fell rather tamely to a low tackle. Harvey was bold enough to try a grubber kick in one raid; it did not come off because the support was not alive to the ruse.

Another downpour drenched the players as they came out again. Harvey made a good break and twice Vollenhoven led raids to the scoreboard corner. Vollenhoven made another bid for the corner and the brawl which followed this was a bad explosion.

Referee Coates rushed in to intervene as fisticuffs began and was himself knocked down. When he had regained his feet and separated the combatants, he pulled out Kilroy and Major to have their names taken. Coslett hit the post with a penalty.' Summing up Ashcroft says 'Smith did not strike up a good partnership with Harvey, nor was he the equal of Smales on the day.' 'About Harvey there will be some reservations but I do not put the blame for the defeat at his door. He is small but alert and nippy and apt to take defences by surprise. What Harvey was not able to show was the clean cut through after the set scrum. Come to think very few regulars in that position are gifted in that way. When play was broken Harvey was as dangerous a raider as any inside back on a day when the competition was not of a high standard.

Eden Thomas in one of the national dailies had as his headline:

HARVEY ONE BRIGHT SPOT FOR SAINTS.

His match report was as follows:

St Helens 7 Huddersfield 10.
These two teams have played many controversial games in the past seasons with both sides having their share of success and failure. On the opening day of the new season, with the pay dispute now happily settled, this was a bitter pill for St Helens players and supporters alike. The introduction of former Lancs and Liverpool star Harvey into the Saints half-back line was a feature of the home play, although his more experienced colleagues, with little exception, gave a drab show in return. The Saints had enough scoring chances in both halves

to guarantee success, but dropped passes, slow thinking and poor backing up brought its own disastrous reward. They were 10-0 down at the interval and although scoring seven points without reply in a second half revival-with an improved try by South African winger Killeen, and a second goal from Coslett—they still have a disappointing show. Booth and Smales scored tries for Huddersfield and Curry kicked two goals.

Arthur Brooks in another daily newspaper had this comment on my play:

Throughout the first half the one St Helens player who was always shining was debut making ex Liverpool RU man Peter Harvey, though winger Len Killeen gained merited reward for some strong running, with a try in the 50th minute . . . Exchanges were sometimes tough between the two packs. There was one sudden flare up in a rain storm involving a dozen players.

The *Sporting Pink* had the headline:

HUDDERSFIELD STEAM ROLLER THE SAINTS

In the third paragraph the writer says

Desperately short of possession in the opening minutes, the Saints defence creaked without wilting, and then whipped viciously back through a red headed firework Peter Harvey, an ex-Lancashire RU cap, who was obviously intent on making a spectacular debut in Rugby League. He ripped away most of the substantial Huddersfield cover before setting Vollenhoven off on a pulse racing 60 yard gallop. The red head bobbed in again when Watson made a titanic forward effort, scything through every tackle and failing only when he was grounded by weight of numbers.

Had I done enough to impress? How were the critics to call this performance? More importantly how would the other players respond?

For the press Henry Tomlinson wrote:

The big question for the Saints Board at their weekly meeting will be to sign or not to sign local trialist Peter Harvey, the Rugby Union international reserve, 23 times a Lancashire player. Discounting the domestic trial games before the season, the directors have but 80 minutes of Harvey's showing against Huddersfield as a guide. For the arrangement was that he should have this one game as a trial and Peter told me today, 'It is now up to the St Helens officials to decide?' Did Peter do enough in this game to persuade Saints to sign him? I think so. For me, the only question is the matter of the fee. On his football he is a very good prospect to solve that nagging Saints worry of quite a few seasons—a good class half-back to go with Alex Murphy. Allowances must be made. This was Harvey's first game in Rugby League football. It was at stand-off—one of the most difficult positions for a 'convert' with so little time in which to make up one's mind. He made four excellent breaks and one, a thread through a three man cover was done with the minimum of space in which to work. And that Huddersfield defence was very good with its smother tactics. They had two well taken tries and a determined defence, to give them a surprise 10-7 win at Knowsley Road against a sluggish Saints. Harvey looks on the light side if one thinks of the last great stand-off at Saints—Ray Price—but he could develop from his present eleven and a half stone. And to be fair to Harvey he did his stint of tackling including bringing down some hefty forwards. He was with Saints on an off day. He made as much as could be expected from a rather orthodox service. It was a pity Alex Murphy had not been with him, for this is the exciting possibility. Alex with his split second movement and timing might have given Harvey the room in which to work. Certainly on this, his first game he did not let the Saints down in a game of missed chances amongst the backs and forwards. He did a great deal better than one could barely have expected.

St Helens *Reporter* 27/08/1963
No Decision on RU Trialist

Yesterday Saints reported 'no decision yet' about Peter Harvey, the Rugby Union trialist, who has received a firm offer from Castleford. I hear that Saints will have to pay between £3000 and £5000 to get him. One of the considerations Saints will ponder over is the number of ex Rugby Union players in their ranks who are not yet fully attuned to the professional game.'

Then he names several RU players who are with Saints, Watson, French, Williams, Coslett, Killeen and Vollenhoven.

Harvey could be faulted in Saturday's game for letting the ball go after the tackle, as is the practise in the amateur code. It takes time to get used to the play the ball procedure too but it was soon apparent that Harvey has ideas and guts.

So the first game was over and I duly went to see the board at their evening meeting. Not the whole board, that never happened, but the Vice Chairman, Mr Dromgoole, who explained that as Mr Cook was still on his holidays and I would have to wait for a decision, 'As the fee involved was much too high' for him to decide. I pointed out that as Mr Cook had not seen the match and that I was not due to play in any others before I signed, the Board would have to advise the Chairman what to do. He told me that people had been impressed with my attacking play, but there were still some doubts about whether I could tackle sufficiently well to play regularly.

I went to watch the mid-week match against Hunslet but did not play.

I did play in the next match which was on the Saturday, but not before my crucial interview with Mr Cook. He had come back from his holidays and I was invited to meet him upstairs, in the same room which I had visited before. There were three people in the room, Mr Basil Lowe (Club Secretary) being the extra one. After the pleasantries Mr Cook asked me to remind him what I was looking for by way of a signing on fee. I asked for £5,000 as I had heard that figure mentioned in relation to Ray French. 'But he was an International. You're not,' was his response. Basil Lowe explained to me that the whole board had met previously and that not everyone was convinced that I was the player they were looking for. I reminded Mr Cook that he had been waiting a long time for this signing and it was not my fault that he hadn't been present at the Huddersfield match. He confirmed that he still wanted to sign me, but he thought at something less than I was asking. He explained that they never gave all the money up front and that I should expect to be paid in instalments. Basil Lowe brought out a contract and explained that once it was signed I would become a St Helens player for life. I thought immediately of the contract which Martin Regan had signed when he went to Warrington after playing for the British Lions; £1,000 pounds a year for each of five years (£5,000).

I accepted £1,500, to be paid immediately, with another £1,000 after twelve matches. I was also to receive first team playing money for the first season, no matter which team I played in, and £500 if I played for Lancashire, with another £1,000 if I played for Great Britain. The last £1,000 would be paid if I managed to get a testimonial. So the magic £5,000 was on the contract. At first Mr Cook had been counting in £50 segments and when I objected and wanted him to count in £500, he said that he usually counted in £5 for local talent, and was prepared to count in £1 notes for some. I was pleased with the deal and determined to make it pay. The next match was against Castleford, who I had turned down. It was played on 28 August 1963. I was immediately at home playing with RU team players beside me.

In the *Reporter* of 31 August Tom Ashcroft wrote:

SAINTS TAKE EARLY COMMAND
Fast moving backs subdue Castleford

It was a matter of some interest that Saints turned out a back division which, Smith apart, consisted of ex Rugby Union types. The best feature of a fast moving game of all out action, which Saints played against Castleford, Yorkshire's most improved team of recent times, on Wednesday evening was sheer cleanliness. Without a questionable incident, hardly a caution, tempers always under control, the teams settled the account on honourable terms.

We scored four tries, all close to the posts, two of them by Keith Northey, and all four converted by Kel Coslett. In his summary about me he wrote:

> Harvey shirks nothing, supports every move and thinks fast which are among the basic attributes of the good club man. He missed one golden chance through getting his legs crossed when virtually in the clear. If he has not taken to the game like a duck to water, he has shown none of the foibles which often confound the new convert.

I remember the break which he is talking about. It was in the second half of the match, playing towards the tunnel, when I broke clear of the cover with only the full back to beat. I was running right to left and my sidestep to beat the full back was poor, I stepped into him and fell over my feet, instead of the first try being under the posts, in front of the Pavilion, I would have to wait for another occasion.

St Helens Rugby Talk by Henry Tomlinson before the match at Swinton:

Expert's view on Murphy and Harvey

'St Helens fans are very keen to have a look at the half-back pairing of the world's best scrum-half, Alex Murphy and the new signing from Rugby Union, Stand-off, Peter Harvey. It has had to be delayed until after the Lancashire Cup Tie against Swinton—George Parkinson is too tough a nut for a newcomer to try his teeth on-but it should be coming up soon and then Saints fans can start making up their minds. Harvey should then get a better chance to show his football skills and to show what he can do with the extra yard Murphy should give him to work. To the present, Harvey in three games, has not had much chance to shine, but he has hinted at some very good football and a quick and nimble pace and wit for the opening. He has at least proved he is not short of 'guts' and courage in taking on the heavyweights crashing through to dangerous positions near the line. But bringing down 16 stone forwards is a forward's job and does not prove a stand-off. The Harvey signing has had a sharp division of opinion about it—from the board to the fans—and from 'too light' to 'full of promise.' I had a word with a man who should know all about stand-off halves, Les Fairclough Junior, son of one of the greatest stand-offs in pre-war days, Les Fairclough, of the late 20s and early 30s. 'Young Les' a regular fan at Knowsley

Road, tells me: 'Considering he came straight into the first team from Rugby Union—and that at stand-off half, Harvey shows a lot of promise. I think he has a very good chance of making the grade, but we shall all have a better idea when he has played with Alex Murphy and when he has had more experience. He looks like a footballer, has plenty of skill and thinks and moves quickly. He could team up well with Murphy and he looks quick enough to 'keep up' with Alex. A lot has been said about his weight—11 stones—but there is not all that much difference between his and my father's playing weight. My father Les was stockier built. But when Harvey has had a season's full training in the Rugby League game and had a close season to fill out, he should not be worried about his weight. At present I would say that he is trying to do too much, trying to be in the game too much. But with experience he will find his place in the team scheme and could be a winner.

So within three matches I had been compared to two of the greatest stand-offs ever to have played for the Saints but the next match was to herald a new position.

Leslie Woodhead reported before the game, first round Lancashire Cup tie at Swinton:

Harvey on wing and Heaton at scrum-half

St Helens have produced two shocks in their team which starts their defence of the Lancashire Cup with a tough first round fixture against Swinton at Station Road. Peter Harvey former Liverpool and Lancashire Rugby Union star, who has had only three professional games is switched to the left wing as deputy for speedy South African Len Killeen who has a knee ligament injury. Young Jeff Heaton, that rugged little scrum-half, who was a first team regular last season during the Saints bad injury patch, is promoted again to replace Wilf Smith who is also nursing a knee ligament injury. The switch in Harvey is made in preference to playing utility back Keith Northey on the wing and bringing in hard tackling Mick Mooney at left centre. Harvey is no stranger to the wing position. Although his established position in Rugby Union was fly-half he also had some great games on the wing and fullback. But this will be his toughest test so far, plunging straight into an important and difficult cup match and probably facing the strong running John Speed. Harvey is on the small side, but his tackling and finishing speed lack nothing. He also has the advantage of knowing centre partners Northey's play, for they appeared in the same Rugby Union sides on many occasions.

As an aside: once more we see that reporters often write rubbish, even though they are the 'experts.' My established position throughout RU, since my school days was centre, with only a few representative matches on the wing. Keith

Lancashire Cup 1963.
Keith Northey gives Harvey an inside pass at Swinton. Bill Major is the Saints player in the foreground left, Dick Huddart can just be seen behind Bobby Fleet, the Swinton player, and Kel Coslett is on Harvey's right in the background.

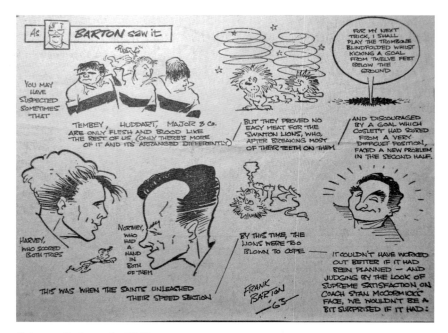

Saints *v.* Swinton in 1963.
Cartoon of Lancashire Cup tie.

Saints *v.* Warrington 1963.
Cartoon.

Northey and I did play in the same school team for many years, but never as a centre and wing partnership. Still they were right to mention my full back play, a regular there in the Bantams and Colts; I last played full back in 1956. Not quite a match for Kel Coslett playing every game for the Saints, and a Welsh International full back to boot, kicking goals from everywhere.

Anyway Leslie Woodhead was able to report after the match:

Gamble pays off richly for Saints

St Helens started their defence of the Lancashire Cup where they left off, with a convincing win over Swinton—their opponents in the last three finals—and the hero of the first round victory at Station Road on Saturday was diminutive left wing deputy, Peter Harvey. St Helens took a calculated risk in switching Harvey to the wing after only three professional games, all in the stand-off half position. But the gamble paid rich dividends; the former Liverpool and Lancashire Rugby Union star played a decisive part in taking St Helens through to a second round home tie against Workington and ending Swinton's fine run of 21 games without defeat.

He goes on to describe the two tries which I scored that day: the first from a Huddart break and a long pass to the wing to send me 'scorching in at the corner.'

> Harvey's second try and the one which really clinched this thrilling clash was a brilliant individual effort. Taking the ball on the burst 30 yards out he beat two men with clever sidestepping then staggered to his feet after a half tackle near the corner flag to sprint over for a try which brought a great ovation.

My actual memory of that match was that a few minutes before the second try, I had to tackle John Speed who hit me directly in the windpipe with his elbow. I went down near the half way line and the trainer ran on with the magic sponge, my throat was throbbing and in fact my vocal chords were damaged, but I stood up and regained my position. Almost immediately Keith Northey passed the ball to me and away I went touching down to great applause. As he dragged me up Keith said, 'You may have scored a better try than that, but that is the most important one you have ever scored.' I'm not sure that is true, but I certainly remember that one. Once more my name was in the headlines, we had broken Swinton's long run of success, and we were marching on towards The Lancashire Cup, and my first medal in Rugby League.

We can easily pass over the fact that I did not ever sing in the church choir again.

These cartoons were typical of the work of Frank Barton and this one looks at the difference between forwards and backs. Drawn about the Lancashire Cup semi-final in which we defeated Warrington 21-14.

In the match programme for the game against Featherstone (16 November 1963) there is this paragraph:

> The Saints, for half an hour in the game against Warrington, played as well as they have ever done. The first quarter was an even battle between the forwards. Then the Saints three-quarters went to town and we were treated to a spectacle that we are always looking for but rarely see. We have had good three-quarter lines since the war, but to find a line of four three-quarters as good as this we have to go back to the days of Ellaby and Hardgrave. Let us hope that Killeen, Vollenhoven, Northey and Harvey will give us other games as good as this.

That was the back line for the match against Featherstone, with Vollenhoven playing centre to Killeen, and Northey to Harvey.

So I signed for the Saints, and after just eight matches, one off the record held by Eric Ashton, I was playing for Lancashire at RL and had won my first medal in the Lancashire Cup Final, and within two months of signing on, had completed my first twelve matches. I went on to play in perhaps the greatest of all Saints teams, with my name appearing on more team sheets than any other player, during the months that I played.

Keighley 4 v St Helens 18 at Lawkholme Lane 31 August 1963.

Tom Ashcroft writes:

The one hand of the scoreboard clock which ticks the minutes off had all but run
the first 40 as the game took on a new character when Smith cut through and
kicked to the posts. Tembey chugged after it and scored by the posts.

My everlasting memory of this match is welcome to Rugby League. Sabine,
playing stand-off, took his chance with me as the innocent newcomer to the
game. I was laid out three times in the first half as I did not know how to cover
up having passed the ball. Tackling late, after the ball had been passed, made me
a simple target and he must have enjoyed the feeling whenever he could. Wilf
Smith, even then an old campaigner, told Cliff Watson that Sabine was hitting
me after the ball had gone. Enough said, and with no more ado, Cliff switched
to the open side of the scrum at the next one so that he could get to Mr Sabine as
I tackled him. He brushed me aside and picked him up: with one movement he
shook him like one would shake a carpet and dropped him to the ground. As the
trainer ran on with the smelling salts Cliff turned to me and said, 'Are you alright
now?' Thus began my real affection for Cliff Watson who became my minder. I
would have Cliff Watson on the team sheet of any game in which I was playing.
Tom Ashcroft makes no reference to any of those incidents but says:

Before the hour was up Keighley were steamrollered out of the game. Fiery
Cliff Watson put in one more charge and this time there were no willing takers.
He barged over to score. Shortly after that Killeen scored in the corner and the
crowd took to the pitch in large numbers, precisely why no one could tell. A
corgi dog with lead attached wandered onto the field and it had to be handed
back to the owner before Coslett could take his shot at goal. The referee blew the
final whistle before the ball had dropped wide.

There is a distinct slope on this pitch and at the lower end of the field the
terraces are unfenced and the crowd can do as they like. Keighley had police
in plenty to control the traffic but few visible to deal with the nomadic habits
of spectators. Fortunately this was another game in which Saints and their
opponents earned acclaim for keeping their tempers under control and taking
hard knocks without flying off the handle.

Harvey worked tremendously hard and lasted better than Sabine [that might
have been because Cliff Watson sorted him out for me] who has the reputation
of being one of the best out halves in Yorkshire. Sabine looked entitled to the
description in the first quarter of the game as he tackled Harvey out of the game
but Sabine did not last [I wonder why?] Harvey tackled all and sundry, went for

loose balls with terrific enthusiasm and generally held his corner.

Saints had to leave out Major and played Huddart in his place. This meant that for the first time I played alongside Dick Huddart and heard that phrase 'Follow me this time.' The long striding Huddart had a knack of flowing through a hole and handing the ball on. I clearly remember running down that hill at Keighley with the wind blowing in my hair. Tom Ashcroft doesn't mention that but did say that Huddart had his best game at thirteen that he had seen.

Programme notes from 16 November 1963.

Saints new players

Transfer news has been big news in soccer. I suppose that Rugby League signings, if not as big are just as important. John Warlow, The Saints recent recruit from Llanelli, had his first game last Saturday, and a most successful debut....He was direct and forceful in all he did.

John maintained that power and energy and became one of the keystone members of a great pack, a pedigree workhorse, and that is intended as high praise.

In the same programme notes it says that Eric Ashton had been appointed coach to Wigan in place of Griff Jenkins and at Leigh Alan Prescott is replaced by Gerry Helme. So both of these great players, Jenkins and Prescott, disappeared into history, early in my career. About this time also there is a newspaper report which tells us that Jimmy Honey has left the Star Inn, Merton Bank and gone to Australia to take up a coaching position there. Peter Metcalfe was coaching Pilks Recs. Two of my schoolboy heroes were moving on, whilst my later golfing teacher, John F. King was in charge of the 'B' and 'C' team at St Helens.

Tom Ashcroft *Reporter* Saturday 4 January 1964. St Helens 6 v Swinton 8.

The Knowsley Road enclosure, often lukewarm in atmosphere of late, was an excited hubbub on New Years' Day as the match between the champions and the challengers achieved the highest expectations.

Looking at the team sheet there is a surprise selection of Keith Northey on the wing in place of Vollenhoven, and I played in the centre. 20,000 spectators watched the match and a great many of them disagreed with the referee Ron Gelder of Wilmslow on some crucial decisions. The match was settled in the end by a fine try scored by Buckley from a pass by Stopford, which most of the crowd called as forward, converted under the posts by Blan. Unusually in this game there is mention of kicking, the ball not the man.

'Saints offered their all however, and made as much use of the kick through as Swinton. This intelligent use of the boot broke up spotting tactics and brought about some fantastic switches from defence to attack by both sides.' The game had everything save the spoils of victory and in the article Ashcroft writes: 'They first had to find replacements for three players of international standing, were not given the rub of the green on two vital decisions on passes, and had the winger Keith Northey groggy for a good part of the game.

This comment is further explained in the piece when he writes:

Murphy's long drop out, pursued by Saints forwards on trial, Warlow and Laughton, pushed the Great Britain fullback Gowers, into the first of several mistakes, and it was from this that Northey made a bid for the corner which ended in his being thrown into touch in goal and being shaken up so badly that he was never the same player afterwards.

To give a flavour of the game I quote another paragraph in the same article.

Saints, in the remainder of this half had one near miss, and the worst of another referee decision. Harvey's kick had Gowers at sea again. The Saints three-quarter chased the ball to the posts and the cover beat him by a nose to the touch down. From this attacking position, the battling Benyon fought his way through and could only roll the ball to Harvey as he was battered to earth. Harvey scooped it up and went over and the referee's refusal produced a howl of disapproval. Individually, Saints had no player of star rating, but there could be warm satisfaction in the way the team as a whole buckled to the task. Harvey, for his opportunistic keenness, and Benyon for the way he held the middle and broke the tackle, can be classed as players who will have a say in Saints future. Murphy tackled his weight and more, but was not the first to find that he could not have all his own way against Parkinson.

The St Helens *Reporter* of Tuesday 28 January carried a report with the sub-heading,

Old Style combined attack pays off handsomely
St Helens 28 Keighley 3

Saints were always looking for new players and this match contained two of them. Bob Burdell was hailed as the possible replacement for Bob Dagnall, but Lance Davies, playing in the centre was not entirely successful. In this game Smith and Murphy played 7 and 6, and I played at 5. It was a match in which I managed to score four tries and have two others disallowed. Tom Ashcroft

Harvey played left wing for Saints *v.* Keighley January 1964.
Cartoon—He scored four tries that day.

says during his review of the match

> The day's big successes were Murphy and Harvey and if there was a vindication
> of my own long held view that these two were in their best positions this was
> it. Murphy, with the ball heeled quickly from the scrums and helped by Smiths
> service, was back to his best form.

In a paragraph headed, 'Too Quick' he wrote:

> Incidents then came thick and fast. Harvey, on the blind side of the scrum was
> ready for Murphy's clever cross kick, too ready in fact. He pinched a flying start
> and the referee would not let him have the try. The little winger's pertinacity
> was rewarded, however, when Major put him through from close range. Even so
> Harvey was able to slip Garfield Owen, which was more than Vollenhoven could
> do after a terrific thrust on the other side.

In the final paragraph he writes about Keighley. 'Todd was easily the
outstanding back and the veteran Owen played well until he was forced to
retire.' Watson broke his arm and Saints switched Ray French to prop for the
first time, and there is comment about the fact that Coslett missed so many
of his attempts at goal. It was the only match played by Lance Davies; if you

don't take your chance you are gone.

Quick on the ball Saints signed Bryan Todd immediately and he is mentioned in the first paragraph of the match report the following week. It was described as a dream debut in the next match away to Hull KR 5 Saints 9:

> It was a marvellous boost for next Saturday's first round of the Cup and almost a dream debut for Bryan Todd, the new centre from Keighley.' 'Todd voted onto Saints books by the opinion of the crowd as much as anything else played his part with gallantry and skill. It was he who largely made the first try of the game with a classic break and a perfect ground kick for the eager Harvey. It was Todd who swung the game right in the visitors favour when, straightaway after the interval, he supported Huddart's break away and bustled his way through a tackle, to charge over for a try, without the assistance of Harvey who again was at his elbow.

Later in the same article, and describing the same try, Tom Ashcroft writes:

> Todd confident in his ability to place the ball to the right length released a grubber, and quick as lightning Harvey flew for the touchdown, the first try of this nature from Saints I can recall without an exhaustive search of the records.

This is an interesting point because Ashcroft goes on to compare 'the dozens of tries scored by Brian Bevan in this way', and our relative lack of such a tactic.

It is interesting for me looking back at these reports to see the tone and perhaps more importantly the teams as they were then. 'Team spirit and the will to win were much in evidence.' I don't remember it ever being different from that, but that match report tells us that Kel Coslett had received a shoulder injury which would put him out of the team and 'having played every match since joining the club,' he would be missed. In the absence of Watson, praise was duly given to the rest of the pack, which for the record was: Bill Major, Burdell, French, Warlow, Huddart, and Ashcroft.

The cup match against Castleford next week will be 'interesting.'

In fact we lost and were dumped out of the Challenge Cup in the first round.

Getting another headline the match report for 18 February reads: 'Todd's Trusty boot wins game of errors and surprises.' The match was against Barrow at Craven Park and I remember it for a single incident. I played on the left wing and for the first time faced Billy Burgess, with whom I had played in the Lancashire RU team. I would say that we were very friendly up to the beginning of the match. Even having played several tough games in Rugby League up to that day I was still very surprised by one incident which happened to me. Every match, though a team affair, has a huge element of man to man marking and it is important to establish some superiority over the person one is playing against, or marking. During this match I tried to run round Burgess, who was very fast himself. He gave me the touchline and I took my chance and ran round the outside, quickly moving into the gap between him and the touchline. He managed to catch me and gripping my shoulders ran me over the touchline, and carried on pushing me straight into the concrete wall surrounding the pitch. When I hit the wall with both arms outstretched he simply said, 'It's a tough game this Rugby League.'

Friendship, it seems has no place on the pitch during a match.

Now in the match report for that game, Tom Ashcroft mentions all four wingers in a way which tells much about the game:

> Barrow took the lead at the end of the first quarter with the best solo try which has been scored against the Saints for seasons. Bill Burgess was the hero of that effort with a swerving run from behind his own line. He covered slightly in excess of a hundred yards to plant the ball between the posts.
>
> In his place was Murray, a local sprinter, who has appeared in the Powderhall, but facing Vollenhoven he did not present the same problems as Burgess did on the other side. Burgess, who is not normally an aggressive or unscrupulous player, did commit one questionable action early in the game when he took Harvey over the touchline, and ran him into the rails. Harvey damaged his hand and the referee would not let him on again for a long spell until the game had been halted. Burgess was paid back in his own coin however after leading a raid and getting the half-back Matthews, away down the middle. As Vollenhoven raced across from the wing to halt this move in great style, Frank Barrow waded into Burgess with a shoulder charge and left him gasping.

They say 'he who laughs last laughs longest' and it was me who scored the final try ten minutes before the end to clinch the win, 'with a defender clinging to my back'. I'd like to think that was Bill Burgess, who did teach me a hard lesson that day.

As I look at the records now, I find that I played thirty-nine times in the first season, twenty-six times at 5, 10 at 6, twice on the right wing and once at right centre. I scored twenty-two tries which equalled Tom van Vollenhoven for that season and bettered Len Killeen by ten. Often when people consider the Saints team of the sixties, they start with Vollenhoven and Killeen, then naturally talk about Alex Murphy, all of them great players, and in the Saints Hall of Fame. Little notice is taken that I actually played twenty-six times at 5, to Len Killeen's fifteen in that season, so I could claim, that at least in Stan McCormick's eye I was a better left wing than him. You see he did not kick any goals that season. It was the injury to Kel Coslett, and the fact that he kicked 140 goals the next season, which brings him to the fore.

Even a direct comparison with Alex Murphy, over the three seasons 63/64/65, shows that I played more games and scored more tries than him. I was always at ease with all of the players, and I look on myself rather like the grease that keeps the engine running. It is very bold of me to make this next comparison, and I duly acknowledge that it is only statistical, but I did also have a better appearance record than Tom Vollenhoven, undoubtedly the greatest winger I ever saw. I admired him so much, that sometimes I would find myself watching him, even when a match was in progress, and wondering how he beat so many men so easily.

In training one day I asked him to teach me to swerve and sidestep, like he did. 'I don't know how I do it; I just know when to go inside and when to go out.' Much of it was change of pace, by which he could force the opposition to get on the wrong foot, to over-balance, which is why there are so many pictures of players laying on the ground, with their arms outstretched. He had tremendous pace, and a flowing running action, with a fifth gear, which was perhaps not as quick by the time I played with him. He was always targeted and by 1963/4/5 he had suffered numerous knee injuries. I said to him that night at training, 'Tom you have it all.' His reply stunned me because he said, 'No Peter, you have it all. Playing with us and being qualified as a PE teacher.' He would have loved that PE qualification, and later perhaps a British passport to go with it.

He has been back a few times, and fully deserves his place in the Greatest 17. The old timers (they call us the black and whites, because there was no colour TV in our day), include Dick Huddart and Cliff Watson, both of whom I played alongside that season, and both in the Greatest 17. We recall that nearly 10,000 supporters came to watch an 'A' team game when Tom van Vollenhoven first came to play at Knowsley Road in 1957. I was playing at Liverpool at the time and Reg Higgins told me, 'The people of St Helens have no idea how good this chap is.' He had played against him on the Lions Tour when Tom had outshone Tony O'Reilly, the pride of the Lions team. I saw Tom play his first game, and played against him in his last, he was outstanding. However, I do know that if I were to say that in Warrington, I would be told that he was not as good as Brian Bevan, or in Wigan, Billy Boston. I watched them both and played against them too (Bevan in a Charity Match), and it will always be Vollenhoven for me. All three are in the Rugby League Hall of Fame and it would be like trying to choose between the brilliance of diamonds. Billy Boston was later known as bouncing Billy, because as he got bigger he sometimes didn't bother to sidestep, but bounced players out of his way. I certainly remember the moment late on in our Challenge Cup Final at Wembley in 1966 when I was faced with the dilemma of tackling him head on. I had maybe half a second to decide what to do and I think that I choose right. I went high and bounced about three yards as he ran right over the top of me, but I slowed him down enough for Ray French to complete the tackle for (with) me. Len Killeen used to say that he marked Boston seven times and he never tackled him once. I don't know if that is a fact but I do know that in that Wembley final, the plan was that Billy Benyon cross-tackled him, as Killeen was to come inside to tackle the centre. I'm not convinced that he ever made a tackle at all during his Lance Todd winning performance, perhaps one to be fair to him.

I like Billy Boston—he is a great bloke. It is true that I have met him in largely social occasions and never had the problem of marking him. I was once due to mark him in a Saints v Wigan Boxing Day match and everyone told me what a terror he was. I was to try to make him run round me or I was to try to make him cut back inside me, so that our forwards could cut him down. I was at a party on Christmas Day, refusing drinks as I was playing the next day. Just about everyone at that party came over to tell me that marking Billy Boston would be a nightmare. As the snow fell and the ground gradually got harder with the biting frost, I convinced myself that the game would be called off. Late in the evening I even had a couple of drinks before driving home. Luckily the game was postponed and I never had 'the pleasure' of marking him at any other time. Thinking about the five hundred and fifty plus tries that he scored, I wonder just how often wingers gave him the outside only to see him skip past them, or gave him the inside to see him clear everyone out of his way like a bowling ball knocking over skittles.

I once went with Duggie Greenall to a presentation at Billy's pub in Wigan and we spent the evening talking about matches they had played on tour.

Saints *v.* Wakefield.
Harvey's first try as a stand-off. The other player is Neil Fox.

Duggie played centre to both Boston and Vollenhoven and Duggie was a great admirer of each one.

If we look at the try scoring record of Brian Bevan, 796 seems an impossible number, but it is real. To say that he scored tries for fun was to state the obvious. He seemed impossible to tackle; he was such an awkward runner, he seemed to run like a crab twisting and turning as he scooted along. But he was very quick too, scoring about a third of his tries by following kicks into the corner. Virtually no one could turn round and catch him. I remember one of his tries perfectly well which he scored against Tom van Vollenhoven in his pomp. I was one of the 39,000 plus spectators watching the Lancashire Cup Final at Central Park in October 1959, a match that was enthralling, though no tries were being scored. In less than ten seconds we wiped our eyes as Bevan ran round Vollenhoven, clearly outside the touch line and corner flag then back in again, within the in-goal area and dived on the ball, just as Vollenhoven kicked the ball away. 'Try' said the referee as about 15,000 Saints fans said no try, but it stood and Saints lost 5-4.

When I talked to people who played with Brian Bevan they said that he very often used to run outside the touch line, when he didn't have the ball and even when he did carry it he sometimes used the touchline as his friend if he saw two or three forwards coming to get him.

7th December 1963. Wakefield 7 St Helens 8
I got this headline on my first visit to Wakefield Trinity: Harvey plays havoc. Jack Bentley in his match report said:

> On the evidence of this first big test at stand-off he could prove the answer to Saints long standing No 6 problem. He has speed and courage and his textbook tackling forced Trinity Test man Harold Poynton into a 'one eye on Harvey and one eye on the ball' attitude which played havoc with Poynton's potential around the scrums.

Describing my first try in the stand-off position, another match report says,

> Harvey is just as effective from stand-off as on the wing. After handling in midfield the little red head raced brilliantly outside of Vollenhoven for the final pass in Saints first try scoring move.

This first try in the stand-off position is all the more memorable for me because I ran outside Neil Fox to score with a dive worthy of Stuart Llewellyn. Fox was one of the greatest players I ever played against, a point scoring machine, big fast and clever; definitely fit to be in the Rugby League Hall of Fame. His favourite move from the scrum was to run inside the standoff and take

St Helens *v.* Swinton.
Harvey scoring against John Stopford.

St Helens *v.* Castleford.
Harvey playing left wing.

the ball direct from the scrum-half running at the stand-off, his size and pace usually forced the line break, causing mass confusion in the defensive line. The alternative strategy of the run around with Harold Poynton, usually left Harold in the clear: a very difficult pair to mark.

I had scored ten tries in sixteen matches on the left wing, twenty-two in the season, with this one from stand-off. My final listings for the season show that I played twenty-six times on the left wing to Len Killeen's twenty, and I played ten times at 6. We both played on the right wing to cover absences by Vollenhoven, Killeen eight times and twice by me. I also played centre to Keith Northey on one occasion. It was New Years' Day 1964 in front of 20,000 people at Knowsley Road. Kel Coslett kicked two goals and Alex Murphy, playing at stand-off, one. No tries were scored and Swinton beat us 6-8. McCormick did not pick that side again, a New Year Resolution which did not work. By the end of the season we had won the Lancashire Cup and the Western Division Championship, Beating Swinton 10-7, but defeat at Castleford 6-13, knocked us out of the Challenge Cup in the first round.

There is one story from the Western Division Championship noted here, that only Alex Murphy and I can tell, because it was the match in which I

Stan McCormick's year. Two trophies on the picture.
Back row: left to right. Northey, Warlow, Coslett, French, Laughton, Smith, Burdell.
Front row: Williams, Vollenhoven, Tembey, Murphy, Killeen, Harvey.
Trophies: Lancashire Cup, Lancashire League.

became the Murphy mouthpiece. The match was to be refereed by Mr Eric Clay who had sent Alex off a number of times and called him a 'yapper'. I was to play stand-off to Alex at scrum-half and was changing right next to him. A number of different people came to Alex to 'remind him who was to referee the game', as if he didn't know. After a few people had spoken to him the vice chairman Cecil Dromgoole came and once more said, 'Now don't go talking to Mr Clay and giving him a reason to send you off.' Alex answered, 'I'll tell you what Mr Dromgoole, I bet you a gallon of beer that I don't talk to him today.' 'Done,' replied Cecil: but as he walked away Alex said to me, 'You can do the talking to Clay to-day.' 'Good afternoon, Mr Clay,' was Alex's greeting to him, but for the rest of the match he used me as the go-between. 'Tell him to keep them on-side.' 'Ask him if high tackles are alright today,' and a variety of other instructions, came from the talkative Alex, but he never directly spoke to Mr Clay. After the match, with us still steaming from the victory, and before we even got to the showers the press descended on us in the changing room. Jack Bentley, Brian Batty *et al*, quizzed him about the victory and Alex duly gave his statement, as he was expected to do; but as they left he turned to me and said, 'Was that alright?' as if I was going to be his mouthpiece for the rest of the day as well! Give him his due, the Vice Chairman of St Helens RLFC came out onto the pitch on the Tuesday evening as we were training, with a five-pint can under his arm. Smiling he said, 'They don't do gallons in a tin.'

In the Western Division final, played at Wigan 16 May 1964, St Helens beat Swinton by 10 points to 7 points. I remember that final for three reasons. First and most of all, because Mr Eric Clay refereed the match and did not allow what I thought was a perfectly good try from me. Playing at stand-off, I broke clear and was tackled just short of the line, but with the ball still not on the ground, I reached over the line and touched down. Try thought I, no try ruled Mr Clay. 'Double movement,' he said. To this day in my mind it was a try. Ray French did score a perfectly good try which won us the match, but it excited Stan McCormick so much that he leapt in the air arms aloft, forgetting that he was in the dug out. He split his skull and had to be carried off on a stretcher to have the wound stitched, but he still had a smile on his face as we had won another trophy.

On our way back from Castleford having lost 11-10, in the last match of the season, Stan McCormick was called to the front of the coach by Mr Cook and told that his contract would not be renewed. 'Do you mean that I am sacked?' 'No Stanley, we are not going to renew your contract.' A puzzled Stan came to the back of the coach with a face which would have suited Oliver Hardy. We all laughed but it was the end of a good season with a lovely person, if not a great coach.

So we started the 64/65 season with Joe Coan in command, no easy training sessions now. From pre-season we were metaphorically flogged. Joe, with

West Park school games day. Three players played for Lancashire RL.
Back row: 4th from right Harvey, 2nd from right Donovan.
Front row: 3rd from right Northey.

stopwatch in hand had us running in separate sets. Forwards and backs, then in competition, forwards against backs, with forwards getting yards in hand in handicap races. No one complained, though quite a few were physically sick when he ran us for the longest time he calculated we would have to play without stopping. In the days of unlimited tackles that could be ten minutes without respite. We learned the lesson with this hard taskmaster – to win we must be fitter than the opposition. Interval training with shorter and shorter recovery time, mixed up with sprinting on the track across the front of the stadium.

I must have been playing well because once more I was selected to play for Lancashire RL senior team, this time as a stand-off.

The date: Wednesday 16 September 1964, the place Blackpool.
Lancashire v Cumberland Kick off 6 p.m.

The most remarkable thing about this match, again played mid-week, was that for part of the match, the midfield trio was Harvey, Northey and Donovan. We were all from the same team at West Park School and now playing, at very close to the highest level in Rugby League. I suppose also in retrospect, some people would argue, that since I was not born in Lancashire, I should never have been selected. However, to state the obvious, I played twice for

Lancashire RL, once on the wing and once at stand-off. That is why Joe Coan used me as a utility player, and I was virtually always on the team sheet.

John Donovan had played at St Helens throughout the 1960/61 season; indeed he played in the Challenge Cup semi-final, but was not selected for the final. If he had been selected he would have played centre to Vollenhoven, and the Ken Large /Tom Vollenhoven try could never have happened. So once more the vagary of selection affects the history of sport. Keith Northey had played for Lancashire RU when he was still at Hopwood Hall Training College, before going on to Carnegie College, Leeds. He was in the England RL squad during the Australian Tour 1963, so he was very close to selection as a test centre. He could also play anywhere in the backs and was a very dangerous attacking player. Apart from saying that it was a lovely sunny evening and I enjoyed playing, I can't remember much, if anything about the match. Playing at Blackpool was a novelty as they had only recently entered the Rugby League.

My head teacher was not pleased at these representative matches and deducted pay every time we played midweek.

Besides making us train much better, Joe Coan took another decision: he made Alex Murphy the club Captain. There had been doubts about whether Alex could keep his head when trouble flared, but Joe saw him as the natural leader on the field. The reward for us as Saints players came in the shape of twenty-one straight wins from the beginning of the season, including a 12-4 win against Swinton in the Lancashire Cup Final on 24 October 1964. It was my twenty-fourth birthday and I was two years older than the average age of the team that day. I played stand-off to Alex Murphy, with Benyon and Northey in the centre berths. Benyon scored a try and Killeen kicked three goals. The other try scorer that day was massive Mervyn Hicks (twenty), yet another Welsh RU player, playing alongside Ray French in the second row, with an effervescent teenage Doug Loughton at loose forward. Cliff Watson was on the bench which shows how strong that team was. The front row of Tembey, Dagnall and Warlow could get us the ball and do the work in the open field. With an average age of twenty-eight they also had plenty match experience behind them.

The flying English RU trialist Tommy Pimblett (twenty-two) was playing his fifteenth game on the right wing as Vollenhoven was having treatment on a damaged cartilage. The ubiquitous Alex Murphy lifted the Cup which was a fore runner of things to come.

Shortly before that winning performance there was this match report.

Tom Ashcroft *St Helens Newspaper* Tuesday 6 October 1964.
Played at St Helens with a match attendance of 12,000.

The headline for this match report was stark. FOUR SENT OFF IN KNOWSLEY ROAD RUMPUS, with a comment below which said, 'Saints showed super skill despite the storm.'

With an almost rhetorical question, 'Why won't teams let us play football?' says coach. (Joe Coan) Ashcroft began his report with a statement which read:

Workington come to Knowsley Road with an underlined brief. As on one or two occasions in the past they were out to knock the Saints off their perch. I think they set out with the best of intentions and were ready to match skill with skill. Regrettably when that did not work and Saints began to get rich rewards for slick handling, the visitors altered the tactics and sparked off the biggest rumpus since heavens knows when. Saints Captain Alex Murphy is emphatic that his side did not touch off the trigger. The coach, Joe Coan complains, 'Why won't these teams let us play football?'

The trouble probably started early on when big John Tembey got an elbow in his face and retired to have four stitches in a gash. The time when Workington really got mad, however, was when slack tackling in the middle enabled Saints to get the ball out to Killeen for the opening try after 15 minutes. The apparent decision then was to knock any Saints player with the ball, off his feet without any equivocation, and the strong-minded men in the home side took the same line. These were the sternest of terms but Saints were still prepared to play the handling game as they did with a super brilliance when Hicks, who had come on for Tembey, slipped a pass as he was gripped in a mid-field tackle. Benyon, Harvey and Northey had the defence on a string as they inter-passed at speed at the approaches to the line. Northey's magnificent try was as salt in Workington's wounded pride. Then the trouble really began.

Martin, one of the toughest forwards in the business, a short while before had been panned out when French fairly charged him in the chest. The scene which brought about their dismissal could have been a reprisal attempt.

Ray French and Workington's Martin who had taken an early dislike to one another, got mixed up in a brawl in front of the main stand as play ran into the middle and they were caught out by the touch judge. Once he had made his report, the referee shooed both forwards off and when they sat on the bench he sent them another reminder that their place was in the dressing room.

The game was still producing passages of flourishing football and such was the movement which brought Harvey a fine try on the brink of half-time and killed the goose for Workington good and proper.

The second half opened stormily. As the referee turned to admonish Hicks for a wild kick at a loose ball, Dagnall, Saints hooker, was laid low amongst a group of forwards while play was stopped. By the time he had been brought round again after attention on the side line, the second major incident had taken place. Foster, a muscular forward held the ball on his 25 and waited for Murphy to go into the tackle. It has been alleged by Murphy that the Workington man butted him.

The clash resulted in a set to and Murphy was held back by the restraining arms of Hicks and Watson. So Foster waded in again. When they were hauled out of the struggling mass they were made to go and the teams were reduced to 11 men each.

The form of Harvey was a revelation and he was able to play his part from beginning to end because he judged the point when further resistance to a tackle was courting trouble. He took his bouncings with admirable self-control and his opportunities with a flourish. Benyon and Northey played very well and Laughton, playing in the centre, had a fine game.

By the time the return match takes place at Derwent Park in February, the memories of this match may have faded.

Somehow I doubt that very much.

I learned long ago, never to wrestle with a pig. You get dirty and besides, the pig likes it.
George Bernard Shaw (probably).

It may not have been the return match that year, because every match at Workington seemed to be the same, but the one I am speaking about had a very interesting story. The game was deteriorating into one long maul, with periodic outbursts of fisticuffs, usually sparked off by the front rows when in the act of scrummaging. These were highly competitive affairs and we had one of the very best hookers in Bob Dagnall. Naturally he was the target for much of the arm wrestling and the crowd booed him at virtually every scrum. I believe it was referee Matt Coates but it could have been Ron Gelder who was instrumental in one of the funniest things I ever saw on a rugby pitch. As the forwards pushed and pulled to gain an advantage and the crowd roared their disapproval, he gave a loud blast on his whistle and raised his arm to beckon Bob Dagnall out of the mêlée. There were neither TV cameras nor microphones, so only a few players like me were close enough to hear the exchange between him and Bob. The referee whilst raising his arm and waving said, 'Make this look good Bob. The crowd think that I am telling you off. How's the missus?' Bob with his head bowed said, 'Champion Matt, never been better.'

'That's good Bob, now go back and get on with the game.' As he said that he pointed to the dressing room and the crowd roared their approval, thinking Bob was getting his marching orders. He had cooled the game down but still the big fellows up front wrestled for dominance.

I will talk more about this style of rugby later.

When I look at my playing record there is one very odd sequence of events. I am going to extend the comments on these matches but first I want to detail the reason why I think that it is an odd sequence, we lost every match.

Date	Team	Half time	Full time	Crowd	Position
16/01/65	Warrington	4-4	4-6	13,471	6
13/02/65	Workington	2-0	3-4	2,934	14
16/03/65	Wakefield	2-6	2-9	14,100	6
20/03/65	Wakefield	2-5	4-5	5,900	2
23/03/65	Wigan	4-7	6-10	18,500	6
27/03/65	Salford	6-9	8-11	3,000	6

These are the matches I played in the first team and I will deal with them all in turn.

The match report for the game against Warrington begins:

The mighty have fallen! The best victory run in the club's annals came to an end at Wilderspool, but this was a defeat without shame for Saints. They simply could not muster up the best brand of forward play and backs had no inspiration.

In a way defeat for Saints must come as a great relief. The defeat of such a record twenty-one wins has been too much of a load on their backs for some weeks now. Their play has been too stereotyped for fear of the interception, or some fatal handling error, which would have earned one or other member of the side, the unenviable distinction as the player who threw the record away.

So no problem there from the local press; not quite true as we shall see. In his match report Tom Ashcroft talks about the close marking of Alex Murphy and the effect that had on the team.

The home scrum-half was certainly never keen to retire. All the more reason, that Murphy should have taken more chances than he did, to get the ball away. He did not make Harvey's task an easy one, yet I am afraid that Harvey may take the rap for another moderate game, in which he was somewhat below the standard of Billy Aspinall, the lively young UGB product.

A more effective partnership in the game would have been Harvey at scrum and Murphy in the number 6 jersey. I have never altered my view that Murphy would do best for Saints at out half. General opinion is against the idea, outside critics revolt at the thought of playing Great Britain's first choice scrum worker anywhere else.

Tom Ashcroft's opinion was not shared by many at that time, but he was correct that I would take the blame and be dropped for the next match, in which Saints beat Whitehaven 16-3. Neither Murphy nor I played, as the halves were Smith and Benyon. I was probably sent to play at Whitehaven with the 'A' team.

For the match at Workington I am down as the 14, sitting on the bench in case any of the backs gets injured. Actually in the newspaper it gives French and Laughton as the two substitutes but in the match report it says that Hicks came on in the second half, so we can't always believe what we read in the newspapers, can we? Since I am not mentioned at all I will talk about some of the events which took place according to the match report.

This match was televised, so many more than the 2,934 spectators saw The Saints go down to a defeat. Goal-kickers so often get the credit for winning matches and, unusually one of the very best, Kel Coslett, got the blame for losing this one. Looking back at his wonderful record one might think a kicker of his ability would not be fazed by tension, but pressure is felt by everyone. The article was decorated with a picture of Kel wearing his Welsh RU Cap and Tom Ashcroft describes how he missed a kick to convert Benyon's try 'from no more than three yards wide of the post.' He then goes on to point out that Kel also missed four other penalties, any one of which would have won the match. Perhaps seeking to apportion blame for the loss Ashcroft says that Tembey should have realised that Coslett was off form, and asked Killeen to kick the goals. As usual, at Workington, it was cold and blustery and the game was a hard one with running battles as the forwards played their 'one at a time ball-rushing tactics in the loose.'

Before I leave this match I want to give two more small pieces from Tom Ashcroft. In a piece headlined 'inquest' he states:

> The question that will arise after this defeat will involve team selection. Was Coslett allowed to make his come-back too early when the man in possession, Barrow, was in tremendous form in the full-back position? Were Saints wise to dispose of Stan Owen, the forward who got the pack handling after a bad spell? Or have Saints hit their peak too early in the season and are they now on the decline?

On the same page it shows Saints in third place after eighteen wins and two losses in the league, having played five matches fewer than Wigan and Warrington who were above them in the table. We know that they had also had four victories to win the Lancashire Cup.

In his follow up piece Ashcroft reports:

> A stormy scene occurred right behind the television cameras during the Saints game at Workington. A highly respected follower Dr J. Chisnall who occupied a seat in the Directors' box close to Alex Murphy, the Saints skipper, was set upon by a number of home spectators, and a police inspector and police constable had

to rescue the doctor from an ugly situation.

Later he says that it had all kicked off after an innocuous remark but at Workington the spectators are apt to flare up quickly.

I suspect that the remark was likely to have come from the Saints skipper, rather than the good doctor who bore the brunt of the attack. Even when he was not playing Alex could cause a storm by some of his remarks about opposition players. On the other hand the popular Dr Joe was a well-known supporter of the Saints and might well have said something injudicious, as he sometimes did; however as a guest of the directors, in the directors' box, he would have felt safe to express his opinion. Dr Joe was very well known and well-liked by all St Helens players and was one of the characters of rugby league.

It does not show in my record (taken from the Saints Heritage Site) where it says that Tony Barrow was selected, but it does show in the local newspaper that I was picked at 14, on Saturday 13 March 1965 at Oldham where we won 15-9. Watson came off the bench when a forward was injured but I was not called on to play. However, I do want to give this match a mention because one of the players who was praised was John Donovan who played centre for Oldham that day. John had played at West Park with me and for Saints throughout 1961, famously being left out of the cup final team. But once more he is getting praise when our centres are not: another case of ex-Saints players playing well against them.

It was just three days later when Saints where beaten by Wakefield at Knowsley Road, and less than a week after that, when Wakefield achieved the double in the home match there.

In the first match at Knowsley Road a crowd of 14,100 people watched as we played a hard-fought but even match against a very talented Wakefield team. I played six to Murphy at seven but for once neither of us took the blame for the defeat.

Ashcroft writes:

The decisive incident of the second half was a remarkable try by Berwyn Jones, Wakefield's flying winger. At that moment Wakefield were without Ponyton who had been dazed by a Barrow tackle. Trinity maintained a steady attack however and Berwyn Jones was served on the Saints 25 by Barlow the reserve hooker. Jones drew clear of Saints cover but seemed to be well covered by Barrow as he went for the corner. A momentary feint to go inside, and sudden acceleration into the smallest gap on the outside, deceived the full back and Jones got the try which put Saints out of the hunt.

We lost 2-9 and the try is remembered by everyone who saw the pace of Jones and the startled look on Frank Barrow's face.

Just four days later we faced Wakefield once more but this time I played on the wing.

The snow fell steadily as we crossed the Pennines, and continued to fall as the game progressed so that the match, which we lost 'by the odd point in a hard slam under vile conditions', was almost cancelled, but they managed to keep the lines clear of the snow.

Tom Ashcroft reported:

> The deciding contribution was once more the finishing speed of Berwyn Jones and the fact that Trinity were able to move the ball by hand from one abortive effort by Coetzer in the left corner to give Jones his chance on the other side.

In this game I was playing on the right wing and marking Coetzer playing on the left wing for Wakefield. Peter Gartland was playing scrum-half to Alex Murphy at stand-off, with Cen Williams and Keith Northey in the centres and Killeen on the left wing.

The backs were all given praise for their efforts in very difficult conditions, but at the same time there is both implied and direct criticism as in these two cases.

> Northey stood up to Neil Fox so that the big Trinity centre never got very far, but was less reliable in defence when it came to dealing with an opponent running in a broken field.
>
> Harvey also had difficulty at times dealing with the fiery Coetzer and missed a tackle or two, particularly when Metcalfe, a strong running Wakefield full back, was coming through on the burst.'
>
> Wakefield are now beginning to use Berwyn Jones as Saints used Vollenhoven in the days of Doug. Greenall and Ken Large and opponents will soon realise that the sprinter needs only a half chance.

Further in his report he praises Frank Barrow for his defensive work but then comes this assertion:

> He ran the ball out strongly, but did not play quite the attacking part in the game as did his opposite number. One of the ways to get the extra man in attack is to use the full back and Saints are not using Barrow in that way often enough.

Let me rewrite those ideas to say that Metcalfe the Wakefield full back caused problems by coming into the line to support his centres, and caused confusion in the Saints' defence as he made the extra man.

But Ashcroft is more open in his continuing criticism as opposed to his comments at the time of the first defeat by Warrington:

> It is by no means certain that Saints will finish on top of the league and less certain
> that they will survive the top 16 play-off and win the championship, which is the
> normal right of the leaders at the end of the season. About the forward play I am
> beginning to think that Saints keenness for signing international rugby union
> pack men is not producing the best results.

He goes on to criticise the very nature of RU forwards and their 'inability to handle the ball' saying: 'Much as I admire the promise and drive of John Mantle, Saints latest Welsh recruit, I have to admit that the uncertainty of his handling in this match caused anxieties.'

Just three days later on the 23 March came the game against Wigan, played at Knowsley Road in front of 18,300 spectators who cheered and groaned in equal measure. It was one of the great memories of the time of unlimited tackle rule that the emotions of the crowd could swing with the possession. Once the ball was gained it could only be lost by an offence or a mistake. The crowd would cheer in unison, and the build-up of that appreciation would mount as the attack got closer and closer to the line. It was rather like following the tanks as our pack rolled forward, and we acted like snipers dodging out from behind them in attempted strikes on the enemy line.

Tom Ashcroft, our ever-present reporter gives us this enlightened viewpoint. 'If ever a team won a match without the ball it was Wigan on this occasion.'

As a regular part of reports the statistics of the hooker would be set upon and comparisons made. Bob Dagnall usually won these battles, and at the time of his injury in this season, the board started to look for his replacement. Not immediately but we can see their efforts.

Paraphrasing the newspaper reports of that match I can say that for twenty minutes of the second half Saints, having reduced the lead to 6-7, threw everything that they had against the opposition, but somehow Wigan's defence refused to crack under the terrific barrage.

An injury to Cliff Hill (who had been signed when I didn't go to them) meant that Ashton came in to stand-off, with Lyon on the wing and Boston played at centre.

I remember Ashton was difficult to tackle because he had long legs, bony knees and was very angular in his general shape. Boston on the other hand was solid and rotund and very powerful indeed. These two players were like tank blockers in the middle of the field and neither Murphy nor I could get round them. One try from the diminutive Parr, their scrum-half, won the game for them on one of the very few occasions they had the ball.

For those people who are keeping count that is four matches in ten days and we had just four more days before the next one.

Salford 11 St Helens 8 played on 27 March 1965 in front of 3,000 people.

I played stand-off to Wilf Smith at scrum-half in this match, Northey and French were the two subs.

Dagnall suffered a recurrence of his shoulder injury in the first half and so Ray French came on and Watson was moved to hooker. Tom Ashcroft reported: 'The injury to Dagnall raises more questions about Saints forward play. This time Watson was far from an adequate substitute against Harper, a St Helens lad.'

As was becoming his usual complaint not only was the blame put on the shoulders of the pack but Ashcroft comes up with a couple of suggestions, citing some of the Salford team who have passed through the St Helens club in the past, and then he specifically says,

> The more I see of the present plight the more does the need for another old stager to think out attacks, suggests itself. There are not many of them about, but Saints could do worse than spend a few hundred pounds to bring back Ab Terry from Castleford. He was recently on transfer at £750. What Owen did for a spell he might also do.

Three trophies with Mackeson tankards 1965.
In one line: Mr Cook, Mervyn Hicks, Alex Murphy, John Tembey, Doug Laughton, Len Killeen, Frank Barrow, Bob Dagnall, Ray French, Mackeson man, Keith Northey, Cliff Watson, John Warlow, Peter Harvey, Cen Williams, Tom Pimblett, Bill Benyon.
Trophies: Lancashire Cup, League Leaders Lancashire League.

At the same time Douggie Laughton was put on the transfer list at £10,500, but as he was about to get married, it seemed that this was his way of getting an additional payment from the Saints, when they took him off the list again.

For myself I was obviously not setting the match alight and again my partnership with Smith was uninspiring, with no breaks occurring in the first half. Joe Coan brought Keith Northey on to see if he could spark a change in fortune.

Ashcroft reports:

> At half time Saints did some regrouping. Benyon was switched to out half where Harvey had played without distinction and Northey took over as partner to Killeen. He was able to effect no improvement and Saints as a whole could produce no flash of inspiration in attack. Their game was sadly lacking in confidence, the result questionably of the recent slump in form and in particular the defeat by Wigan when so much effort was put in for no return.
>
> Playing under difficulties against an opposing scrum-half who handled the ball far more, Smith came out of the game rather better than most. There were times when he got his own backs moving smartly, but these are days when the other inside backs cannot buy a break for love nor money.

This whole article was written under the headline, 'Saints just haven't any confidence' and the sub title, 'Let's hope they have reached the low watermark.'

During that season (1964-65) Joe Coan's first in charge, we won The Lancashire Cup, The Lancashire League and the New League Leaders Trophy for coming top of the League. However, we did not win the League Championship because

The Championship final Saints v. Halifax 1965.
Harvey played right wing. Harvey, Kellett Halifax, Laughton, Renilson Halifax and Alex Murphy all heading for the try line. Notice the ring side seats.

we were beaten in the Final by Halifax, who had managed only seventh place in the table.

There is a saying that a team has got to lose before it learns to win. Of course winning is a habit, but to lose a Championship Final was such a bad experience, we all learned a great deal. Not least Joe Coan, who had made us work very hard in the week leading to that match, he never did that again. We had left too much energy on the training ground. The record shows that Fogarty, one of their second row forwards won the Harry Sunderland Trophy. I remember that he kicked us back into the right hand corner over and over again. I was playing right wing and was continuously running back to field the ball, rather like they do today, but then it was unusual to kick the ball downfield. As always our forwards carried the ball back but we did not have the snap and crackle at the back to score enough tries. This is a commentary and not a criticism; for after all I was an integral part of what for us was a great disappointment.

I do not know what happened to Cen Williams, who I believe was a great centre, but he wasn't picked for that match. Instead, for the only time in that season (and for the rest of his playing career), Tom van Vollenhoven was picked to play centre. Now Tom had played centre in Rugby Union and was a truly great player, both in attack and defence. I played right wing to the great man that day, a reversal of Mr Cook's offer to me. Keith Northey played in the other centre position with Len Killeen outside of him. Wilf Smith and Alex Murphy were at 7 and 6 so it was a very experienced back line. Still their centre John Burnett managed to score two tries and the right wing Jackson one. I marked John Freeman and I know that I played well but neither of us managed to score. One of the 20,776 spectators that day was Tom Owen, a persistent critic and regular letter writer. His letter says:

> Beaten by three tearaway breakaways of a very ordinary side! Allow for more dropped passes than the Saints had dropped all season; persistent and deliberate Halifax off-side at the scrums and play the ball, plus a persistent intent to knock or snatch the ball out of every Saintly hand—and you still have the old, old fault of forwards with head down, bash and batter charging.

Perhaps the unusual set up of the three quarter line was the reason for those breakaways and the poor handling. We will never know, but it never happened again, that the great Tom Vollenhoven played centre to me.

From the Eric Thompson Corner, Tuesday 9 June 1965. *Evening Post and Chronicle*:

> Alex Murphy collected that fourth Trophy for St Helens yesterday at Headingley

after an afternoon of seven's rugby—The Wills Golden Rugby Ball.

Hit on the back of the head with a stone thrown from the crowd Mr Eric Clay, the referee said that had he turned his head he could have been blinded. Saints collected £25 a man for their victory. The Saints team included Northey, Murphy, Killeen, Hicks, Laughton, Mantle and Harvey which was a team big up front and quick at the back.

We didn't play many 7 a-side tournaments but they were great fun both in RU and RL, though playing in half a dozen matches is very tiring and fitness is a key element. So even on a bright sunny afternoon of fast open rugby, someone decides to throw things at the players once more. This time it was the referee Sergeant Major Eric Clay who needed the stitches, and it was us who consoled him.

CHAPTER 17

Teammates and Trophies

Traditionally when people talk about, 'The great side of the sixties,' they can only name about half of them. For example Bill Major was the club captain in the first two seasons I played. He played loose forward, as did Duggie Laughton, who was magnificent until he suffered major knee damage. Mervyn Hicks a giant of a second row, who left for a career in Australia, was dynamic in handling and tackling. Few people talk about John Tembey, and almost laugh at his roly-poly appearance. He was a fine prop forward, a good ball handler and jolly quick as well, good enough to Captain the side against Australia, and play for Great Britain. I remember running out of the tunnel behind John, both of us were joining in with the Beatles, Twist and Shout, which was a popular song of the day, singing at the top of our voices. Rothery Radio must have been playing the music that day, so we did not have our usual 'March of the Gladiators.' Tembey began as a centre at Haven and was a good break-maker in his own right.

Both Wilf Smith and Jeff Heaton, good enough to play in the Lancashire Cup Final, before I came, and get into the Saints' Past Players' Hall of Fame, after I left, found that they could not get a regular first team place while I was there. Stan Owen, that hard headed campaigner from Leigh, bought to teach the new Rugby Union forwards how to play rugby league, played just thirteen times in the year he was with us. Mick Mooney and Bryan Todd were bought to provide the rough tough centre, some of the board thought was essential. They were not needed.

In my opinion the silky skills of Keith Northey and Cen Williams or the virtuosity of Alex Murphy was much better to watch. Billy Benyon, Frankie and Tony Barrow, all brought the tough rugby league approach to the backs and to some extent kept out the sheer pace of Tommy Pimblett, who was the quickest of all local talent in a straight race down the wing. David Wood, unusually for us was an Australian, who had many fine games in the centre, and local boy Dave Markey was talked about as a possible big centre, but played most of his matches as a second row, or loose forward. There were also players like Bob Burdell, who seemed for a time to have gained the no. 9 spot, or at least shared it with young Joe Egan, before the old headed Bob Dagnall, heeled them off, before he was finally replaced by Billy ('Sos') Sayer, as his speed about the park deserted him.

This competition for places was one of the reasons which made it one of the greatest sides ever: that there was tremendous competition for every position can be seen by the names of those transferred in, and out. Jimmy Mustard, Peter Goddard, Mervyn Hicks, Dick Huddart, Keith Ashcroft and Doug Laughton, all played and gave way to John Warlow, John Mantle, Joe Donegan, Joe Robinson, Brian Hogan, Freddie Hill, before Albert Halsall and Geoff Hitchin came in to get a place in the Cup Final team, in 1966. There were no prepaid contracts so every player was literally as good as his last game. No one got paid in advance and the coach was never in the position to have to play anyone.

Joe Coan had the luxury of rotating his pack and the backs, giving people a rest, and certainly covering from injury, without powering down the team. Players like Ian Jones, Peter Gartland, even Ken Kelly and Frank Ward were on hand but got little chance of playing during the 65/66 season.

I remember a game at Castleford, such a difficult place to win at, in August 1965 when David Wood was playing one of his earliest matches. He scored a try with a trick which I have only seen on the training ground. He pretended to pass the ball with one hand, but instead passed the ball around his body, without ever letting go, and then he reached out and placed the ball over the line. It was a sunny day with a very good crowd cheering their team in great waves. The tries by Coslett from fullback, and me from the wing were greeted with reasonable applause, the charging runs down the wing of Tom Pimblett brought much delight, but Wood's try caused a riot. The crowd began to boo and shout obscenities, and then they started to throw whatever was to hand, including lumps of concrete. It really got out of hand but the referee, Eric Clay, stood his ground and the try was allowed.

As a postscript to that event there is a private story. My brother John was at that match, having travelled down from Catterick Camp, where he was stationed with the Army. He was in uniform as he was hitchhiking which was quite normal in the sixties. Seeking a lift on the team coach after the match, he was sitting by the open door when a barrage of sods and mud was thrown at us. He, and his uniform, was covered with mud. I don't think either he or his commanding officer saw the funny side of that day.

There is little point in quoting from every game in which I played, but it is worth looking at the development of the team I joined.

I well remember Stan McCormick complaining that there were too many Rugby Union players in the team, and it is also possible that some of the local rugby league players agreed with him. It is certainly true that the coach did not get to pick the players who were given to him, and that the teams he picked, had to be submitted to the board for ratification. Despite what was being written about the flowing rugby played by 'The rugby union types', there was a faction somewhere that wanted a big rough tackling centre, in the Don Gullick mould.

In my second season, when I played largely at stand-off (6), the discussion was so often about the quality of service to Vollenhoven and Killeen on the wings, and how it could be improved. I am guilty in this book of not recognising that there was already a great side in the sixties, that being the one which won the Challenge Cup in 1961. The reason is that I was so engrossed in my own playing career, that I did not watch the Saints much during the period 1959-1963. However, there are many people who to this day believe that the 1961 team was better than the 1966. As always in sport that is a matter of opinion. I played with Vinty Karalius just once, when he captained the Lancashire RL team which I first played with. This legendary figure played little part in my life, and it is quite possible that he did not know who I was, but I did play with him and noted the authority in his voice and the command of his presence. Eric Ashton told me the story of the test match in Australia in which Alan Prescott broke his arm. Besides allowing me to carry the hod for Harry Pilling, I wanted to know how it came about that Prescott managed to play a whole match with a broken arm, when I would have expected the notorious Aussies to tear him apart as he carried on. He looked at me sternly and said:

'You are forgetting about Vince Karalius.'

'I know that he played a great game that day in defending his captain.'

'You have no idea what happened but I will tell you. At the beginning of the second half when Prescott had refused the management option of leaving the field, Vinty called the Australian pack together and faced them all. 'Alan has broken his arm but because we are two men down already he will be playing on. If any of you put him in hospital I will personally see to it that you will follow him on a stretcher.' They believed him. Why wouldn't they?'

There are many tales of Vinty saying jump and others asking how high, but this one is the most telling. Vincent Peter Patrick Karalius is also in the Rugby League Hall of Fame for his wonderful playing career. I heard him speak at a presentation for Alex Murphy and he was a gentleman, but never on the pitch where he was 'The Wild Bull'.

I know that Vollenhoven was quicker in 1961 than later, when a variety of injuries slowed him down, but I saw him in his prime and knew him very well. I did not go to Wembley in 1961 and so saw the famous Large-Vollenhoven try on television. So I don't enter the debate, but I certainly joined a club with a great recent history. Brian McGinn played centre in that great team and he was still there when I signed in 1963. For me he is the epitome of only being as good as your last match. Once he had sustained an injury and been replaced he was forced to come back through the 'A' team. This meant losing money as 'A' team pay was less than he could earn by working on a Saturday, so he stopped playing. This reminds us of the original break from Rugby Union when they objected to 'broken time' payments for players. David Markey has told me of his dilemma because a glasscutter at Pilkingtons could earn more on a Saturday than the 'A' team pay, even if they won. Not being a regular player in the first team had a consequence for those playing 'A' team rugby over a period of time.

In his book *The March of the Saints 1945-1985,* Alex Service the club historian, chooses to draw a line between Stan McCormick's coaching time and that of Joe Coan:

> The super-fit Saints under the captaincy of Alex Murphy made a remarkable start to the season with 21 straight wins including a 12-4 Lancashire Cup final victory over seemingly perennial opponents Swinton.

But later in the season he recalls that a near 40,000 crowd saw Wigan beat us 7 points to 4. At the end of the season we lost the Championship Final 15-7 to Halifax. So despite winning three trophies that year, there was a feeling that it could have been better. Alex Service says that the only bright spot for Saints fans, in the defeat, was the encouraging display of John Mantle, the club's latest recruit from Welsh RU.

I recall a conversation in our home dressing room at Saints, when I was asked my opinion of John Mantle, because I had played with him at Loughborough. The directors who had gone to see him play in the Cardiff v Newport match, thought that he was a bit slow for RL, what did I think? 'Simple, he is quicker than any forward I have seen playing, including Dick Huddart.'

I had played with Huddart in my first season, possibly his last in the English game, but what a great player he was. With that comparison I was not surprised to see John Mantle in the Saints dressing room shortly after. In all there were sixteen ex-Rugby Union players on the list of players who played with me in 1965/6 and Joe Coan had to manage them all, as well as the eighteen players steeped in Rugby League.

Before I move on I want to put before you this criticism known to Alex Service as the Bash and Batter Blues. Despite the three trophies, we were heavily censured for what Tom Owen (nemesis to Ray French) regularly wrote about 'the old fault of forwards with head down, bash and batter charging.'

So the directors decided to do something about that, in an effort to make the game more interesting for spectators. During the same match where they were looking at John Mantle, they saw the Bob Prosser, David Watkins partnership in progress and decided that they wanted the pair at St Helens. It is quite possible that the signing of Bob Prosser was a sprat to catch a mackerel, but

I don't think they were prepared to pay nearly £15,000 to prove a point. However, as well as strengthening even more the powerful pack, with Mantle, by bringing Bob Prosser to the club pre-season, the directors showed that they were aware of a wider problem. They were thinking the unthinkable, when and how they would replace Alex Murphy. He was undoubtedly the greatest scrum-half in the world and in Joe Coan's words, 'better than any of the other players in any position.' So it was a matter of finding the best position for all of the players at his disposal. I am not looking at this from a purely personal point of view because I was on the team sheet as many times as anyone else, during the three seasons to September 1966, playing in virtually all of the back positions.

Of the thirty-six matches that Alex played in 1963/4, the season I started, he played twenty-two times at 7 (scrum-half) and thirteen at 6 (stand-off), with two matches at 3 (right centre). The following season he played twenty-nine times at 7 and five times at 6. These were the two seasons, one under Stan McCormick and one Joe Coan, when the team was being criticised for 'bash and batter forwards.'

In my opinion Alex Murphy was a great scrum-half and I owe so much to him as a guide and mentor, but he was not the easiest of players to play alongside. There were two reasons for this, one he was not only a brilliant individual player, but he was also very brave and courageous. He would take on the opposing pack, often to the detriment of his fellow backs. The other would be his tendency to react to situations, rather than carry out pre-planned moves, which he had called for everyone else. This was a most frustrating habit. As Captain and leader of the team, he would call a set play and six other backs would deploy to carry out that plan. If he changed his mind and did something off the cuff, everyone else was left trying to catch up with him, which was nearly impossible, even if you knew what he was doing. Earlier I wrote about the smooth flowing rugby sometimes produced by the Saints when Alex was not playing. We always missed his impudent, fiery and magnificent breaks. His trademark from being a seventeen year old was the break direct from the scrum, on both the open and blind side. He could take off in an instant and leave everyone trailing in his wake, he was impossible to catch at club and international level. He could make me look majestic, if I managed to follow his lead, but so often I got the ball when he had decided that there was nothing more that he could do himself. So often his presence was a contributing factor to the seven-man rugby played by St Helens.

In 1965/66 season, Joe Coan had a new piece to add to the armoury, an unknown player in Bob Prosser. When Bob first came to the Saints in pre-season his level of fitness was not at the same standard as the rest of the first team, but he persevered and soon began to run for as long as everyone else.

What Bob brought with him, and it was revolutionary at the time, was the spin pass. Playing stand-off to Bob, I was guaranteed a long flat pass from the base of the scrum. Also because he did not attempt to break, it was produced either on the right or left side as had been called. This meant that all of the backs were brought into play, every time the ball got into his hands. Was he better than Alex Murphy, decidedly not, but he was certainly easier to play with.

Alex Service, in a report of Prosser's first match against the New Zealand touring side, says:

> Prosser gave an immaculate service to his stand-off Peter Harvey, who, along with his three-quarters served up a feast of attacking rugby which delighted the 11,000 crowd. Prosser's capacity for opening out the game proved to be infectious and the second half was a stirring spectacle with the Saints receiving rapturous applause for great scoring movements.

During that season Bob played twenty-five times at 7, but still there was more innovation to come. Again to quote from Alex Service's history of the Saints, Joe Coan is quoted as saying,

> I was never allowed to influence transfers, but this lad Bishop was the exception. I said at the time that he was the best in the league and could do a job for us. He always wanted to play. The best players are those who play in the most matches.

I know, from a source very close to Tommy Bishop, that when he signed for the Saints, he thought that he would be playing at stand-off. So having got him to the Saints, Joe Coan was left with perhaps the biggest tactical decision of all time. Eminent commentators have said that Joe had no tactical knowledge, and yet he takes the decision to bring in another scrum-half, having already seen the effect that Bob Prosser had on the team.

In the season 1965/6 the Saints board were preparing for the departure of their Captain. Alex Murphy played 8 out of his first sixteen appearances at 7 and the other eight at 6. He first played at 3, centre to Tom van Vollenhoven on 17 December 1965, before the transfer of Tommy Bishop was complete. He played a further twenty times wearing the centre jersey, culminating in two Cup Finals in a single week in May.

Tommy Bishop came to St Helens and his first match was at stand-off to Bobby Prosser, I played on the wing at Wakefield and they beat us by a considerable margin. The match report was quite clear – the St Helens pair did not match the Wakefield half-backs.

This is my version of what happened the next Saturday.

Wakefield Trinity 0 St Helens 10
Challenge Cup First Round
26 February 1966, at Belle Vue, Wakefield

The official banged on the door expecting it to be opened; the coach ordered the kit man to keep it closed. They want the team sheet someone demanded. 'When I'm ready,' said Joe Coan 'they can wait till we walk out on the field.' Thus began, possibly the match of my life. The Challenge Cup tie at Belle Vue, Wakefield, was a win against the odds as they had beaten us 20-12 the week before. They had a very powerful pack and excellent three-quarters, cup winners playing at home and full of confidence. A world-class centre, Neil Fox was in his pomp and tourist, Harold Poynton, was the ringmaster of the side with his ball play and astute run-around passes. I was stand-off and my instructions were clear and to the point, 'Smother Poynton, I don't want to see him pass the ball,' said Coach Coan. This was the first match that Tommy Bishop played for the Saints at Number 7 and with Alec Murphy marking Neil Fox, in the centre; I was to be a human torpedo, man-marking Poynton. No expansive match this; 'kill the game' were my orders. I'm sure Harold felt me like an overcoat as I managed to tackle him out of the game. Everyone else did their job and we won ten points to nil, with Bishop scoring under the posts and Vollenhoven getting his customary try, both converted by Killeen. The prize was Wembley 1966 and the great 21-2 victory against Wigan.

Once more Joe Coan had pulled a master-stroke, by switching the half backs and delaying the publication of the team, they had no time to respond. We rarely see man marking anymore; it is difficult, takes lots of concentration and a great deal of energy. Joe knew that I had enough ability to trust me with that role, and he did.

Wakefield was always a difficult team to beat and I remember two incidents from other matches against them that involve Berwyn Jones, who was an international flyer from Loughborough. When we talk about speed, we are thinking about rugby players who are quick, and then we meet up with an international sprinter who is ten yards quicker than that. I remember one match at Knowsley Road when Frank Barrow gave Berwyn the touchline when he was hemmed in the corner by the paddock. Berwyn scorched past Frank and was under the posts when he picked himself up having grasped at the air. We often talked about that experience but I had one which was even worse in my eyes. We were playing at Wakefield and I broke through towards the halfway line with Len Killeen on the left wing outside me. A two on one, should clearly have led to a try for us, but it was not to be. Berwyn started running backwards as I tried to draw him in, he checked to tackle me and I passed to Killeen who was clear. Not clear enough as Berwyn opened the after burners and caught him in less than twenty yards.

Alex Murphy played in his testimonial match at Knowsley Road with virtually 30,000 spectators present, many of them sitting on the top of the Pavilion and many more sitting on top of the Edington Stand. How many of them could have guessed that it was his last Derby Game at Knowsley Road? I am convinced that Alex himself already knew, because he told me so. 'We are just pieces of meat to them (directors) and they will sell us when they want to.'

I should have heeded his warning but I didn't. It was my last Derby game too.

The one occasion Alex played at stand-off that season, produced one of the most spoken about, match-ending incidents, of all time. In the Challenge Cup third round, a tough-as-teak Hull KR came to Knowsley Road with little expectation of winning. I was sitting on the bench next to Joe Coan and the game was dying away from us, as they had scored a converted try late in the game. There was nothing Joe could do, except exhort his players for one last push as the clock ticked away. The score was tight at 10 points to 7, but the Saints needed a try at least to tie the game, as they fought their way to the 25-yard line in front of the posts at the Pavilion end. Cliff Watson was tackled, and when he got up to play the ball, the opposition player quite deliberately went off side and was penalised. Cliff, knowing that this was a ploy to run the clock down, kicked out at the player, and Mr Clay sent Cliff off. The time was indeed up, but a Hull KR player kicked the ball away in another time wasting incident. Referee Clay made him go and bring the ball back to the spot where he had given the penalty.

Joe Coan told me to get to the dressing room to console Cliff. By the time I got to the entrance to the tunnel, Alex was about to take the penalty. Knowing that two points would not suffice, he kicked the ball high in the air, with deadly accuracy, clearing the cross bar and falling right into the arms of full back Cyril Kellett. It is amazing what pressure can do. Normally he would have taken that kick safely into his hands, but with three St Helens players flying towards him, the ball passed right between his outstretched arms, onto the pitch in front of him. Billy Benyon dived in there, but Alex Murphy got to the ball a fraction before him, to touch down. All three players slid over the line, Kellett bowled over by the other two. Murphy jumped up to claim the try, and Mr Clay, unsighted as he was behind the advancing players, looked to his touch judges, both standing by their corner flags, before awarding the try, under the posts with an easy conversion to come. I was the closest person, not on the pitch, in fact I was within a single pace, and the players slid right to my feet, as I stood right in the tunnel entrance.

It is true that a great many of the crowd had gone home thinking that the match was lost. It is equally true that the match was overtime, but as the referee was the sole timekeeper, he had added time, for the time wasting of the Hull

KR players. So the path to Wembley had been partially cleared, and a whole generation of supporters will tell you that they were there. Ray French, lagging well behind in the chase, has written that the ball was over the dead ball line. Sorry Ray, it was by the time you got there, but Mr Clay was big enough to make the decision, without any reference to squares in the air. He pointed his finger and blew his whistle, try. Then we have the classic Alex Murphy quote when told that it wasn't really a try, 'Just look in the paper in the morning.'

I was in the big bath with everyone else, and it wasn't only the water that was hot. Cyril Kellett could not deny dropping the ball and the arguments among the players were about the time wasting and the added time, and the fact that neither touch judge had indicated that the ball went dead. Kellett was well inside the field of play and the ball went through his hands in front of him, it had to be in play when Murphy and Benyon dived on it. True it did squirm out afterwards. Those heated exchanges in the bath, with the brooding presence of Cliff Watson, sent off but not penalised, were to be continued in the next match with Hull KR in the Championship semi-final, just seven days before Wembley.

I had sustained concussion in the match at Oldham, where I played on the wing, as Tommy Voll was carrying an injury and was unfit to play, and the Bishop-Prosser experiment continued, with Prosser at stand-off. Due credit is not given to Joe Coan for his tactical awareness and in particular his man management. For example in this game he took Prosser off at half time and moved me to stand-off, so that Tony Barrow could have a run out on the

Wembley 1966. The Saints walking out in number order after the Captain.
Mr Cook (Chairman), Murphy (Capt.), Barrow, Vollenhoven, Benyon, Killeen, Harvey, Bishop, Halsall, Sayer, Watson, Mantle, French and Warlow cannot be seen.

wing. He knew that I could fill any position in the back line, but he also knew that he might need Tony Barrow at Wembley or in the Championship Final at Swinton the week after. I was wrapped up in cotton wool and sitting in the stand, when the revenge seeking Hull KR came to Knowsley Road, just seven days before Wembley. In a very hard fought match, no one took a backward step, and as the battle ended with a huge altercation, the referee blew for time rather than send half a dozen off.

So it was that we all gathered at Knowsley Road on Monday morning to be taken to Southport 'for special training'. The fact is that in the days of part time rugby, it was more about controlling what the players were doing, and getting them away from their place of work, rather than any special training. In fact, Joe Coan had learned the lesson of us leaving too much on the sand hills of Southport, for us to repeat that exercise. Instead, we trained with a gentle run out on both Monday and Tuesday, before Joe went back to the Knowsley Road ground, to present his team to the board. On the Tuesday evening we had dinner in the Prince of Wales, and Joe gathered everyone together afterwards, so that he could announce his team for the final at Wembley.

I was named at six, with Tommy Bishop at seven and Alex Murphy at three, with Billy Benyon at four, Vollenhoven and Killeen on the wings, with Frankie Barrow at full back and Tony Barrow on the bench with Jeff Hitchin. We had a massive, but highly mobile pack with a front row of Cliff Watson, Billy ('Sos') Sayer, Albert Halsall, hard running and tackling, Ray French and John Warlow, with John Mantle trusted with the loose forward position. There was real disappointment for Kel Coslett and Bob Prosser, who were with us all of the time, and very much part of the squad. Also with us was Bob Dagnall who was very much still part of the squad, which he had played with until the New Year. We were all told most solemnly, that night would be the last night that any drinking would be tolerated before the Final. We made the best of it, and I vividly remember writing myself a letter when we came in, (I've still got it) and how it is so difficult to read because of the scrawling handwriting.

We left Southport and went down to London on Friday, spending no time at all in sight seeing, as that had been the lesson learned from previous finals, when teams had dissipated their energy, wandering around London, instead of concentrating on the match.

We walked around Wembley an hour or so before the game and the single thing that I remember, apart from the sheer size of the stadium, is that there was a box of green sawdust ready to cover any patches which might appear in the 'perfect turf'. The Football World Cup was still to come.

The long walk out of the tunnel and the line-up and presentation before the match is so unusual that it makes a joyful memory. The huge ovation given to all of the players is made from the pent up emotion of fans, willing their side to succeed. Standing waiting for the whistle blast to kick off, I looked at

Killeen try at Wembley.
Boston walks away as the team celebrates the Killeen try.

Mantle try at Wembley.
Mantle scores the try, Vollenhoven and Harvey are the other two Saints players in the move and in the picture.

'It's ours!' Murphy with the cup.
Halsall, Watson, Mantle, Barrow, Murphy (with the Cup), Sayer, Warlow, (Hard hat), Bishop (with Teddy Mascot), Harvey, Killeen, Benyon. 'We got what we came for.'

Above left: Wembley dressing room.
Harvey with Teddy Mascot. Bishop in the background, he was a great success in Australia, but no-one knows what happened to the Teddy Bear.

Above right: Wembley big bath. Frank Barrow, Peter Harvey and Billy Benyon all smile for the camera. Actually there were another five or six in that bath, the picture has been edited.

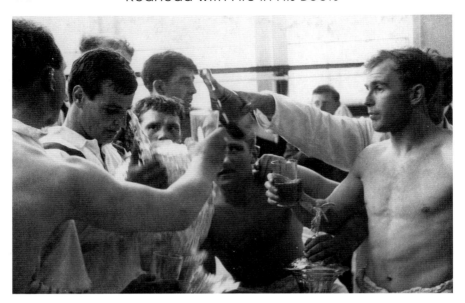

Wembley Celebrations. Wembley Dressing room Champagne flows, hardly the right word as there were only two bottles. Harvey at the right of picture.

Cliff Hill and promised myself that I would come out on top in our personal battle. Once more I can tell you that Joe Coan had given each player specific responsibilities. I was to distribute the ball quickly to the centres, mark Cliff Hill and also cut off Ray Ashby when he tried to come into the line from full back. We were all told that Eric Ashton was playing with a pain killing injection in his ribs, so he would be tentative, and we had to tackle him hard.

We can pass over the match which we won 21-2. I can honestly say that I was not aware of the 100,000 crowd until about twenty minutes from the end when we had won and I suppose I relaxed. In the match that really mattered we stopped Billy Boston from scoring yet another try, though as I have said elsewhere, that was not down to me. Killeen actually scored his diving try, from a kick through by Billy Benyon into the Boston corner. I also remember taking a loose ball going towards Tom van Vollenhoven and giving him a reverse pass as he went inside to meet up with Big John Mantle who crashed his way over for the first try.

We managed to make sure that Wigan did not score a single try, largely because we had a swarming defence, with players flying back to cover anyone who had managed to break through the line. The one exception to this was Frankie Barrow's tackle on Trevor Lake, a very dangerous winger who was very quick. He broke down the left touchline and had evaded our cover till he was clear to the fullback. Frank set him up and cut him down with a brilliant tackle, as he tried to run round him.

What I do remember is that we were hustled off the ground by the men in hard hats, only managing to get half way round the ground, and not even near where our wives and families where sitting.

We met up with our wives at the Dinner in The Russell Hotel. The first course was vichyssoise, a classic ice-cold soup, and the serving was met by a chorus of, 'The soup's bloody cold.' Having tasted it before at Rugby Union dinners, I was able to tell them that it was supposed to be like that. I can still see the cut on Billy Benyon's mouth as he dribbled the soup down his chin, and later the brandy that he asked for to kill the pain. He had been 'clothes lined' by one of the Wigan props and needed stitches in his divided lip. Our ladies were present as we ate and no doubt they were a very civilising influence. Ruth looked very smart indeed in her cream suit, set off with the red rose of Lancashire in her lapel. We were all determined to celebrate our win and were going 'on the town'. We had 'come up for the cup' and we had won, so it was time to celebrate. Our party was about six or eight of us, with our wives happily alongside, we all piled into taxis, with Ray French taking charge, as he had done all week. He said, 'Take us to the best club in town,' and we duly arrived at Churchill's, where the top-hatted doormen greeted us happily.

Having paid an exorbitant entrance fee, we were ushered to a table which was a long way from the stage, and shuffled into the seats in semi darkness. Billy Sayer, that connoisseur of London life, had ordered some drinks and when faced with the outrageous bill and before everyone was settled came out with the immortal line, 'Are we going or are we staying?' pronounced with his classic Wigan accent. Acknowledging that the prices were ridiculous we all got up and left. Of course the doormen at first refused to refund the entrance fee, but looking at more than half of the St Helens pack, they relented and handed back the money, until it came to me walking out behind them. 'Sorry,' they said 'there is none left for you.' The fact that they stood seven feet tall in their top hat worried me not one jot. 'Cliff, he won't give me my money back.' I said. 'That's because I have already got yours, so come on, get into the taxi.' By now it was getting late when we were dropped off, and as we all wondered around, someone suggested that we have something to eat, and thus it was that we finished up in The Golden Egg in Leicester Square for our posh night out in London.

Then on the Sunday morning we were at Mass, yes, Alex and Alice, the two Barrow boys and their girlfriends, Ruth and I, were all in church on the Crompton Road for the 10 a.m. Service. I don't remember what we did for the rest of the day, other than to tell you my heels were blistered and I could hardly walk; the result of new boots for the final, not totally worn in. We did go to the Eamon Andrews show on the Sunday night. Cassius Clay was the most important guest, but the camera did pan across us as he talked to Cliff, Ray, the two Johns, Mantle and Warlow, 'You guys look like you can handle

The Championship Final in 1966. Saints *v.* Halifax ended in a punch up with many players involved. Mrs Cotton can be seen striking a player with her umbrella. This led to the banning of ring side seats.

your selves, do you fancy your chances in the ring?' I'm not sure which one of them said it but the reply was certainly given. 'You bring the ball out against us and we will see how you go on, OK.'

As an aside, Stan McGowan of Ellison's Travel who had done all of the travel arrangements and was watching the programme, as live, on TV in St Helens, but in fact one hour later, in real time, was worried. His comment was simple, 'They are going to miss their train home.' That was the teachers among the team, Ruth and I, Alice and Alex, Helen and Ray French, John Mantle and his wife, were all booked on the overnight sleeper from Euston, as we had to go to work in the morning. Such is life, even for cup winners.

Of course it was far worse for losers, we teachers would have lost a week's pay, and been paid the princely sum of £8. Not to mention no homecoming, and the adoration of the Town Hall crowd, and best of all, the life-long honour of playing in one of the greatest teams ever.

This was a cup winning side that knew, not only how to play rugby, but also how to stay relatively sober for the next cup final in a weeks' time. We were so confident, that even without Tom Vollenhoven, with a badly sprained knee, we had a strong replacement in Tony Barrow, who had been waiting for this chance to shine. Halifax had triumphed in this match the season before, but this time we had a secret weapon in Albert Halsall. Having never scored for St Helens before, he managed to score a hat trick, all with strong bursts of great pace. Len Killeen also scored three tries and kicked six goals, but was beaten to the Harry Sunderland award by our outstanding prop forward, Albert. The game was hard fought, but we were clearly much quicker, and the Halifax

The Town Hall Steps. 'Alex Murphy holds the Cup aloft as I look on with Ray French and Frank Barrow behind me. Such a great feeling, definitely one to remember.'

Championship Trophy 1966 Dressing Room.
Warlow, Hitchen, Sayer, Killeen, French, Mantle, Bishop, Murphy, Frank Barrow, Benyon, Harvey, Watson, Halsall, Bracken (Physio). Tony Barrow also played but is not on this picture.

pack was over run.

This match might be remembered for the all action fight during the second half, when most of the players were dragged in, but the most unusual combatant was Mrs Cotton, who once more came onto the pitch wielding her umbrella. The problem is that people remember the fight, and not the rout, which was the main cause of the punch up. The Halifax players just could not hang on to the Saints players as they flew hither and thither, with real pace and power. There were no complaints about bash and batter forwards that day, though they did both with panache. I have reviewed both finals on video and the Saints look to have an extra two men, they are so much faster than the opposition.

The Wembley win, according to the newspapers was as a result of gamesmanship by our captain Alex Murphy, hoodwinking the referee into giving Wigan too many penalties. The fact is that penalties were very even and largely for the same offences, kicking at the play the ball, off side on occasion, and technical offences in the front row. We made much better use of the penalties than they did. Who can forget the 60-yard penalty which Len Killeen put over? As he passed me on the pitch, the supremely confident Lenny said, 'What do you think?' I said that I thought that he should kick it into the corner but he replied, 'I'm going to put it over the sticks.' And he did. Far fewer people remember that he tried to kick another one from a similar position in the second half, to see it go sailing outside the upright, but way over the crossbar.

The homecoming from the Wembley success was a magnificent parade through the town, standing on a platform on top of one of Stan Magowan's coaches, (Gavin Murray's) now famous as Ellison's Travel. We were cheered to the rafters and given a civic reception, and this time it was me standing on those Town Hall steps, with all of my teammates, beneath the clock my parents had passed before I was born, waving to the crowd, just as my boyhood heroes had done in 1956 and 1961.

No civic reception after the Championship Final, nor one to rival the rumbustious 1964/5 affair, when only Halifax and St Helens players turned up to the'Mackeson's Trophy Celebrations at the old Manchester Racecourse, when 'we few' drank enough beer and spirits for the eight teams that were expected to attend. It was definitely the biggest end-of-season party ever, never to be forgotten by those who were there, but then again, not to be remembered by some. In fact a very little known story, from me brings my season to a close.

In my working life I was still at St Bedes, teaching PE, and in particular coaching schoolboy football. Now that the rugby season was over, a very close friend, invited me to play in a big match for his works team, who were playing at home against fierce opposition. I was into football, and we had season tickets to watch the World Cup group matches to be played at Everton very shortly. We drove up to a park in Preston and he met me and introduced

Saints with Four Cups in 1966.
Back row: Coslett, Sayer, Dagnall, Watson, Warlow, Mantle, T. Barrow, Hitchen.
Front row: Halsall, Benyon, Bishop, F. Barrow, Vollenhoven, French, Harvey, Prosser, Killeen.
Trophies: Harry Sunderland Trophy, League Leaders, Lancashire League, Challenge Cup, Championship Trophy, and Lance Todd Trophy.
Because of the fall out with Alex Murphy (Capt.) he did not come to this photo session and the Club refused to put him in an inset.

me to his fellow players. I was guesting again, this time to play on the right wing, at football. 'We get changed here,' he told me, and I started laughing as he pointed to the back of the hawthorn hedge, which was the 'dressing room'. 'You do realise that the last two games I played were The Challenge Cup at Wembley Stadium and The RL Championship at Swinton?' Anyway we won the match and he was delighted.

We did go and watch those games at Goodison Park, and I loved Portugal v North Korea, when Eusabio turned a lost game into a win, but in particular was fascinated by the Brazilians. I was coaching football on the school fields, by the roundabout in Ormskirk, when the Brazilian team bus pulled up, and the players spilled out. One of them took out a cine camera and started to film the lesson in progress. After a little while the footballers all waved goodbye, and went on their way. I watched them playing later, and I have thought, somewhere in Brazil there is an old film of me teaching football. In my dreams it was Pele who filmed it and waved to me, as he flashed that lovely smile.

Actually I didn't watch England win the World Cup here in England. I did see the match on television, in a café bar in Avignon France, as I was in charge of sixteen teenage boys on a canoeing expedition, down the River Rhone to Marseille with PGL which became a quite famous company in later years. I was really surprised that the French patrons supported the Germans. I thought that we had supported them when it really mattered, but what do I know?

Alex Murphy changed clubs as he knew he would. There was much argument about the transfer fee to be paid if he was to continue playing either here or in Australia.

I changed schools in September 1966 and went to Prescot C of E, because I wanted to have experience teaching in primary school. I carried on at the Saints, playing the role of utility player, covering any back position as needed. Therefore it was not unusual to be picked on the right wing against Whitehaven, when Tom van Vollenhoven was indisposed, and had to sit on the bench. I scored four tries that match, and was feeling very pleased with myself until the next training night, when I found, not only was I not in the first team, but I was reserve in the 'A' team. I went to see both Joe Coan and Steve Llewellyn (A team coach) for an explanation, but was told that they were not allowed to pick me. I went to see Basil Lowe the club secretary and he said, 'The best thing that you can do is phone Brian Batty (RL writer for the *Daily Mail*) and tell him you will never play for the Saints again, nobody retires on our books.'

The record shows that the Saints bought Peter Douglas from Barrow to

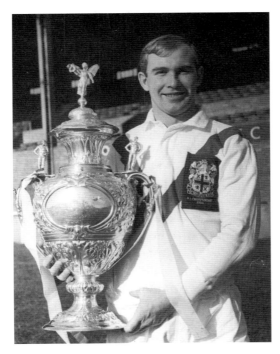

'Just for me.' Peter Harvey holds the Challenge Cup in 1966.

replace me and I played just three more games before being ignored altogether, kicked into the long grass for telling them that I wanted to concentrate on my real career. It was not what I had hoped for, but The Saints had decided that the four try performance, was the equivalent of going in the shop window, and they wanted some other club to come in for me. So much so that within my dealings with Basil Lowe, I was told, 'If anybody comes in for you with £1000 and 100 books of Green Shield stamps, they can have you, and you can have the Green Shield stamps.' Cutting but true.

During the evening of the Wembley dinner celebrations I had said publicly, in open conversation that I was hoping to retire at the end of the next season. I did not realise just how commercial the Saints actually were. My contract with them was for life, but their contract with me was until they wanted it to end. I was 'put into dispute' with the club as I didn't want to go to any other club. I wanted to retire at the end of the season, not seven games into it.

What happened happened, and I take solace from the fact that in Barry John's autobiography, he tells of how the Saints approached him in 1968. We know that Frank Myler, was bought from Widnes in a deal which cost Ray French his captaincy, and Dave Markey any further progress at St Helens. I don't know what would have happened if I had not been open about what I wanted to do at the end of the 1967 season, but I do think that I would have played until 1968.

I want to refer to Barry John as I have just read his autobiography. He too was at Gwendraeth Grammar School, as was Ken Jones who I referred to earlier. But unlike Jones, he was not chosen to play for the Welsh Schools, and he is quite bitter about that. He tells how he was not selected for the Welsh under 15's, nor the under 16's the next year. His invitation to play for Llanelli came when he was 18, but he was never picked for the Welsh School XV. He was brought up in a council house, and his father was a miner, so there are parallels with me there; though I actually never lived in a council house, we had shared accommodation with my auntie and cousins.

Then he tells how he was first selected for Llanelli and then Cardiff, and how that was just like playing for both Liverpool and Manchester United at football. Such nonsense, I played with Cen Williams who played for Cardiff, and he never made those kinds of comparisons, though Bleddyn and his brothers were all players there. Nor did John Warlow who was at the Scarlets (Llanelli) at the same time as Barry John arrived, suggest such a comparison. He worked hard both at St Helens and Widnes and is rightfully in our Hall of Fame.

I am more than intrigued at some of the passages in his book 'Barry John the King.' In one of them he tells of a meeting with the Wigan RL club who went to his college to offer him terms. 'As I sauntered out with my ten and a half stone frame, looking grey faced and with bags under my eyes, I could see in the faces of these men that they were thinking 'So why the big fuss about him then?' Remember they were accustomed to dealing with the big strapping men who played the hard game of rugby league, week in week out.'

He politely explained that he wanted to get on with his studies, but I think he always remembered the big strapping men who played such a hard game. On the same page he tells how he nearly signed for St Helens when he had come back from the Lions Tour with a broken collar bone in 1968. That is of great interest to me, because I had already been forced out of the St Helens team then, and they were looking at Barry John as a possible replacement. He says they offered him 'a tempting package' centred on a signing on fee of £8,500, and as an extra sweetener a part-time job as a teacher. He was out of work and needed a job.

'I travelled to a second meeting in a Hereford Hotel, had the contract put in front of me and was handed the expensive fountain pen. I considered my unemployed situation and thought 'if this is what people think of me I might as well go north'. My hand holding the fountain pen hovered over the contract and just as I was about to sign, I pulled it away and asked for another week to think about the offer. When I got home I realised, 'BJ you're being a coward by taking the easy way out'. There is nothing wrong with going to rugby league, providing it is for the right reasons. But I was going for the wrong reasons, and in the next few days I told St Helens, 'Thanks but no thanks.'

Once more he was being a coward thinking of the hard men he would come up against. He wants to turn that round to suggest he was doing a brave thing in not signing as a professional.

He tells of how he was on the dole with no sign of a job, when 'quite out of the blue' he got a job offer from Cliff Morgan, the main director of Sportsnight, with David Coleman as the presenter.

Now this is where I take issue with Barry John. I do not believe for one minute that he would have made the grade in rugby league. Far from being the King he would have been cut to pieces by the tackling, so he was right not to sign. Cliff Morgan was himself a target for St Helens and went even further than Barry John, before dipping out, or some might say coming to his senses. Wilf Smith, that warrior from Parr, was a regular Saints player when Cliff Morgan was introduced to the players in the dressing room at Knowsley Road, at the end of one training session. He had signed for the club (allegedly) and they expected him to play within a fortnight. Perhaps like Barry John he decided to change his mind at the last minute.

Despite the totally wrongful view taken by the Rugby Union to these approaches, no player was ever let down by the rugby league clubs that approached him. I know of one high ranking member of the hierarchy, an England prop forward who had played three trials before deciding rugby league was far too hard a game to play. He is still enjoying a great deal in business terms with the rugby union, whereas he would have been an outcast had he signed as a 'professional' player. Not Fran Cotton, who never looked like a rugby league prop: even though his father had played for the Saints and captained Warrington RLFC in the past, and his brother David who actually did play with us at that club. Fran does seem to understand the easy relationship which exists in the North, as opposed to the South and Wales.

The life of a rugby league player was hard work, not much recreation, either on or off the pitch.

Barry John's claim says, 'In the end, rugby gave me that opportunity as an adult to mix with celebrities and be invited as guest of honour to the grandest functions and bashes.' This would not have come to pass had he signed as a professional in the 1960/70s.

He claims that Gareth Edwards was the best scrum-half in the world. That can only be the world of rugby union, as Alex Murphy is recognised as the greatest-ever once you get north of the Mersey.

In fact one of the chapters of Barry John's book, in a chapter headed 'Boot Money' which tells us a great deal about sham-amateurism, he talks about setting up 'a professional rugby circus' funded by American Money. This was to be called World Rugby, and included the top 50 players in the world. No wonder professional Rugby Union came to pass, despite howls of protest from some sources.

He also talks about being paid (sponsored) by various companies to wear their boots, and that he had contracts with more than one of them. The great St Helens team which won four cups in the 1965/66 season, was the first 'professional team' to get a sponsor, not for boots, but we all did get one string vest with the offer of a second one at half price - not much of the Manchester United or Liverpool about that offer. Incidentally Alex Murphy, who both was and is a rugby league legend, had a personal friendship with Bobby Charlton, which meant that we did on a few occasions meet him socially. He was always very nice, but I would never claim to have known him well. I do remember one visit by Ron Yeats, the Liverpool centre half, to what was a tough match at Knowsley Road. He asked what we got paid to play, and was astounded to hear that the wages for that match was £20 less tax. He said that he would not go on the field for £1,000 a match, and when he stood next to Mervyn Hicks he looked like a beanpole, rather than his nickname of 'telegraph pole'.

One early evening I went into our local hostelry, The Seven Stars, where I met Alex Young, the famous Everton player, and we shared a pint together. I did not know how famous he was, and he had no idea who I was. I asked him what he was doing in our neck of the woods, and he replied quite truthfully that no one took any notice of him here; unlike Liverpool, where he would have been mobbed apparently.

One other Welsh stand-off that I do admire is Jonathan Davies. I have never met him but I remember once, when Widnes came to St Helens sometime in the 1980s, and they played him in the centre to try to hide him from the brutal tackles. Duggie Laughton was their coach and he knew that Knowsley Road was a very difficult ground for visitors. Davies tried to run round Ian Pickavance who was a hefty defender. Ian flattened him and Davies had to be helped to the touchline for lengthy treatment. Still, and this is what I admire, he came back into the centre position, and late in the match skated round Pickavance and scored a great try in the corner. He did that kind of thing many times in his career. I heard Duggie Laughton recently on television talking about contracts, first for Martin Offiah and then Jonathon Davies. He said that he signed Martin on a ten year contract at ten thousand pounds a year for ten years: now that's inflation to upset Alex Murphy all over again. Then he signed Davies at £150,000, money that Widnes never had, so he had to sell the contract to Warrington, where Jonathan played some seasons.

Having signed for the Saints I gave up any notion of returning to Rugby Union, as I definitely would not have been made welcome. There is one exception to that rule which I want to talk about, and it concerns Lancashire County RU. I don't know who took the decision, but on the occasion of the 100th Anniversary of the first county match, all players who had played for Lancashire, were invited to a Grand Dinner. I'm not at all sure when the event took place, but once more I think that it was in Blackpool in 1981. There was a table of players who had gone to rugby league, and we were happy to be there, if rather remote from the union types. There was a very important exception to this which occurred well after the speeches and amidst much flowing bitter. I met up with Richard (Dick) Greenwood, and we got talking about the way I thought rugby union could be improved. Dick Greenwood and I had played together in the Lancashire Schools, but our paths had separated when I signed for St Helens. I'm not sure whether he was actually coaching in the England RU set up then, or if that followed, but the gist of our conversation was about coaching.

I was, as the earlier part of this book pointed out, a Loughborough qualified PE specialist, who had also coached a professional rugby league team, as well as played at the highest level. Our conversation was about the changes which I envisaged in RU if it wanted to gain more spectators. There is no doubt that RU has always been a game for the player, whereas RL has always tried to entertain the crowd. The simplest rule change took two players off the field to create more space for a passing game, in which tries could be scored.

So there was Dick defending the RU position and me, without any responsibility at all, saying what I though should change. I suggested many changes and these are a few of them:

Change the rule on kicking directly into touch which would cut down on the line outs.

Look at the way that the back row linked with the three-quarters. Remember that had been my thesis. In the simplest terms have big back row forwards running at the players in mid field. Stop the forwards all running into the break down and slowing the re-cycling of the ball.

Change the standard practice of the day which was to align the backs with the corner flags.

Bring the stand-off up flat thus giving more options for players to run off him, because they would be closer to him, and he could pass both inside and out.

The effect of these changes would mean that all of the players could play across all of the pitch, and not be constantly chasing the ball around wherever it went. But that would look like rugby league he said, and of course I agreed with him.

I never went as far as to say take two players off the field to create more space, but he could see that RU players would have to be much fitter to play the game I was talking about. He also said, 'It is a pity that you can't come to help with the coaching in the Lancashire set up.' I'm not saying that I would have done that, but the fact remains I would not have been allowed to do so, but I was right in all of the predictions.

Earlier in this book I talked about Sean Edwards and Joe Lydon, who managed to make it to the England schools teams. Both are now coaches in the international set up, along with Andrew Farrell and many others who were rugby league players. People like Mike Ford and Phil Larder who were employed as defence coaches, and took the game on wards as the changes occurred. Perhaps the most famous English World Cup winning coach was not a RL player but was a Loughborough Qualified PE teacher, now Sir Clive Woodward.

I started this section with Dick Greenwood and I will end with his son Richard Greenwood, who I don't believe that I have ever met, though I have seen him very often on television. A big centre, as I predicted in 1962, who is talking about the game in terms that I would certainly understand, because the changes I was talking about have now come to pass: obviously not because I predicted them, but because they are better for the game. I have spent many an afternoon watching an England match at Twickenham before 1990, when the crowd had little to shout about. Then along came Jason Robinson, one of the first cross-code internationals, 'Billy Wizz' zipped through the defence and the crowd erupted in appreciation. He was a joy to behold, though such a loss to RL. Such transfers are becoming commonplace and it is difficult to imagine those conversations about holding your head up high by staying an amateur, rather than 'selling your soul' by taking the money to become a professional.

CHAPTER 18

Gone to the Wire

I stopped training and 'retired', six months before I wanted to. In fact in the summer of 1967, I was approached by Warrington who thought that I was a 'good buy', even for a short term. The Saints got their fee, but I didn't even get the stamps! Saints even took the 'new boots' which I had now broken in, and I imagine Walter Jones taking the brass tacks out as he converted them for someone else.

I made my debut on 6 September 1967, for Warrington and was very happy to be the utility player they expected. Within a few weeks of my arrival, I played against the Australian Touring team as a scrum-half, in the absence of Parry Gordon. This just shows my versatility, as I had played against three international touring teams, Australia twice and New Zealand once, each time in a different position, wing, stand-off and scrum-half: four counting the second half at St Helens, when I played in the centre when Mooney was carried off, and Arthur Johnson came on: the first substitution in rugby league, in this country.

I was to bring some additional experience into what was quite a young side. Jackie Fleming, one of the 'past player coaches', we talked about earlier, wanted me as a playmaker, but picked me as a centre when we made it to the Lancashire Cup Final a month later. Played at Wigan against St Helens, it had an explosive start for me. I drove my car to the ground, rather than go to Warrington and travel with the coach, taking Ruth with me. I distinctly remember watching my dad walking from the tunnel at Central Park, all the way round the pitch to his ringside seat, at the other end of the ground. We kicked off and within two minutes, at the very first scrum, Bill Benyon came away with the ball running outside Jackie Melling my co-centre. I grabbed at Alan Whittle, who I was marking, whilst watching Benyon. Just as I turned back towards Alan he wacked me in the face. The full force of my turning head and his blow knocked me onto the ground, stunned, and for the first and only time in my life, I lay with a broken nose. I was walked from the field into the dressing room and someone sent for an ambulance. My father arrived in the dressing room, having walked all the way back from his ringside seat, to console me, and look after me. The match progressed and eventually it was a 2-2 draw. For me the difficulties were only just beginning. We waited in the Wigan Infirmary for a couple of hours, because there had been a major road accident on the M6. Then the doctor decided to send me home, giving me an appointment for the following Tuesday. When my dad and I got back to the ground, both coaches had left and luckily for me Basil Lowe was prepared to bring me back to St Helens. Ray Ashby, an old friend from Carr Mill, and an adversary from Wigan, showed true friendship by driving my car and taking Ruth to her mother's house, where my son Simon was. I arrived about seven o'clock with a very disfigured face, and demanded by telephone, that the Warrington Club Doctor do something about it. When I arrived, by appointment at the Whiston Accident and Emergency Unit, I was greeted by an ENT specialist, Mr Wipak still in his off duty dress, who told me to go back home and prepare for a stay in hospital. He would operate on the Sunday morning as I had had something to eat and drink, and so he couldn't perform the operation then and there.

I was in hospital till the Wednesday and had to wear a mask at night for about ten days. Somehow I think that the whole business would have been handled better in later years.

I got back into the side and by the middle of November. I was the regular stand-off as Willie Aspinall, who had played for Great Britain on the 1966 Australian Tour, and played the first thirteen games of the season, picked up an injury which was to keep him out for about three months.

I held that position for twenty two of the remaining twenty seven matches. I enjoyed being the playmaker, and perhaps for the first time in rugby league, commanded the ball. That concept, of getting first option on the ball, and dictating play, rather like the quarter back in American football was a dream come true. If at the same time you are playing behind a pack which is dominating the opposition, you are able to drive the whole pack around the pitch, and have the backs flying around at your command. We won nineteen of those matches and the teams who beat us were St Helens and Leigh, each three times, Halifax twice, Wigan and Castleford once. So we were not quite in the very top bracket, but I found the team spirit and camaraderie to be excellent.

It is much more difficult if the pack is being rolled over and you are continually on the back foot. The concept of the gain line is really quite simple; you either go backwards or go forwards at each play the ball. Because the ball has always to be passed backwards, it gives one the conundrum of having to pass backwards but still be able to go forwards. The play the ball is always as close as one gets to the gain line, as soon as the acting half back passes the ball the team is going backwards. At the time that I was playing for Warrington there were packs of forwards who would 'roll over' ours. Their defensive line being too powerful for our forwards to break through, and consequently pressure was always on the half-backs either to try to break close to the play the ball, or to kick over the heads of the on rushing forwards. The deeper the backs lay the more ground we lost when trying to get the ball to the wingers. When I tried to explain this strategy to the teachers who came on the summer school, they were amazed how simple the game actually was. Forwards like Cliff Watson punched holes close to the play the ball, we didn't have a Cliff Watson in the team. John Mantle and Dick Huddart would run out wide and get round the close defence. We didn't have either of them in our team. We did have Brian Brady who took on the direct route play and Ken Parr who tended to play at first or second receiver, but because he handled the ball more than anyone else, tended to make more mistakes. Ray Clarke was in the Duggie Laughton mould but not quite up to the same standard. Brian Briggs and Cannon worked hard in the second row and both were good ball carriers. But we had no destroyers in the team. Keith Ashcroft was a ball handling prop with David Harrison as an experienced hooker. The team had lost Charlie Winslade from the season before, and he had been one of the strike weapons, breaking close to the gain line and feeding Willie Aspinall to release the backs.

We had Tommy Conroy and Keith Affleck sharing the full back role and I must tell the story of my first return to Knowsley Road. Both Keith Affleck and I scored tries that day and Keith kicked three goals but we still lost 17-12. Before the game when we were in the very cramped away dressing room, the first time that I was ever in there, Keith came over to me to ask about Tommy Voll. He said 'If Tommy Voll breaks through and he has me one on one, which way will he go?' My reply rather upset him, 'Any way he wants to because you won't get anywhere near him.' In the event Tommy broke clear down the right wing and came inside to stop Keith in his tracks, shimmied away round him on the outside and ran round under the posts to score. The only way to stop Tommy Voll scoring was to deny him the ball. We had two very good wingmen in Brian Glover and Tony Coupe, both strong runners and surprising quick as well. There was also an excellent centre in Jackie Melling, who was hard and quick in the rugby league mould, partnered by either Joe Pickavance or Bill Allen.

Jackie Melling scored twenty one tries that year and I scored only three. Parry Gordon got seven more than me, but I did drop five goals in the season. Still I was adding experience if not firepower to the armoury.

I have never complained about the greatest difference in Rugby Union and Rugby League and that would be the strength of the defence and the quite viscous tackling. To illustrate the point I will tell the story of my first encounter with David Watkins, or more accurately his first encounter with me. When St Helens brought Bob Prosser from Newport there were plenty of people who expected David Watkins to follow him, after all he was the Welsh stand-off and highly regarded in that position. As I indicated earlier St Helens were happy with me at stand-off, and were not prepared to pay the £15,000 which it would have cost to replace me. However, Bobby Prosser had made it quite clear that he thought that David Watkins would make an excellent rugby league player were he ever to 'come north'. He said that David Watkins was quicker than Alex Murphy over five, ten and fifty yards. I could not quite believe that but respected Bob enough to give it credence. So when the day came for me to play against David Watkins, he having signed for Salford, I was quite certain that I was going to have a hard time in catching him. I knew that he was a stand-off with both acceleration and a side-step off either foot, so he would be very difficult to tackle, if he ever got clear. So we had to plan to defend as a team, no simple man marking here. Brian Glover was playing in the centre and I told Brian that I would shut off the inside break, by running on an inside curve, and give him the outside break. I knew that Watkins would try to run round me, as no doubt he had done to others many times before. So at the first scrum I stood directly against him and begun to run the inside curve as I wanted to. I was shouting 'You can't run round me you're not quick enough.' He of course was determined to show me that he was quick enough and ran the outside curve. He was looking at me as he tried to get clear, suddenly wallop! Brian Glover hit him on his blind side, as we had

Warrington v. St Helens Challenge Cup 1969.
Peter Harvey (6) is passing to Ken Parr with Barry Briggs in support outside him. Parry Gordon, Len McIntyre and Brian Brady are also in the picture. Saints players left to right are Alan Whittle, Tommy Bishop, Kel Coslett and Bill Sayer.

planned. Welcome to Rugby League David. Brian stood over his unconscious form, 'Now twinkle, twinkle little f…..g star,' he said. The only stars there at that time were in Watkins's head. Welcome to rugby league David, no one told you about the 'treatment' dished out to new RU players.

I give great credit to David Watkins. He learned quickly and Salford gave him the opportunity to play both wing and full back, from where he could use his pace to find space for his lightning breaks.

In my first season at Warrington, besides playing scrum-half against John Smith and the Australian Touring side, I played three times on the wing, once in the centre and twenty two times at standoff, and I was the named substitute three times.

I had been accepted into the team of players, many from Wigan and a few from Warrington with Willie Aspinall and Brian Glover both from St Helens, though neither had played for the Saints. I travelled regularly with Brian Glover over to training and he talked about his time alongside the great Brian Bevan. What a phenomenal player but a really odd character. It was very difficult for players to come to terms with his idiosyncrasies and his taciturn behaviour. Brian claimed that he would arrive well before everyone else and take up his place in the corner of the dressing room and start taping himself up. Every joint had to be taped, each toe, ankle, knee and finger, shoulders and thighs, he looked like a mummy, before he went out to play. But boy when he played he was the daddy of them all. He did not join in with the noisy youngsters, but that may well have been because he was so much older than most of them. Born in 1924 he was just nine years younger than my dad, and he was playing rugby league when I was just one year old. In September 1946 he turned out for Warrington in a Lancashire cup tie against Salford and scored his first try in this country. The war was recently over and I was still in infant school, perhaps crying over the smack against my legs. He had a long and magnificent career and played in perhaps the most famous team that Warrington ever had, certainly until the coming of Alex Murphy. Bevan finished his time with Warrington in 1962, and was still playing for Blackpool in 1963 when I decided to turn professional. Little wonder that Brian Glover thought Brian Bevan was somewhat remote from the other members of the team.

In my final season I was picked in forty out of the forty three matches, thirty one times at 6, three at 2, one at 5, and the remaining five at 14, covering the backs as substitute. Coached by Joe Egan, supposedly one of the great rugby league coaches, but far from that, we won twenty five games and lost nineteen.

I regularly played at stand-off to Parry Gordon at scrum-half and I found him a joy to play with. Having been beaten three times by St Helens the year before, and already three times before Christmas in the final season, we were

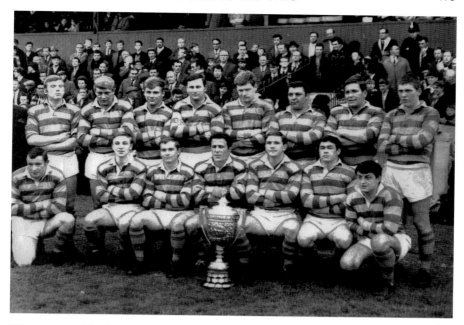

Warrington with the Lancashire League Trophy 1968.
Back row: Billy Churm, Ray Clarke, Peter Carrington, Geoff Bootle, Ken Parr, Brian Glover, Brian Brady, Barry Briggs.
Front row: Keith Ashcroft, Parry Gordon, Peter Harvey, Willie Aspinall, Jackie Melling, Tommy Conroy, John Coupe.

drawn to play them again in the third round of the Challenge Cup. It was 1 March and we were at home at Wilderspool. I agreed with Parry that we should switch markers and I man marked Tommy Bishop who played scrum-half. Though they were the stronger side we managed to beat them in a very low scoring game 4-2. I remember waves of St Helens forwards pouring over us, with Bishop prompting and pressing as always, but I stuck to him like a limpet, tackling my heart out. No sitting back on the chariot that day. They probably remember a Saints' player dropping the ball over the line, but I prefer to think that we fought for our lives, and deserved the touch of good luck.

We went on to play in the Challenge Cup semi-final, played at Wigan, but unfortunately lost to Salford 15-8 on 22 March 1969. During that match, which was very tense as Rugby League Cup semi-finals should be, I do remember one particular tackle, out of the twenty or so that I would have made. They had bought Colin Dixon from Halifax and he was having an exceptional game in the middle of Central Park. I flew into my version of Duggie Greenall's 'mammy' tackle but failed to knock him out. As I stood up he gripped me by the shirt and dragged me towards him, I turned round looking for protection from our forwards. He laughed, 'You are not playing for the Saints now, and you are on your own, so beat it.' That is perhaps a polite version but the warning was very clear. He got the penalty and I got the warning. We lost the match. David Watkins, who had been very circumspect throughout the game, passing rather more than was normal to avoid the tackle, came over to shake hands. He said, 'I have a suspected fracture of the cheek bone and didn't want to get mixed up with your tackles.' Thanks David I admire you for that. Salford went on to lose to Castleford, in the final at Wembley, with a young loose forward called Malcolm Reilly winning the Lance Todd trophy.

I started my second season at Wilderspool with some doubts as to whether I was to carry on playing; being substitute back for four out of the first six matches with two matches on the right wing with a try in one of them. Joe Egan wanted me as a stand-off and he paired me with Parry Gordon saying that we were well suited to each other's play. I'm not sure what that meant but I do know that playing outside of Parry was the dream I spoke about earlier. If only we had the pack to take us forward. We did have one new prop forward in Ken Halliwell, who had played with the successful Swinton side. He was uncompromising in his approach and stiffened the front row enormously. Parry scored twenty two tries that year, I got three, play maker not a try scorer, still it takes all sorts to make a team. Jeff Bootle kicked 125 goals and scored seven tries playing full back or wing.

We did win one cup when we were awarded the Lancashire League trophy and I have included the picture. We also won another trophy with quite interesting consequences, but few people will remember the Mackeson Golden Ball. Partly as a result of the St Helens dominance of the Mackeson Trophy Competition over the previous two seasons, they changed the rules, and as so often with rule changes, without thinking them through. Basically it was a very simply idea, The Mackeson Company constructed a very large Golden Ball which would be competed for every week. One team would have the ball, which would be taken out onto the pitch before the game, and if that team won that match, the ball would be retained. A prize of £25 would be given to the winning team, and the ball taken back to the winning club each week. Warrington won the Golden Ball very early in the season and the players decided that they would put the £25 into a kitty to be shared out at the end of the season. The ball was too big to fit into the coach and had to go into the boot, with the kit baskets being moved into other spaces. The rules were rather like conkers - the winners took the Golden Ball and the money. We somehow kept on winning the Golden Ball, losing it and winning it back again, and eventually there was £365 in the kitty. Now that does not seem a great deal of money today, but it was worth at least £3,650 if you can think about inflation. That was the Warrington players' kitty for their day out in Blackpool at the end of the season. Fit young men released from training regimes, rules and regulations! You need not ask if a good time was had by all.

Thinking about Blackpool there is a tale to tell. One Saturday when the

Saints had been playing at Blackpool we stayed late for a few beers. On arriving back at the coach there was a drunken Saints supporter wondering around, looking lost and forlorn. There were no other coaches on the car park. One of the Barrow boys, showing real concern asked him where he lived and on being told Blackbrook, invited him onto the coach, and we were to take him home. On arrival at Blackbrook, they carried him to his front door, holding him up as they knocked. The next door neighbour, awakened by this knocking after midnight, opened his upstairs window and said, 'It's no good knocking there, they have gone to Blackpool on their holidays.'

At the end of the second season with Warrington they acceded to my request to go back into education, and I went on to Liverpool University for three terms, to take a Diploma in Special Education. When I returned to Warrington I was two stones heavier and no longer quick enough to play top class rugby league, and so I didn't go down for the first dozen games. They had lost twelve out of the first seventeen matches, Joe Egan retired as coach saying, 'No one could coach donkeys like them.' I applied for the position and became the coach, taking on a failing team, just when the club were in the worst financial situation they had ever been.

Joe Egan had left a group of players, not very different from those I had played with, just over twelve months before. The one exception, who I never met, was Bobby Fulton, who had appeared and left, like a meteor in the night sky, and the other Brian Glover, who had transferred to St Helens. The players were insulted by being called donkeys, but I insulted them far more on the first training night after our two defeats at the hands of Salford and Leeds, when they had conceded ninety eight points to only eight scored.

I remember taking them into the old wooden shed at Loushers Lane. Once upon a time it had been a sparkling sporting pavilion, but now it was fit for these, dispirited, downhearted, ramshackle, jumble of rugby players, who had lost their confidence and pride, and consequently their ability. The rain beat down heavily, drumming a tattoo on the roof. My voice was raised into the most shocking rant in an effort to transmit to them, just how bad I thought they had become. 'You are players who have proved that you can play rugby, I have played beside you and know how good you are, but the last two games have been a disgrace, to you, to your jersey and your club. This is it, there are no other players coming, there is no money in the bank, I can't get rid of you, so you will have to buckle down from this moment on, or we will be a laughing stock, now and forever.'

In fact there were thirty one players on the Warrington books that year and we were expected to play two teams (first and A) every week. Ron Mather, the 'A' team coach, and I sometimes had to pick up amateur players from their homes if we were short, and we often were.

As any decent Coach would do, I set about changing the training methods, to try to get something like a standard of fitness to play the game. These players all knew how to play, but they needed organising, making back into a team, relying on each other to make tackles, never throwing in the towel, never accepting defeat. Progress was slow but we gradually got better, beating Rochdale Hornets in the first round of the Challenge Cup so that we travelled in hope to Salford in the second. We had a side, unchanged from the week before, when we had beaten Oldham 23-9, and I was confident that we had turned the corner.

What I remember about that match is that we totally dominated the scrums, but every time we took the ball on their put in, by the efforts of our front row Larkin, Harrison and Brady, the referee blew and gave them a penalty. It was such a show of bias that I confronted him after the match. I totally understand the frustration with the referee, shown by coaches. I still feel that the referee is the most important person on the pitch, because of the decisions which he gives, and equally those he doesn't give.

One of the most important people at Warrington was Jack Hamblett who was just about everything behind the scenes. 'Grounds man, kit man and general factotum' is the way rugby league historian Robert Gate describes him. I like to think of him as a friendly chap who would do anything for anybody. He revelled in the tales of Harry Bath, Brian Bevan and Gerry Helme but had to draw back ever so slightly when Jackie Fleming was on the scene. One apparently mundane task was that he washed all of our training kit. That was one difference from the Saints which I did appreciate, as the training kit there had to be taken home and washed by the players, or more likely their wives. Our kit was spotless, sweet smelling and left out ready for us to wear, thank you Jack, you looked after us so well. The plight of the club could be described in a single picture, that of one of the fallen goal posts which lay rotten on the passageway. The paint was peeling from it, the top broken of and the bottom, rotten where it had been standing in the ground. Like the team it was weak and there was no money to repair it. Just picture it lying there; it is an image which I will never forget.

As the season came to an end, Mr Ossie Davies bought out the entire board and took complete control by himself, helped by the former club secretary, Phil Worthington, with one other director, Brian Pitchford, who worked mainly in South Africa. His infusion of money was too late for me, but he did introduce Alex Murphy as the new Manager before we ended the season. I stayed on at Warrington and completed the pre-season training with the players, and to this day players who completed that, tell of the impact it had on them. For many of them it would be the last hurrah, as Alex used his new power, and new money to build a team, which would be successful. There is absolutely no doubt that his influence on the field, was of paramount importance. He continued with his philosophy of making sure that no mistakes were made, and by his own brilliance, raised the standard of those around him. He gradually brought players from Leigh, his former club, who understood his methodology, and with an introduction of Welsh players, including John Bevan, Mike Nicholas and Bobbie Wanbon; he built the most substantial team seen at Wilderspool in two generations.

He is a genius, has spent his life playing and working in Rugby League and still to this day supports players, both young and old, and is a great advocate of the game. I look forward to seeing his statue outside Wembley Stadium, an honour thoroughly deserved.

At the schoolboy finals at Langtree Park, the new home of the Saints, only last season (2012), there were five past players in attendance to support the youngsters, Geoff Pimblett and I (Secretary and Treasurer) Kel Coslett, as life President, Eric Chisnall with Alex Murphy OBE, there to present the trophies. I have not given Alex Murphy OBE, member of the Rugby League Hall of Fame, his full title throughout this book because he earned that honour, over the whole of my lifetime. I know from many sources, which it is right to keep private, that he performs as many charitable acts as he played matches in rugby league. Many of them for groups of people and some of huge benefit to individuals, I can only say that it has been a privilege to know such a character.

CHAPTER 19

Life away from Rugby

My own situation was changing rapidly by this time. Marriage to Ruth Twist in 1964 when I was still at the early stages of my rugby league career was following our intended pathway. Then the births of Simon and Louise in 1965 and 1968 were natural and well planned events. Our third child Rachael, born in 1971, came at a time that was even more eventful and in some ways the least stable for all of us.

I started an Open University course hoping to pursue a degree in Mathematics. At the same time I was taking on the coaching role at Warrington Rugby League Club, and for good measure, I left teaching to go to work for *Encyclopaedia Britannica* (EB), where I was part a team of teachers who developed multi-media learning techniques, using materials published by that company, and sold the idea to schools. I enjoyed all of these changes and gained vast experience from them all, each being self-directed and a joy to undertake. I could, and perhaps should, write chapters for each of these experiences, but I will simply say that I learned a great deal from all of them.

By April 1973 all of those experiences were in the past and I returned to teaching classes of children in schools in the normal manner. A revolution had taken place at Warrington when Mr Oswald (Ossie) Davies, bought out all of the other directors and hired Alex Murphy as his first team coach with me as coach to the 'A' team. I had worked for *Britannica* for some time and then as a self-employed consultant meeting, head teachers in their schools every day of the week.

My original career path intention was to become a Lecturer in Physical Education and work in Teacher training. By now I was far more interested in becoming a head teacher in my own school. But first I had to begin again at the bottom of the ladder, having jumped off it to go to work at Britannica. I took a job as a supply teacher in St Joseph's Peasley Cross for a period of one term, the only time that I worked for St Helens Local Education Authority.

My experience with *EB* told me that I should get some work time in an Infant School, and I knew of two schools in which I wanted to work. One of them, St James Orrell, did not have a post which I could apply for, the other Cherryfield Co. Infants, in Kirkby did. I applied to Miss Nicholls the head teacher, who I had visited, as a representative of *EB*, on a number of occasions. She was told by the staffing officer in Kirkby, that he did not think it right, that a male member of staff should be appointed to an infant school.

Think about it, I had been a head of Department in a Secondary school, taught both infants and juniors for five years, been at University for one year, worked at *Encyclopaedia Britannica* for two years, played rugby for St Helens and Warrington, coached a professional rugby league team and the Staffing Officer thought it wrong that I was trying to teach in an infant school.

I had worked at Prescot C of E, which was a Primary School, and had taken the special needs children throughout the school, but it was thought that I should not be appointed to an infant school. Miss Gwen Nicholls being the person she was, appointed me anyway BUT on a probationary contract so that they could watch me teach for three months. I went in as a probationer (having already served nine years in schools) and was promoted through scale one, two to three in the next two years. I had the most wonderful learning experience with my two main mentors - Ann Gordon who taught in the classroom next door, and Maureen Haworth who was in the classroom on the other side. Like two book ends they supported me, and guided me through the travails of vertical streaming and teaching ITA. (Initial Teaching Alphabet). I thank all of those wonderful ladies who worked there at Cherryfield Infants, but I learned so much from the two next door to me. In addition to supporting me as a teacher, Maureen was the Deputy Head of the school and being Deputy to Miss Nicholls was, I should think, a very stressful experience. Gwen to her friends, and only when invited, she was quite a formidable lady!

One day perhaps I will write about teaching and she will figure as someone who had her own way of doing things. She was not married, a spinster of a certain age, a magistrate, bred Siamese cats, and did not come into school until 10 o'clock in the morning, and always went home at 2 o'clock on the day which had best suited her hair appointment. But stick up for her school, did she ever! Put her with Mr Cyril Prescott, the Head of the Junior School and one time Chairman of the National Union of Teachers, and they would have taken on a battalion of Education Officers never mind one staffing officer.

So in two years I was ready to apply for positions as a Deputy Head teacher myself. Mr Boardman, the head teacher at Whiston Willis Junior School saw in me the stuff of a future head teacher. Someone who was willing to stand up for his beliefs, with a wide experience of children and an understanding of matching curriculum to individual needs, in effect, someone like himself. My two years at Cherryfield Infants, which was in Kirkby, a notoriously difficult place to teach, with very challenging children, had been spent on my own learning experience and also working on another university course about Gifted and Talented Children, this time at Lancaster University.

Mr Boardman was the boss, my boss, and never in the four years I was Deputy to him did he call me Peter, or I call him Maurice, it would not be proper. However, he was the most open minded and progressive of head teachers and we developed timetables and specialist teaching throughout that school. As an aside, and perhaps to show just how wrong staffing officers can be, for the first two years of my time at Whiston Willis Junior School, I was paid via Whiston Willis Infant School. At the end of each month I used to go down to the Infant School and sit in the staffroom and have a cup of tea. I would chat to the staff, and the head teacher would come in and hand me my pay slip, every month for two years, after which she insisted that I was being counted on her staffing lists, and so had to tell them at the office that I was actually employed in the Junior School. Yes still separate schools in those days in the 70s.

Ruth had joined me at Cherryfield and had brought Rachael with her in the mornings. Rachael got used to the rough and tumble of the Kirkby kids and more than held her own, which we were very happy for her to do, but when she began to talk like them and use words like 'Purple people eater,' which came out in a strong sounding Scouse voice, we thought it might be time to get her back to St Julie's in Eccleston. Now that Rachael was in school, Ruth taught at St Julie's for a year before looking for a promotion herself and going to Windle Pilkington School in the middle of St Helens.

Then in 1979 I became head teacher at Millbrook County Junior School and within two years took over the amalgamated Infant and Junior School when that happened, I think in 1983. Then I moved to Eastcroft County Primary in 1985 and took on the worst school, in the worse authority in the country. Well that is what the statistics would suggest, but after surviving having half the school burnt down in an arson attack, with the great help of a truly gallant staff, we all got to grips with turning the school around into a very successful one.

At Millbrook I met the very talented Steve Palin and together we produced Cross Curricular Learning materials for *Encyclopaedia Britannica*. This published material helped to pay for the financial support needed to put Louise and Rachael through University. My son Simon worked hard to gain experience in the world of logistics and commerce and all three have responsible jobs in their chosen fields of employment.

When I won the Captains Prize at Grange Park Golf Club, my father told me the story of how once he had hit a golf ball when he was courting my mother. He went 'Up the braes' and stood looking at a person teeing off. I don't suppose my Granddad even did that, when he was discharged from the army with severe wounds in 1917. So perhaps I might be excused for the wonderful delight which I felt when I caddied for my son Simon when he won The Presidents Prize a few years ago. I managed to play golf to a handicap of five, so Mr Blackadder, my tutor at Loughborough, might have been reasonably pleased with me.

I should mention ten years in Lions International from about 1975 when I was delighted with the motto 'We serve'. A charter member of St Helens Lions in 1975, I became zone chairman and Deputy District Governor in 1981. As a club we set up the St Helens Half Marathon, in which runners of all types ran for Charity. The present St Helens 10k run is a successor to that event.

I have worked as the Treasurer of the Deafness Resource Centre in Dentons Green Lane since about 1999 and been the Treasurer of the St Helens Past Players Association (now St Helens RFC Players' Association) for more than 25 years.

Past Players Association.

'Those who drink from the well should always remember the people who dug it.'

This quotation I have taken from the Warrington Past Players Association and it epitomises the role of Past Players. None of them, no matter how good they were, can compete with the present generation, simply because of advancing years. Not that the modern day player is necessarily better than those from the past, but they do owe the foundation of the clubs to others.

I have been a member of the Saints Past Players since the inception over thirty four years ago. I have enjoyed all aspects of the work, all purely voluntary, and am delighted to say that successive chairmen of the Saints have encouraged us all to stay closely in touch with the mother club.

At the first meeting I was able to talk to Alf Ellaby, who confirmed that it was him who had tried to get me to sign for Castleford, and I became good friends with Jack Arkwright, the legendary prop forward from the 1930's. In meeting heroes like Duggie Greenall and Alan Prescott, and listening to them recount tales of their time at the Saints, definitely gives us the feeling of passing on the baton to the next generation. It takes probably ten years for a player to realise that they are now past players. Far longer if they insist on playing on in the lower teams and the various veteran's groups who want to benefit by their experience. I met John Donovan a few years ago and he told me that he had continued playing until his 65th birthday. Apparently many people play for a few years, some at the local open age clubs and others at various rugby union clubs.

Come what may, at some stage, everyone stops playing, and becomes a past player. The axiom 'the older I am the better I used to be' can be applied to everyone, but I find that most people just accept that as each past player wore the same shirt, there is a common bond. I am a member of two past players associations, St Helens and Warrington, and I am proud to stand next to every one of the players who are fellow members. The banter, which was a daily occurrence in playing days, still exists and genuine friendship thrives in the spirit and warmth of social occasions. I say that because I know that relatively few players actually go to watch matches any more.

It is very difficult for a former player to become a spectator, even more difficult to become a fan. Watching other people play, rarely stirs the emotion which is evident in true fans.

In my case it took maybe ten years and I missed most of the matches in the 1970s and so did not enjoy the spectacle of Kel Coslett at loose forward, or captaining the side from prop. Neither did I see Geoff Pimblett, one of the younger members of our Carr Mill fraternity, blossom into his role in the Eric Ashton backed Cup Winning side which did so well. However, I did come back and was a season ticket holder for many years, sitting alongside Ruth in 'D' Stand, during the 80s. Besides watching the matches, we were aware of the blind people, who came with their friends and sat on the back row, listening to a match commentary.

When the new corporate boxes were opened, I took a share in the number one box with Big Mike Hewitt of Burtonwood Plastics, and a number of other business people. It is indeed a different way of enjoying a rugby match, but I have to admit that I really did get used to it.

Then maybe about 1995 I was asked to share in the commentary for the Blind, and once more I was back in the stands watching, but now doing some analysis, to add to the work of Mike Kennedy, the main commentator, Steve Manning who is very knowledgeable about BARLA and young players, and Denis Whittle the well-known independent reporter. The little box at the back of 'B' Stand, had begun life as the home of commentators for a hospital broadcast, situated next to the Radio Merseyside position, on the shelf at the back of the stand. It shook when the fans stamped their feet, during those exciting times of the late 90s and early noughties. I have been a proud commentator for about fifteen years now and commend the St Helens Club for providing this service for so long.

Run by Geoff Ward, in conjunction with the goodwill of the club, the Blind or partially sighted, whether registered or not, are able to go to matches with their friends and enjoy the day out. In the new stadium people can sit in a seat of their choice, and be informed by a specialist team of commentators, throughout the match in progress. Though I am not always part of that team now, I fully commend it to all those who would benefit, and perhaps extend the years of enjoyment which Macula Degeneration threatens to overtake.

Last year when the Saints moved into their new stadium at Langtree Park, we met with the Chairman Eamonn McManus, who has been a long-time supporter of the Past Players Association, and reviewed the way forward in the present day playing structure. Steve Leonard (Leo) was given the role of being the interface between the club and the players, past and present. Our committee agreed to become a Players Association, partly to try to overcome the known fact that when players left the Saints we often had difficulty keeping in touch with them. This is especially true of those who are transferred to other clubs, and then retire from there. So rather than wait until a player retires before offering membership of our association, we decided to offer membership of The St Helens Players Association on the day that a player plays his first match for the Saints. By this means we hope that all players will feel part of the Players Association and be able to enjoy the friendship across the age groups.

As a member of the committee I have had the honour and privilege of accepting and assessing those players nominated to become a 'Hall of Fame' member. Candidates for this honour are nominated by the general membership and a discussion takes place as to how the nominee compares with the accepted criteria, which include outstanding ability and a playing career of around 200 first team matches. Exceptional coaches and chairmen have also been nominated and accepted, because we recognise that a successful club must have many facets.

Looking at the list of members of our 'Hall of Fame,' we see the names of so many outstanding players, and I am proud to say that I knew them all, and played with many of them. Perhaps if I had managed to play for two more seasons, I might have been able to join them.

CHAPTER 20

Saints Greatest 17

As the sun set on the halcyon days at Knowsley Road, we were set the task of picking 'the Greatest 17'. With the last long season drawing to a close, but just in time for the wonderful climax, we completed the impossible task. Not quite the labours of Hercules, and in fact with a great deal of agreement, Ray French MBE, and I, representing the Past Players, sat around a table with club chairman Eamonn McManus and (CEO) Tony Colquitt, in the presence of Alex Service (Club Historian) and Mike Appleton (Media Manager), and over a pot of tea and some biscuits, debated the relative merits of the names put before us for a *considerable* amount of time!

Friends on and off the pitch. Alex Murphy, Alice Murphy, Tom Van Vollenhoven, Ruth Harvey, Peter Harvey.

Not one single fan agreed with all of our selections, though a great many agreed with most of them. No doubt every one of the readers of this book would have picked someone other than our composite 17, it is also true that individually each of those present might not have selected every one of the 17, and plenty of other names were discussed and argued for. To get a consensus within a couple of hours must have been more difficult than picking a tour party, but we managed to do that.

The names appeared in the programme for the final match when Castleford Tigers were the fitting opponents. I watched from the restaurant, where I was MC for the evening and as the final quarter of that final match drew close, the tension was palpable. We would win the match, but would we have sufficient points difference to take us to the play-offs? I found myself doing a match analysis, as I have so often done working with the team doing the commentary for the blind, a service possibly unique to the Saints for 25 years. With the last play of the match, captain fantastic Keiron Cunningham, crashed over the line, right under the posts, to widen the gap enough for the fans to bring the house down, one more time.

The play offs were achieved and once more a Grand Final beckoned. Old Trafford is a magnificent venue and we, Past Players, have been present at every final, obviously enjoying most those which we have won. If it has to come down to a drop goal, there was no one more reliable than Sean Long, to win us the match. The Super League Grand Final has been a tremendous end of season occasion and the setting at Old Trafford makes it a truly northern occasion, welcomed by everyone present.

On a slightly different note, but for me even more spectacular, because it really was unique, was the occasion at which the St Helens RLFC honoured 'the Greatest 17.'

The shadows had grown so long on the old lady of Knowsley Road, and the walls were literally falling down, with fans picking up whatever they could retrieve, when a huge marquee was raised linking the playing surface to the grandstand. The club had employed specialist organisers for the event and I must say that as Ruth and I entered the Marquee, it felt a truly magnificent setting. Though it sounds mundane, they even got the toilets right, and believe me that was bringing rugby league into the twenty-first century.

The one thing that the organisers got wrong was that they did not trust Ray French MBE, with the job of Master of Ceremonies. There is no one who can interview rugby players with the skill and panache that Ray brings to the occasion. To hear him talk to Tom van Vollenhoven, Alex Murphy, Cliff Watson and Dick Huddart, all of them teammates from the sixties, would have been worth a TV documentary. A conversation between Ray, George Nicholls and Chris Joynt would have been peer assessment of the highest order. I have

Alex Murphy with Ruth Harvey.

Dick Huddart and Cliff Watson both legends of RL both here and in Australia.

Alan Rooney and Peter Harvey match commentators at Langtree Park.

heard Ray speak to Keiron Cunningham, bringing out the family background which has him stamped through with pride, so often hidden when the light is too brightly shone on him. The relatives of Duggie Greenall, Alan Prescott and Vince Karalius are all comfortable in Ray's friendly presence, and would have been delighted to say more about their famous kin. The two Pauls, Newlove and Wellens, together with Sean Long make a trio who can speak for their generation, all still immersed in the game, to which they have brought such class. That brings me to Paul Sculthorpe, who might have made the 17 at either 13 or 6, both iconic shirts in the pantheon of the St Helens club. Believe me a fight for the number 13 shirt between Paul and Vince would have been a sight to behold, but no contest between Paul and the one true veteran Leslie Fairclough to take the number 6.

I want to quote from the programme honouring the greatest 17 and see how easy it is to forget players.

Leslie Fairclough played between 1922-1931. With 355 appearances scoring 84 tries and kicking 3 goals.

Although slightly built, he became the fulcrum of the Saints and Great Britain teams for a decade. He had great hands, acceleration, swerve and a fine kicking game, which enabled him to both score tries and create them in abundance for the likes of Alf Ellaby and Roy Hardgrave. He was a sure tackler too and excelled in the 1928 Australian Tour, when a host of Australian Clubs were big admirers and would have signed him for a king's ransom. Yet Leslie stayed loyal to the Saints and was awarded a testimonial, which he shared, on his insistence, with his scrum-half partner Walter Groves. This says it all about the nature of the man.

I think that we should find a place for him as a proper stand-off.

In this quotation it mentions Elf Ellaby, said to be the first Saints 'superstar', who has been a legendary figure, virtually throughout the twentieth century scoring 280 tries in 289 appearances, mentioned by Tom Vollenhoven as possibly the finest winger ever. Both played on the right wing so we do not have a left wing in this 17, but as we agreed on the day, we could not fit everyone in, and this team was special enough to be considered the very best.

'Time has my lord a wallet on his back, wherein he puts alms for oblivion, good deeds are good deeds past, forgot as soon as made.' A speech to Achilles reminding him that what we do, we leave behind us and the past fades a fact which we should heed as we try to keep the memories bright by retelling the stories over and over. Thus it is with most players, few remain within the memory, but those that do, stand out as their halos are polished by popular acclaim. It is impossible to say who was the greatest Saint of them all, but Alex Murphy says that the St Helens team of 1966 was the finest that he ever played in. I played in that team too, just a footnote in the history of the game, and hopefully with the work which I have done since, leaving a footprint.

Statistics Part One
Rugby Union Record

It should be noted that some of the statistics represented here may be incomplete and approximate. It is the best I can do in the circumstances. I have listed, for example, 19 games for Liverpool, but the Club Historian (Mr Barker) told me many years ago that I had played 35 times. Club games at the time had a 'friendly' status.

Seasons 1958/59 and 1959/60

Date	Home team	HS	Away team	AS	Venue
11/04/1959	Liverpool	14	New Brighton	0	Aigburth
18/09/1959	Liverpool	13	Taunton	0	Aigburth

1959/60: 30 matches (approx) for St Mary's College playing mid- week and Saturdays.
Liverpool won the Northern Sevens at Northern
ULIESA Tour to Holland

Season 1960/61

1960/61: 30 matches (approx) for St Mary's College playing mid-week and Saturdays.
23/11/1960: Reserve for North West Counties v South Africa at White City (Manchester)

Date	Home team	HS	Away team	AS	Venue
24/09/1960	Cornwall	9	Lancashire	8	Falmouth
08/10/1960	Ulster	29	Lancashire	0	Ravenhill
22/10/1960	Lancashire	27	The Rest	3	Manchester
05/11/1960	Cheshire	11	Lancashire	9	Birkenhead

12/11/1960	Durham	12	Lancashire	11	Hartlepool
19/11/1960	Lancashire	6	Northumberland	3	Fylde
26/11/1960	Lancashire	3	Cumberland/West		Vale of Lune
10/12/1960	Lancashire	10	Yorkshire	10	Waterloo
17/12/1960	Liverpool	8	Manchester	0	Aigburth
14/01/1961	Harlequins		Blackheath LC		Twickenham
21/01/1961	London Scottish		Blackheath		Old Deer Park
04/02/1961	Liverpool	6	Sale	3	Aigburth
18/02/1961	Liverpool	6	Bradford	9	Aigburth
11/03/1961	Liverpool	11	Abertillery	3	Aigburth
01/04/1961	Bedford	11	Liverpool	3	Bedford
03/04/1961	Liverpool	9	Saracens	3	Aigburth
10/04/1961	Liverpool	27	Rugby	3	Aigburth
15/04/1961	Leicester		Liverpool		Leicester

Season 1961/62

Date	Home team	HS	Away team	AS	Venue
05/09/1961	Cheshire XV		Lancs Pres XV		Chester
07/09/1961	Presidents XV		Sale XV		Macclesfield
30/09/1961	Cornwall	3	Lancashire	3	Redruth
07/10/1961	Lancashire	0	Ulster	11	Waterloo
11/10/1961	Loughborough		Birmingham Uni		Loughborough
14/10/1961	Manchester Uni		Loughborough		Manchester
18/10/1961	Loughborough 2nd XV	12	Old Lutonians	3	Loughborough
21/10/1961	Maesteg		Loughborough		Maesteg
28/10/1961	Lancashire	23	The Rest	0	St Helens
01/11/1961	N. Staff Uni.		Loughborough		N. Staffs
04/11/1961	Lancashire	0	Cheshire	11	Waterloo
08/11/1961	Loughborough		Cambridge Uni		Loughborough
11/11/1961	Lancashire	3	Durham	11	Manchester
15/11/1961	Birmingham Uni		Loughborough		Birmingham
18/11/1961	Northumberland	8	Lancashire	6	
20/11/1961	Whites		Colours		Carlisle (ET)
22/11/1961	Leicester Uni		Loughborough		Leicester
25/11/1961	Cum/Westmoreland.		Lancashire	8	Workington
29/11/1961	Loughborough		Bristol Uni		Loughborough
02/12/1961	Whites		Colours		Penzance (ET)

06/12/1961	Nottingham Uni		Loughborough		Nottingham
09/12/1961	Yorkshire		Lancashire		
10/01/1962	Liverpool Uni		Loughborough		Liverpool
13/01/1962	Nottingham RFC		Loughborough		Nottingham
20/01/1962	Birmingham RFC		Loughborough		Birmingham
27/01/1962	Oxford Uni Greyhounds		Loughborough		Oxford Uni
31/01/1962	Loughborough		Leeds Uni		Loughborough
03/02/1962	Loughborough		Middlesex Hosp.		Loughborough
14/02/1962	St.Lukes College		Loughborough		Old Deer Park
21/02/1962	Loughborough		St Johns Cambridge		Loughborough
24/02/1962	Oxford RFC		Loughborough		Oxford
03/03/1962	Loughborough		Worcester		Loughborough
08/03/1962	Leicester RFC		Loughborough		Leicester
10/03/1962	Loughborough		Wolverhampton		Loughborough
14/03/1962	Standard RFC		Loughborough		
17/03/1962	Rhymney RFC		Loughborough		Rhymney
23/04/1962	UAU		Bristol		Bristol
24/04/1962	UAU		Abertillery		Abertillery
28/04/1962	Hartlepool Rovers		RAF (RF. Oakes Mem)		Hartlepool

Season 1962/63

Date	Home team	HS	Away team	AS	Venue
01/09/1962	Wigan RUFC	5	President's XV	11	Wigan
15/09/1962	Liverpool	3	Old Birkonians	11	Aigburth
22/09/1962	Liverpool	5	Roundhay	11	Aigburth
26/09/1962	Lancashire	8	Surrey	3	Waterloo
29/09/1962	Liverpool	9	Broughton Park	3	Aigburth
06/10/1962	Ulster	23	Lancashire	6	Ravenhill
13/10/1962	Fylde	3	Liverpool	6	Fylde
20/10/1962	Nuneaton	6	Liverpool	11	Nuneaton
27/10/1962	Liverpool	10	Halifax	3	Aigburth
03/11/1962	Cheshire	12	Lancashire	19	Birkenhead
10/11/1962	Durham	3	Lancashire	8	Blaydon
17/11/1962	Sale	5	Liverpool	6	Sale
24/11/1962	Lancashire	5	Cumberland/West	3	Fylde

Date	Team 1	Score	Team 2	Score	Venue
01/12/1962	Whites		Colours (played)		Carlisle (ET)
08/12/1962	Lancashire	3	Yorkshire	30	Waterloo
15/12/1962	Lancashire	6	Northumberland	0	Manchester
22/12/1962	Probables		Possibles Res. trav		Torquay (ET)
12/01/1963	England		The Rest Res trav		Twickenham
19/01/1963	England		Wales (Reserve)		Twickenham
09/02/1963	England		Ireland (Reserve)		Dublin
23/02/1963	England		France (Reserve)		Twickenham
09/03/1963	Lancashire	3	Yorkshire	6	Twickenham
16/03/1963	Headingley	6	Liverpool	16	Headingley
21/03/1963	Whites		Blues		Leicester (TT)
30/03/1963	Rugby	0	Liverpool	5	Rugby
02/04/1963	Birkenhead Park		Liverpool		Birkenhead
06/04/1963	Liverpool	6	St Helens	3	Aigburth
13/04/1963	Liverpool	21	Hull & East Riding	3	Aigburth
15/04/1963	Liverpool	6	Saracens	17	Aigburth
20/04/1963	Liverpool	22	Wilmslow	6	Aigburth
26/04/1963	Eric Evans XV	36	St Helens Recs	0	Ruskin Drive

ET: England trial
Res trav: Travelling reserve
TT: Tour trial

Statistics Part Two
Rugby League Record

St Helens RFC 1963/67

Honours

League Championship Winner 1965/66 Runner up 1964/65
Challenge Cup Winner 1965/66
Lancashire League Winner 1964/65; 1965/66; 1966/67
Lancashire Cup Winner 1963/64; 1964/65
Floodlit trophy finalist 1965/66
League Leader's trophy 1964/65; 1965/66
Lancashire representative (2) 1963/64; 1964/65

Major Final Appearances

Season	Comp	Date	Venue	Pos	Saints	Opp
1963/64	LCF	26/10/1963	Swinton	5	St Helens 15	Leigh 4
1963/64	WDCF	16/05/1964	Wigan	6	St Helens 10	Swinton 7
1964/65	LCF	24/10/1964	Wigan	6	St Helens 12	Swinton 4
1964/65	CF	22/05/1965	Swinton	2	St Helens 7	Halifax 15
1965/66	FTF	14/12/1966	St Helens	14	St Helens 0	Castleford 4
1965/66	CCF	21/05/1966	Wembley	6	St Helens 21	Wigan 2
1965/66	CF	28/05/1966	Swinton	6	St Helens 35	Halifax 12

LCF: Lancashire Cup final; WDCF: Western Division Championship final;
CF: Championship final; FTF: Floodlit Trophy final

Overall Club Record

Season	Apps	Subs	NPS	Tries	Points
1963/64	39	0	0	22	66
1964/65	28	2	5	13	39

1965/66	36	4	7	8	24
1966/67	9	2	4	5	15
Totals	112	8	16	48	144

Apps: Appearances; Subs: Substitute appearances; NPS: Non-playing substitute.

In the 1960's two players were picked to cover injuries in all the forward and back positions, if there were no injuries the substitutes did not play.

Match by Match Statistics
(When my name appeared on the team-sheet)

Match by Match: 1963-64

MN	Date	Comp	Pos	Home Team	HS	Away Team	AS
1	24/08/1963	Lge	6	St Helens	7	Huddersfield	10
2	28/08/1963	Lge	6	St Helens	20	Castleford	11
3	31/08/1963	Lge	6	Keighley	6	St Helens	18
4	07/09/1963	LC1	5	Swinton	2	St Helens	12
5	14/09/1963	Lge	5	St Helens	40	Hull KR	5
6	16/09/1963	LC2	5	St Helens	28	Workington	4
7	21/09/1963	Lge	5	Halifax	13	St Helens	5
8	23/09/1963	LCSF	5	Warrington	14	St Helens	21
9	28/09/1963	Tour	5	St Helens	2	Australia	8
10	05/10/1963	WDC	5	St Helens	19	Barrow	15
11	12/10/1963	Lge	5	Leeds	2	St Helens	10
12	19/10/1963	Lge	5	St Helens	11	Hull	10
13	26/10/1963	LCF	5	St Helens	15	Leigh	4
14	02/11/1963	Lge	5	St Helens	19	Warrington	8
15	16/11/1963	Lge	5	St Helens	11	Featherstone	11
16	30/11/1963	WDC	5	St Helens	16	Liverpool City	0
17	07/12/1963	Lge	6	Wakefield	7	St Helens	8
18	14/12/1963	Lge	6	St Helens	12	Halifax	13
19	28/12/1963	Lge	5	Workington	0	St Helens	5
20	01/01/1964	Lge	3	Swinton	8	St Helens	6
21	04/01/1964	Lge	5	Salford	5	St Helens	15
22	11/01/1964	Lge	6	St Helens	10	Hunslet	12
23	25/11/1964	Lge	5	St Helens	28	Keighley	3
24	01/02/1964	Lge	5	Hull KR	5	St Helens	9
25	08/02/1964	CC1	5	St Helens	6	Castleford	13
26	15/02/1964	WDC	5	Barrow	10	St Helens	14
27	22/02/1964	Lge	5	St Helens	6	Leeds	14
28	29/02/1964	Lge	5	Warrington	10	St Helens	17
29	07/03/1964	Lge	5	Huddersfield	11	St Helens	16
30	14/03/1964	Lge	5	St Helens	14	Workington	8
31	30/03/1964	Lge	5	Swinton	7	St Helens	10
32	08/04/1964	Lge	5	Featherstone	19	St Helens	12
33	18/04/1964	Lge	5	Liverpool City	7	St Helens	32
34	22/04/1964	Lge	2	Wigan	13	St Helens	22
35	25/04/1964	Lge	2	Widnes	8	St Helens	19
36	01/05/1964	WDCSF	6	St Helens	22	Oldham	11

37	06/05/1964	Lge	6	Hull	9	St Helens	17
38	16/05/1964	WDCF	6	Swinton	7	St Helens	10
39	27/05/1964	Lge	6	Castleford	11	St Helens	10

Match by Match: 1964-65

MN	Date	Comp	Pos	Home Team	HS	Away Team	AS
40	14/08/1964	GC	6	St Helens	22	Swinton	2
41	22/08/1964	Lge	14	Leigh	6	St Helens	19
42	24/08/1964	Lge	6	St Helens	28	Rochdale	4
43	29/08/1964	Lge	6	St Helens	29	Widnes	6
44	31/08/1964	Lge	6	Whitehaven	5	St Helens	15
45	05/09/1964	LC1	6	Liverpool City	11	St Helens	41
46	12/09/1964	Lge	14	Blackpool Borough	5	St Helens	37
47	14/09/1964	LC2	6	Barrow	11	St Helens	22
48	19/09/1964	Lge	7	Rochdale Hornets	6	St Helens	17
49	26/09/1964	Lge	6	Featherstone	15	St Helens	30
50	29/09/1964	LCSF	6	Warrington	8	St Helens	10
51	03/10/1964	Lge	6	St Helens	32	Workington	6
52	10/10/1964	Lge	6	Blackpool Borough	9	St Helens	31
53	17/10/1964	Lge	6	St Helens	25	Featherstone	12
54	24/10/1964	LCF	6	Swinton	4	St Helens	12
55	31/10/1964	Lge	6	Oldham	6	St Helens	22
56	07/11/1964	Lge	6	St Helens	26	Warrington	10
57	14/11/1964	Lge	3	Hull KR	12	St Helens	25
58	21/11/1964	Lge	3	St Helens	37	Barrow	3
59	19/12/1964	Lge	6	St Helens	10	Leigh	7
60	01/01/1965	Lge	2	Swinton	5	St Helens	11
61	09/01/1965	Lge	2	St Helens	23	Liverpool City	3
62	16/01/1965	Lge	6	Warrington	6	St Helens	4
63	13/02/1965	Lge	14	Workington	4	St Helens	3
64	16/03/1965	Lge	6	St Helens	2	Wakefield	9
65	20/03/1965	Lge	2	Wakefield	5	St Helens	4
66	23/03/1965	Lge	6	St Helens	6	Wigan	10
67	27/03/1965	Lge	6	Salford	11	St Helens	8
68	09/04/1965	Lge	14	Liverpool City	0	St Helens	11
69	17/04/1965	Lge	14	Widnes	2	St Helens	14

70	19/04/1965	Lge	6	St Helens	16	Swinton	5
71	21/04/1965	Lge	6	Huddersfield	6	St Helens	20
72	24/04/1965	CPO1	6	St Helens	23	Barrow	7
73	30/04/1965	CPO2	14	St Helens	24	Hull KR	6
74	15/05/1965	CPOSF	14	St Helens	10	Wakefield	5
75	22/05/1965	CPOF	2	St Helens	7	Halifax	15

GC: Gallie Cup

Match by Match: 1965-66

MN	Date	Comp	Pos	Home Team	HS	Away Team	AS
76	14/08/1965	GC	2	Swinton *	11	St Helens	9
77	20/08/1965	Lge	6	St Helens	15	Halifax	4
78	24/08/1965	Lge	6	Rochdale Hornets	9	St Helens	17
79	28/08/1965	Lge	6	Castleford	15	St Helens	19
80	30/08/1965	Lge	6	St Helens	30	Whitehaven	5
81	04/09/1965	Lge	6	Warrington	2	St Helens	11
82	10/09/1965	LC1	6	St Helens	7	Swinton	8
83	15/09/1965	TM	6	St Helens	28	New Zealand	7
84	27/09/1965	Lge	6	Widnes	4	St Helens	9
85	01/10/1965	Lge	14	St Helens	23	Oldham	17
86	05/10/1965	FT1	14	St Helens	25	Leigh	19
87	09/10/1965	Lge	6	St Helens	18	Barrow	14
88	16/10/1965	Lge	6	Salford	11	St Helens	15
89	23/10/1965	Lge	6	St Helens	43	Workington	4
90	30/10/1965	Lge	6	Barrow	10	St Helens	15
91	09/11/1965	Lge	5	St Helens	11	Huddersfield	4
92	13/11/1965	Lge	6	Workington	3	St Helens	7
93	16/11/1965	FT2	6	St Helens	21	Leeds	9
94	19/11/1965	Lge	14	St Helens	19	Rochdale	7
95	27/11/1965	Lge	14	St Helens	9	Wakefield	9
96	04/12/1965	Lge	6	Whitehaven	2	St Helens	4
97	07/12/1965	FTSF	14	St Helens	9	Swinton	5
98	14/12/1965	FTF	14	St Helens	0	Castleford	4
99	17/12/1965	Lge	6	St Helens	21	Blackpool	9
100	01/01/1966	Lge	6	St Helens	16	Salford	3
101	08/01/1966	Lge	6	Oldham	13	St Helens	9
102	29/01/1966	Lge	14	Halifax	2	St Helens	5
103	01/02/1966	Lge	14	St Helens	9	Widnes	4

104	05/02/1966	Lge	4	Blackpool Borough	11	St helens	25
105	14/02/1966	Lge	4	St Helens	17	Leigh	2
106	19/02/1965	Lge	14	Wakefield	20	St Helens	12
107	26/02/1966	CC1	6	Wakefield	0	St Helens	10
108	01/03/1966	Lge	6	St Helens	22	Warrington	6
109	08/03/1966	Lge	6	St Helens	16	Liverpool City	2
110	12/03/1966	Lge	6	Huddersfield	7	St Helens	8
111	19/03/1966	Lge	6	St Helens	16	Swinton	4
112	23/03/1966	Lge	6	Leigh	5	St Helens	6
113	26/03/1966	Lge	6	Wigan	17	St Helens	8
114	02/04/1966	CC2	14	St Helens	12	Hull KR	10
115	08/04/1966	Lge	6	St Helens	17	Wigan	10
116	11/04/1966	Lge	6	Swinton	20	St Helens	6
117	16/04/1966	CCSF	6	Dewsbury	5	St Helens	12
118	22/04/1966	Lge	6	St Helens	10	Swinton	15
119	25/04/1966	Lge	14	Liverpool City	3	St Helens	28
120	30/04/1966	CPO1	3	St Helens	35	Warrington	7
121	07/05/1966	CPO2	2	St Helens	15	Oldham	10
122	21/05/1966	CCF	6	Wigan	2	St Helens	21
123	28/05/1966	CPOF	6	Halifax	12	St Helens	35

Match by Match 1966-67

126	27/08/1966	Lge	4	St Helens	42	Salford	7
127	29/081966	Lge	6	Wakefield	28	St Helens	15
128	03/09/1966	LC1	6	Rochdale Hornets	16	St Helens	18
129	07/09/1966	FT1	14	Salford	10	St Helens	19
130	10/09/1966	Lge	14	Liverpool City	12	St Helens	35
131	12/09/1966	Lge	5	Barrow	9	St Helens	15
132	14/09/1966	LC2	14	Wigan	11	St Helens	9
133	17/09/1966	Lge	14	Blackpool Borough	14	St Helens	23
134	24/09/1966	Lge	14	Rochdale Hornets	17	St Helens	17
135	30/09/1966	Lge	2	St Helens	35	Whitehaven	12
136	07/10/1966	Lge	14	St Helens	25	Blackpool	6
137	18/10/1966	FT2	6	St Helens	11	Swinton	9
138	02/11/1966	Lge	2	Leigh	29	St Helens	5

Representative Rugby

County Championship
02/10/1963
Cumberland (13) 13 Lancashire (8) 8
At the Recreation Ground, Whitehaven
Attendance: 6,000

Lancashire team: Ray Ashby (Liverpool City); Peter Harvey (St Helens), Keith Northey (St Helens), Alan Buckley (Swinton), Trevor Simms (Oldham); Frank Myler (Widnes), Graham Williams (Swinton); Bill Robinson (Leigh), Bill Sayer (Wigan), Edgar Bate (Widnes), Laurie Gilfedder (Warrington), Jim Measures (Widnes), Vince Karalius (Widnes)

County Championship
16/09/1964
Lancashire (0) 11 Cumberland (11) 13
At Borough Park, Blackpool
Attendance: 1,500

Lancashire team: Ken Gowers (Swinton); Brian Glover (Warrington), Keith Holden (Warrington), John Donovan (Oldham), John Stopford (Swinton); Peter Harvey (St Helens), Graham Williams (Swinton); Danny Gardiner (Workington), Len McIntyre (Oldham), Ken Roberts (Halifax), Harry Major (Oldham), Dave Parker (Oldham), Doug Laughton (St Helens)
Subs: Keith Northey (St Helens), Ken Halliwell (Swinton)

Warrington RLFC 1967-1969

Major Final Appearance

1967-68 Lancashire Cup final at Swinton. Warrington 2 St Helens 2
Played in jersey number 2

Overall Club Record

Season	Apps	Sub
1967/68	27	3
1968/69	34	6
Totals	61	9

Match by Match 1967/68

MN	Date	Comp	Pos	Home Team	HS	Away Team	AS
1	06/09/1967	Lge	14	Warrington	14	Liverpool City	5
2	23/09/1967	Lge	6	Warrington	9	Widnes	7
3	27/09/1967	Lge	14	St Helens	17	Warrington	12
4	30/09/1967	Lge	7	Warrington	7	Australia	16
5	07/10/1967	LCF	4	Warrington	2	St Helens	2
6	11/11/1967	Lge	6	Warrington	15	Liverpool City	13
7	14/11/1967	FT1	7	Hull KR	12	Warrington	13
8	17/11/1967	Lge	6	Castleford	26	Warrington	15
9	24/11/1967	Lge	5	Barrow	10	Warrington	17
10	12/12/1967	FT2	14	Warrington	2	Castleford	14
11	16/12/1967	Lge	6	Warrington	13	Swinton	9
12	23/12/1967	Lge	6	Doncaster	3	Warrington	16
13	26/12/1967	Lge	6	Warrington	0	Leigh	9
14	30/12/1967	Lge	6	Whitehaven	2	Warrington	10
15	06/01/1968	Lge	6	Warrington	37	Blackpool	3
16	20/01/1968	Lge	6	Rochdale H	2	Warrington	8
17	03/02/1968	Lge	6	Leigh	11	Warrington	5
18	13/02/1968	Lge	6	Warrington	10	Salford	8
19	17/02/1968	Lge	6	Warrington	18	Whitehaven	6
20	20/02/1968	Lge	6	Swinton	2	Warrington	13
21	01/03/1968	Lge	6	Salford	6	Warrington	14
22	06/03/1968	Lge	6	Warrington	6	St Helens	12
23	09/03/1968	Lge	6	Warrington	29	Barrow	2
24	16/03/1968	Lge	6	Liverpool City	9	Warrington	7
25	23/03/1968	Lge	6	Warrington	23	Rochdale H	13
26	08/04/1968	Lge	6	Oldham	5	Warrington	23
27	13/04/1968	Lge	6	Warrington	13	Wigan	6
28	15/04/1968	Lge	6	Leigh	6	Warrington	7

| 29 | 19/04/1968 | Lge | 6 | Warrington | 12 | Hull | 9 |
| 30 | 24/04/1968 | Lge | 6 | St Helens | 20 | Warrington | 0 |

Match by Match 1968/69

MN	Date	Comp	Pos	Home Team	HS	Away Team	AS
31	17/08/1968	Lge	14	Bradford N.	9	Warrington	29
32	24/08/1968	Lge	14	Warrington	32	Blackpool	16
33	31/08/1968	Lge	2	Warrington	24	Wakefield T	20
34	02/09/1968	Lge	2	Warrington	16	Widnes	18
35	06/09/1968	Lge	14	Salford	14	Warrington	3
36	14/09/1968	Lge	14	Leeds	24	Warrington	8
37	24/09/1968	Lge	6	Warrington	25	Huyton	7
38	27/09/1968	Lge	6	St Helens	24	Warrington	11
39	05/10/1968	Lge	6	Warrington	22	Whitehaven	2
40	11/01/1900	Lge	14	Widnes	7	Warrington	21
41	18/10/1968	Lge	2	Warrington	12	Swinton	25
42	26/10/1968	Lge	6	Wakefield	22	Warrington	15
43	29/10/1968	FT1	6	Warrington	30	Halifax	12
44	01/11/1968	Lge	6	Warrington	12	Salford	8
45	08/11/1968	Lge	6	Rochdale	9	Warrington	10
46	19/11/1968	FT2	6	Warrington	18	Huddersfield	5
47	23/11/1968	Lge	6	Warrington	5	St Helens	20
48	29/11/1968	Lge	6	Warrington	48	Doncaster	5
49	04/12/1968	Lge	6	Rochdale	8	Warrington	10
50	10/12/1968	FTSF	6	Warrington	6	St Helens	29
51	18/12/1968	Lge	6	Warrington	9	Leeds	16
52	01/01/1969	Lge	6	Wigan	18	Warrington	23
53	05/01/1969	Lge	6	Blackpool	7	Warrington	16
54	11/01/1969	Lge	6	Warrington	21	Workington	18
55	14/01/1969	Lge	6	Leigh	2	Warrington	2
56	17/01/1969	Lge	6	Swinton	18	Warrington	5
57	28/01/1969	CC1	6	Warrington	5	Huyton	2
58	01/02/1969	Lge	6	Whitehaven	9	Warrington	19
59	22/02/1969	CC2	6	Warrington	19	Huddersfield	8
60	01/03/1969	CC3	6	Warrington	4	St Helens	2

61	04/03/1969	Lge	6	Salford	33	Warrington	10
62	15/03/1969	Lge	6	Warrington	14	Barrow	18
63	22/03/1969	CCSF	6	Warrington	8	Salford	15
64	29/03/1969	Lge	6	Doncaster	9	Warrington	23
65	02/04/1969	Lge	6	Warrington	18	Huyton	8
66	05/04/1969	Lge	6	Barrow	13	Warrington	23
67	07/04/1969	Lge	6	Warrington	7	Leigh	22
68	09/04/1969	Lge	6	Warrington	14	Bradford	32
69	12/04/1969	Lge	14	Warrington	17	Wigan	26
70	19/04/1969	Lge	6	Workington	38	Warrington	10

Bibliography

John, Barry, *The King, Autobiography of Barry John* (Mainstream Publishing Company Ltd, 2000). Permission to use extracts.

Gate, Robert, *Rugby League Hall of Fame* (Tempus Publishing, 2003).

Service, Alex, *The March of the Saints* (Self Published, 1988).

Griffiths, John, *Centenary History of the ERFSU* (England Rugby Football Schools Union, 2003).

Lancashire County Rugby Football Union Centenary 1881-1981 (Commemorative booklet).